MW01689385

The following study guides by Dawn Apgar are also available to assist social workers with studying for and passing the ASWB® examinations.

Bachelors

The Social Work ASWB® Bachelors Exam Guide: A Comprehensive Guide for Success, Second Edition

Test focuses on knowledge acquired while obtaining a Baccalaureate degree in Social Work (BSW). A small number of jurisdictions license social workers at an Associate level and require the ASWB Associate examination. The Associate examination is identical to the ASWB Bachelors examination, but the Associate examination requires a lower score in order to pass.

Masters

The Social Work ASWB® Masters Exam Guide: A Comprehensive Guide for Success, Second Edition

Test focuses on knowledge acquired while obtaining a Master's degree in Social Work (MSW). There is no postgraduate supervision needed.

Clinical

The Social Work ASWB® Clinical Exam Guide: A Comprehensive Guide for Success, Second Edition

Test focuses on knowledge acquired while obtaining a Master's degree in Social Work (MSW). It is usually taken by those with postgraduate supervised experience.

Advanced Generalist

The Social Work ASWB® Advanced Generalist Exam Guide: A Comprehensive Guide for Success, Second Edition

Test focuses on knowledge acquired while obtaining a Master's degree in Social Work (MSW). It is usually taken by those with postgraduate supervised nonclinical experience.

Dawn Apgar, PhD, LSW, ACSW, has helped thousands of social workers across the country pass the ASWB® examinations associated with all levels of licensure. In recent years, she has consulted in numerous states to assist with establishing licensure test preparation programs.

Dr. Apgar has done research on licensure funded by the American Foundation for Research and Consumer Education in Social Work Regulation and has served as chairperson of her state's social work licensing board. She is a past President of the New Jersey Chapter of NASW and has been on its National Board of Directors. In 2014, the Chapter presented her with a Lifetime Achievement Award. Dr. Apgar has taught in both undergraduate and graduate social work programs and has extensive direct practice, policy, and management experience in the social work field.

Social Work ASWB® Advanced Generalist Practice Test

170 Questions to Identify Knowledge Gaps

Dawn Apgar, PhD, LSW, ACSW

SPRINGER PUBLISHING COMPANY

Springer Publishing Company, LLC
11 West 42nd Street
New York, NY 10036
www.springerpub.com

Acquisitions Editor: Debra Riegert
Compositor: diacriTech

ISBN: 978-0-8261-3434-9
ebook ISBN: 978-0-8261-3435-6

19 20 21 22 / 5 4 3 2

Publisher's Acknowledgment: Springer Publishing Company recognizes that the ASWB® is a registered service mark of the Association of Social Work Boards and has applied this service mark to the first mention of the association in each of the chapters in the book and its cover. The Association of Social Work Boards neither sponsors nor endorses this product.

Library of Congress Cataloging-in-Publication Data
Names: Apgar, Dawn, author. | Association of Social Work Boards.
Title: Social work ASWB advanced generalist practice test : 170 questions to identify knowledge gaps / Dawn Apgar, PhD, LSW, ACSW.
Description: New York, NY : Springer Publishing Company, LLC, [2018]
Identifiers: LCCN 2017044821 | ISBN 9780826134349 | ISBN 9780826134356 (ebook)
Subjects: LCSH: Social workers—Certification—United States. | Social service—United States—Examinations—Study guides. | Social service—United States—Examinations, questions, etc.
Classification: LCC HV40.52 .A7348 2018 | DDC 361.3076—dc23 LC record available at https://lccn.loc.gov/2017044821

Printed in the United States of America.

To Bill, Ryan, and Alex

You remind me what is important, support me so I can do it all, and always inspire me to be a better person

Contents

Introduction

Despite social workers' best efforts to study for and pass the Association of Social Work Boards (ASWB®) examinations for licensure, they can encounter difficulties answering questions correctly that can ultimately lead to challenges in passing. Social workers who struggle with standardized test taking or have failed the ASWB examinations find themselves at a loss in finding resources to assist them in identifying the mistakes they made and strategies for correcting these errors. The focus of test preparation courses and guides is usually the review of the relevant content and supplying some study and test-taking tips. However, when these resources do not result in passing the ASWB examinations, social workers do not know where to turn for help.

Often, social workers will turn to taking practice tests in an effort to gauge their readiness for the ASWB examinations. In addition, they will try to use them to identify gaps in knowledge and errors in problem solving that prevent desired outcomes. Such an approach is understandable because there has been a void in available diagnostic resources. However, for several reasons, use of existing practice examinations is not usually helpful.

First, it is difficult to identify specific content that is used by test developers to formulate actual questions. For example, many practice tests do not provide the rationales for the correct and incorrect answers. In addition, they usually do not let social workers know which specific ASWB content areas were being tested (e.g., Human Development, Diversity, and Behavior in the Environment; Intervention Processes and Techniques for Use Across Systems; Intervention Processes and Techniques for Use With Larger Systems; or Professional Relationships, Values, and Ethics). In addition, the

ASWB competencies and corresponding Knowledge, Skills, and Abilities statements (KSAs) that form the basis for question development are also not included. Thus, when questions are answered incorrectly, social workers do not know which knowledge in the ASWB content areas, competencies, and KSAs is lacking so they can go back and review relevant source materials.

Based on a practice analysis conducted by ASWB, which outlines the content to be included on the exam, content areas, competencies, and KSAs are created. Content areas are the broad knowledge areas that are measured by each exam. The content areas structure the content for exam construction and score reporting purposes. When receiving exam scores, failing candidates are given feedback on their performance on each content area of the exam. Competencies describe meaningful *sets* of abilities that are important to the job of a social worker within each content area. Finally, KSAs structure the content of the exam for item development purposes. The KSAs provide further details about the nature and range of exam content that is included in the competencies. Each KSA describes a discrete knowledge component that is the basis for individual exam questions that may be used to measure the competency.

Having ASWB content areas, competencies, and KSAs identified is critical in order to make practice tests useful for diagnosing knowledge weaknesses. The following example illustrates the usefulness of having this material explicitly stated.

SAMPLE QUESTION

A social worker at a community mental health agency is doing a home visit to a client as he has not gotten his medication refilled as prescribed. The social worker learns that he has not been taking it for several weeks due to a belief that it is not helping alleviate his thought to "just end things." In order to assist the client, the social worker should FIRST:

- **A.** Accompany the client to his next appointment with the psychiatrist to see if another medication can be prescribed
- **B.** Explain to the client the importance of taking the medication as prescribed
- **C.** Conduct a suicide risk assessment
- **D.** Ask the client if he has suggestions for other strategies that may assist him

ANSWER

1. C

Rationale

Social workers have an ethical duty to respect and promote the right of clients to self-determination. However, there are times when **social workers' responsibility to the larger society** or specific legal obligations supersedes their commitment to respecting clients' decisions or wishes. These instances are when, *in the social workers' professional judgment*, clients' actions or potential actions pose a serious, foreseeable, and imminent risk to themselves (including the risk of suicide) or others (in general or aimed at identifiable third parties—duty to warn).

The client's thoughts to "just end things" may be an indicator of suicide risk. The social worker should FIRST assess the degree of risk that is present to determine whether the client is safe without use of the medication and can wait to discuss his concerns with his psychiatrist at a future appointment or needs to be treated immediately, voluntarily or involuntarily.

Knowledge Area

Unit II—Intervention Processes and Techniques for Use Across Systems (Content Area); Biopsychosocial History and Collateral Data (Competency); The Indicators and Risk Factors of the Client's/Client System's Danger to Self and Others (KSA)

If this answer was missed, social workers need the rationale for the correct response choice in order to identify the need to review materials related to intervention planning, which is the content area being assessed. Specifically, this question focused on determining competency with regard to assessment methods and techniques related to identifying indicators of client danger to self or others (KSA). Reviewing the risk factors and signs associated with suicide would be a useful place to start. In addition, refined literature searches on behavioral, emotional, and psychological warning signs would produce more targeted information to fill this information gap.

Most practice tests will not help direct social workers toward these resources as they do not provide the ASWB content areas, competencies, and KSAs being tested. They also do not give valuable information on the topics as a way for social workers to understand the rationales for the correct answers and why the others are incorrect.

Second, practice tests rarely explicitly identify the test-taking strategies that must be used in order to select the correct answers from the others provided. Even when rationales are provided on practice tests, the test-taking strategies that should be generalized to other questions are often not explicitly stated. This void makes it difficult for social workers to see problems that they may be having in problem solving, outside of content gaps.

For example, in the sample question, social workers must be keenly aware of the client's thoughts to "just end things" as delineated by quotation marks. These thoughts may be an indication of suicide risk.

There is also a qualifying word—FIRST—used, which is capitalized in the question. The use of this qualifying word indicates that more than one of the provided response choices may be correct, but selecting the one that precedes the others is what is being asked. When clients are potentially suicidal, social workers must FIRST assess for risk.

This tool was developed to assist social workers in identifying their knowledge gaps and difficulties in problem solving by providing critical information including the knowledge area being assessed and the test-taking strategies required in order to answer questions correctly.

Social workers should use this diagnostic practice test to identify:

- Question wording that is important to selecting correct answers
- Key social work concepts that are being assessed
- Useful problem-solving strategies and themes
- Mistakes in logic
- Content areas, competencies, and/or KSAs that require additional study

This exam is not intended to be a study guide, but does contain important social work content related to the KSAs. This diagnostic practice test helps social workers who are struggling to find answers about what mistakes they are making and what they need to study more. It can be used in conjunction with existing study guides that provide an overview of needed social work material, such as the second edition of *Social Work ASWB® Advanced Generalist Exam Guide: A Comprehensive Guide for Success* by this author.

Social workers must understand their learning styles and use available resources to fill in existing content gaps through the use of visual, auditory, and/or hands-on materials. Most social work content is available for little or no cost. There is no need to purchase expensive products as there are many educational materials available for free. However, it is important that social workers make sure that these resources are rooted in the values and knowledge base of the profession, as well as produced by those providing legitimate instruction. There are no tricks or fast facts for the examination that can replace learning and understanding a topic. The application of material requires being able to relate it to various case scenarios or vignettes.

Recommendations for Using This Practice Test

Actual ASWB test results are based on 150 scored items and an additional 20 questions that are not scored because they are being piloted. These pilot items are intermixed with the scored ones and not distinguished in any way. Social workers never find out which ones are scored and which questions are being piloted.

In an effort to make this diagnosis as similar to the examination as possible, it contains 170 questions, the same number as the actual exam, proportionately distributed within the four domains—Human Development, Diversity, and Behavior in the Environment (39 questions); Intervention Processes and Techniques for Use Across Systems (54 questions); Intervention Processes and Techniques for Use With Larger Systems (31 questions); and Professional Relationships, Values, and Ethics (46 questions). These proportions mirror the distribution of questions across these domains on the actual ASWB® examination.

The best way for social workers to use this practice test is to:

- Complete it after you have studied yet are still feeling uncertain about problem areas
- Finish it completely during a 4-hour block of time as a way of gauging fatigue and length of time it will take to complete the actual examination
- Avoid looking up the answers until after you have finished completely

- Generate a listing of content areas in which you have experienced problems and use it as the basis of a study plan employing other source materials to further review the concepts
- Generalize the test-taking strategies for future use on the actual examination

This practice test is to be used as a diagnostic tool, so social workers should not worry about getting incorrect answers, but should view them as learning opportunities to avoid common pitfalls and pinpoint learning needs. On the actual ASWB examination, the number of questions that social workers need to correctly answer generally varies from 93 to 106 of the 150 scored items. Since this diagnostic practice test is 170 items, 20 questions would need to be randomly removed (4 from Unit I, 6 from Unit II, 4 from Unit III, and 6 from Unit IV) to determine if the overall number correct falls into this range.[1] Since many social workers who do not pass find themselves "just missing" these pass points, the value of identifying content gaps and difficulties in problem solving is tremendous because it can result in additional correct answers on the actual test.

1 Because different test-takers receive different questions, raw scores on the actual exam—the actual number of correctly answered questions—go through an "equating process" to make sure that those receiving more difficult questions are not placed at a disadvantage. Equating adjusts the number of items needed to answer correctly up or down depending on the difficulty levels. This diagnostic practice test has not gone through the equating process, which is why the number of correct answers needed to "pass" using ASWB standards cannot be determined.

Practice Test

170-Question Diagnostic Practice Test

1. Grounding techniques used with clients who are experiencing flashbacks of past traumatic events primarily aim to:

   A. Connect clients with the present so that they do not have additional negative effects associated with reliving their past traumatic experiences
   B. Help clients put their past traumatic experiences into perspective by discussing them in the context of all of their significant life events
   C. Assist clients to understand the triggers for their flashbacks so that they can be reduced or avoided in the future
   D. Teach clients coping skills to reduce the emotional, physical, social, and other impacts of trauma on personal well-being

2. A client tells a social worker that she has been communicating with her recently deceased son. The client states that she has an altar in her home at which she leaves daily food offerings. She is hopeful that her son will return to the home sometime in the future to visit her. In this situation, it is MOST important for the social worker to:

   A. Determine if the client is at risk for self-harm
   B. Assess the client for psychotic symptoms
   C. Understand the mourning rituals of the client's culture
   D. Identify coping strategies which can assist the client in dealing with her loss

3. Universality in group dynamics is BEST defined as the:

A. Expansion of personal knowledge and skills through hearing diverse perspectives
B. Release of strong feelings to others about past or present experiences
C. Enhanced self-concept which comes from helping others
D. Recognition that there are others with similar feelings, thoughts, and problems

4. A client reports feeling very frustrated by his wife's behavior. She becomes upset when he is quiet at the dinner table, but constantly criticizes him when he speaks. The client is experiencing a:

A. Paradoxical directive
B. Negative feedback loop
C. Double bind
D. Metacommunication

5. Which is NOT a goal of treatment when working with clients who have experienced complex trauma in childhood?
A. Removal of and protection from other sources of trauma
B. Recognition that recovery is possible and can occur quickly
C. Separation of residual problems from those which are uncontrollable
D. Acknowledgment that the trauma is real and undeserved

6. A social worker who provides counseling to clients in a job training program is charged with evaluating the program's effectiveness. The social worker finds that 80% of clients get jobs and keep them for a year after graduation. The social worker is assessing an:

A. Outcome
B. Impact
C. Output
D. Input

7. A client who was briefly admitted to the hospital after a panic attack is being discharged with a prescription for a benzodiazepine. Which of the following medications has been recommended?

A. Prolixin
B. Lithium

C. Prozac
D. Ativan

8. The primary goal of working with enmeshed families is:

A. Enhancing information exchange between members
B. Creating appropriate emotional bonds between members
C. Establishing clear boundaries between members
D. Improving communication channels between members

9. A school social worker is asked by a funder to conduct an evaluation of a youth services program. The evaluation is based on personal interviews with middle school children who are participating in the program. After explaining the nature, extent, duration, and risks of participation, what documentation will be needed in order for the social worker to ethically conduct the evaluation?

A. Written consent from the children's guardians
B. Written assent from the children and consent from their guardians
C. Written consent of the children
D. Written agency permission as the children's guardians already consented to service participation

10. Due to an agency closure, a social worker has referred a client to a new provider. With the client's consent, all relevant treatment information has been transferred. The social worker and client have also had several joint meetings with the new provider to discuss ongoing client needs. Several weeks later, the social worker learns that the client has had no contact with the new provider despite numerous outreach attempts. The social worker feels strongly that ongoing treatment is needed. The social worker should:

A. Seek consultation to determine if steps in the referral process inhibited continuity of treatment
B. Send a termination letter with the discharge plan and contact information of the new provider
C. Meet with the client to determine whether new issues have emerged that have prevented follow through
D. Contact the client about the risks involved with not following through with the referral

11. When social workers contract with supervisors who are not employed in their agencies, all of the following documents are necessary EXCEPT:

A. Contractual agreements between social workers, supervisors, and agencies
B. Authorization by agency decision makers allowing supervisors to provide clinical supervision
C. Monthly progress reports prepared by supervisors
D. Verification from regulatory bodies that disciplinary action has not been taken against supervisors

12. When clients have co-occurring mental health and Substance Use Disorders, which statement best describes the appropriateness of taking psychotropic medications?

A. Psychotropic medications should never be taken for co-occurring disorders as they are contraindicated.
B. Psychotropic medications can only be prescribed if clients understand the side effects.
C. Psychotropic medications are part of accepted treatment protocols for co-occurring disorders.
D. Psychotropic medications have not been adequately studied in clients with co-occurring disorders, making their appropriateness questionable.

13. Who has the ultimate responsibility for selecting models of social work supervision?

A. Administrators
B. Supervisees
C. Supervisors
D. Funders

14. When making a determination of the needed level of care for an older adult client who will be moving from home into a residential setting, it is MOST helpful to assess the ability to:

A. Adapt to life changes
B. Manage medical problems
C. Complete cognitive tasks
D. Perform activities of daily living

15. During an assessment, a social worker learns that a couple spends little time apart despite having problems which have caused them to seek treatment. The wife feels lonely when her husband travels for work as she has few friends outside the marriage. The husband states that he is "smothered," but gets jealous easily, causing him to contact his wife frequently throughout the day. The husband reports that he is often unhappy as his wife seems miserable, while the wife states that she is frustrated as she is just trying to find ways to make her husband more content. In order to address the problem, treatment should focus on:

A. Assisting the wife to develop a stronger sense of self-worth in the marriage
B. Finding out more about past intimate relationships of both the husband and wife
C. Helping the husband and wife to better understand each other's feelings
D. Differentiating roles and boundaries for the husband and wife in the relationship

16. A social worker has additional information on a client situation that he would like to add to the record. It helps clarify discussions which took place with the client during the last session. In order to handle this situation properly, the social worker should:

A. Ask his supervisor about agency protocol related to management of client records
B. Add the material to the previous case note as it clarifies material presented in the last session
C. Record the information as a new, separate entry in the record with a reason for its addition
D. Refrain from documenting it in the record as it was not collected during a session with the client

17. A client is referred to a social worker as she has been repeatedly hospitalized due to medication noncompliance. During the assessment, the client admits to frequently missing doses of her prescribed medication. This behavior has resulted in numerous inpatient stays which she complains are both costly and adversely impacting her quality of life. Which is the BEST question for the social worker to ask?

A. "Why haven't you been able to take your medication as prescribed?"
B. "Can you think of any advantage of having to stay in the hospital?"
C. "What are some of the reasons for skipping your medication?"
D. "How can I help to ensure that your medications are taken properly?"

18. When is family therapy best introduced in the treatment of clients with Substance Use Disorders?

A. Concurrently with clients' acknowledgments that substance use problems exist
B. When there is a recognition by clients that there is family dysfunction
C. Immediately after clients complete detoxification
D. Once clients are stable in their new patterns of behavior

19. During a session, a client discloses to a social worker that she was sexually abused by her father when she was an adolescent. The client has never confronted her father and does not want the social worker to disclose the information as there is no legal duty to report the abuse since the client is no longer a minor. The client reports that she sees the father regularly and he poses no current threat to children given a significant decline in functioning. In order to handle the situation ethically, the social worker should:

A. Arrange to meet with the father to formally assess the risk for re-offense
B. Seek supervision to determine whether to keep the information confidential
C. Report the suspected abuse to the child welfare agency
D. Respect the client's wishes by keeping the disclosure confidential

20. All of the following are appropriate reasons for seeking feedback from a client during the beginning phase of treatment EXCEPT:

A. Ensuring an understanding of what is going to happen during treatment
B. Focusing the treatment on a client's feelings and thoughts

C. Emphasizing that treatment is a mutual and reciprocal process
D. Conveying an interest in a client's views

21. The structured inequality of entire categories of people who have different access to social rewards as a result of their status, power, and wealth is known as:

A. Social stratification
B. Discrimination
C. Institutional malfeasance
D. Cultural difference

22. Which of the following documentation practices of supervisory sessions is MOST appropriate in social work?

A. Supervisory records should solely be maintained by supervisors as they are legally responsible for the delivery of services by supervisees.
B. No records should be kept by either supervisees or supervisors in order to maintain client confidentiality.
C. Supervisees must maintain records of supervision sessions for licensing and other regulatory bodies.
D. Supervisees and supervisors should maintain separate records of each session with both parties being able to access the other's notes as needed.

23. A newly hired social worker in an agency setting learns that he will simultaneously be supervised by more than one person. In order to minimize conflicts in this situation, the social worker should:

A. Develop a memorandum of understanding with the supervisors
B. Meet with the supervisors simultaneously at all times
C. Review the professional code of ethics with the supervisors
D. Understand the personal values and beliefs of the supervisors

24. The primary goal of court-ordered competency restoration is for clients to:

A. Identify ways to provide restitution for actions which have harmed others
B. Develop or regain ability to participate in legal proceedings

C. Serve legal sentences which have been imposed, but not served due to mental impairment
D. Identify legal standards which may apply to conduct based on mental disorders

25. Which of the following is NOT a condition often cited by courts that must be met in order for information to be considered privileged?

A. Harm caused by disclosure of confidential information outweighs the benefits.
B. Written records are kept documenting confidential material.
C. Parties involved in the communication assumed that it was confidential.
D. Confidentiality is an important element in the relationship.

26. A client tells a social worker that she is having problems with her teenage daughter's behavior. The daughter has begun to violate strict rules set in the home. The client, who is frustrated with this disobedience, states that she often does not speak to her child for days as punishment. The client does not understand why the girl questions the rules and does not behave as expected. Based on this description, which style of parenting is the client likely using?

A. Permissive
B. Authoritative
C. Uninvolved
D. Authoritarian

27. A couple seeks assistance from a social worker as they are having problems in their marriage. While they have been happily married for about 10 years, the wife complains that issues have arisen in the last year as her husband frequently telephones his mother after the couple argues. The wife states that she now feels uncomfortable around her mother-in-law and is worried that her mother-in-law has a negative opinion of her based on her husband's conversations. The husband insists that he has tried to work out issues directly with his wife, but needs his mother's opinion to successfully resolve his feelings. This family dynamic is known as:

A. Role reversal
B. Triangulation
C. Entropy
D. Oedipal repression

28. Delusions of reference are BEST defined as:

A. Insisting assertions are correct despite contradictory evidence
B. Becoming disoriented with regard to person, place, and/or time
C. Believing neutral stimuli or communications have personal meaning or messages
D. Attributing personal failure to external factors that cannot be controlled

29. Which statement is NOT true about couples' relationships using a developmental model?

A. Each developmental stage is more complex than the next.
B. There is an invariable order to the stages of development.
C. Each developmental stage is based on the preceding one.
D. Developmental stages may be skipped based on individual maturity.

30. A mandated client questions the confidentiality of specific documentation which is generated as part of treatment. The social worker should:

A. Suggest the client speak to legal counsel to determine whether this material is privileged
B. Review the court order with the client to determine what documents have to be released
C. Seek supervision and/or consultation to better understand specific confidentiality standards
D. Explain that consent will be obtained prior to generating any documents to maximize client confidentiality

31. What is considered best practice in treating pregnant women who are addicted to heroin?

A. Continued use of heroin under medical supervision
B. Discontinuation of all opioids immediately
C. Participation in intensive therapy and social support
D. Enrollment in a methadone maintenance program

32. A social worker employed at a nursing home notices that a client with Alzheimer's disease experiences heightened delirium during the evening hours with improvement during the day. This phenomenon is referred to as:

A. Folie à deux
B. Dementia
C. Sundowning
D. Neurodegeneration

33. A social worker is assisting a client to cope with depression after a stroke. The client reports having difficulty meeting his basic needs and suggests having his daughter come to the next session to discuss his current problems as she lives nearby and is supportive. In this situation, the social worker should:

A. Determine whether other family members or friends should be included in the meeting
B. Explain that including her in sessions is not allowed due to confidentiality standards and their limits
C. Ensure there is an agreement about the meeting purpose and what information will be shared
D. Identify what specific activities of daily living the client is having problems completing

34. A hospital social worker being supervised by a professional of a different discipline finds that she is having difficulty with a social work practice issue. In this situation, the social worker should:

A. Seek supervision from another social worker
B. Contact the hospital administrator to request a new supervisor
C. Consult self-help resources to identify possible solutions
D. Determine how the issue would be handled in the supervisor's discipline

35. Performance monitoring in social work agencies does NOT aim to:

A. Identify key aspects about how a program is operating
B. Determine whether program objectives are being met
C. Justify the need for service delivery to meet target problems
D. Suggest innovations based on unachieved results

36. A social worker is counseling a client who suffers from depression and has recently been hospitalized for a suicide attempt. During a therapy session, the social worker notices that the client appears significantly more cheerful than she has in past weeks. The client reports that she feels better generally without citing any specific reasons for her improved affect. In this situation, the social worker should FIRST:

A. Document the observations in the client's file
B. Conduct a suicide risk assessment of the client
C. Ask about changes which have taken place in the client's life in the last week
D. Praise the client for the progress that she has made since her hospital discharge

37. A client tells a social worker that she believes that a mother should always be available to assist her children and the primary caregiver in the home. However, she often has to work long hours at her job in order to advance her career. The client loves her work outside the home, but is distraught at her inability to parent in the manner that she desires. The client is experiencing role:

A. Reciprocity
B. Conflict
C. Complementarity
D. Confusion

38. A social worker charged with giving a case presentation provides background and demographic information on the client, the reason for the presentation, and the interventions delivered. The supervisor would consider this case presentation to be:

A. Inappropriate because a case presentation should never contain demographic information
B. Comprehensive if the theoretical basis for the intervention modality chosen is included
C. Incomplete because it did not include the nature of the problem
D. Acceptable as a basis for collaborative discussion because as all of the required elements are included

39. In order to promote economic justice, social workers should advocate for which taxation structure?

A. Proportional
B. Flat

C. Regressive
D. Progressive

40. The goal of attending behavior by social workers is to:

A. Determine the scope and severity of client problems
B. Assist clients to identify alternatives which result in change
C. Encourage clients to speak openly about their concerns
D. Explore barriers which have impeded client progress

41. What is the MOST critical factor in the selection of an appropriate intervention?

A. Available resources
B. Past service history
C. Agency setting
D. Presenting problem

42. A social worker, who is meeting with a 10-year-old boy and his mother notices what appear to be burns on the boy's legs. After the social worker asks about the markings, the mother provides an explanation that does not seem plausible. The social worker suspects that the burns resulted from physical abuse in the home. In this situation, the social worker should:

A. Contact authorities without disclosing the suspicions to the mother or child
B. Question the child alone to determine who is the perpetrator of the abuse
C. Ask the mother for evidence to support her explanation
D. Report the suspicions to the authorities with the mother and child present

43. A social worker receives a referral from a high school guidance counselor for a student who has received a full scholarship to college, but decided not to attend due to family responsibilities at home. Both school officials and the social worker feel that the student is making a mistake as it is unlikely that she will be able to attend college without the current scholarship opportunity. In order to effectively work with the student, the social worker must:

A. Understand the extent of the family responsibilities which prevent her attendance
B. Determine the short- and long-term career goals of the student

C. Acknowledge the differences in values that may exist between the student and school personnel
D. Identify the natural and other supports that are available to the student and her family

44. Which action is BEST supported when Gender Identity Disorder, Gender Incongruence, and Gender Dysphoria are viewed using a medical model?

A. Treating these disorders concurrently with medication and therapy
B. Eliminating them as mental health diagnoses
C. Exploring the mind–body connection associated with gender nonconformance
D. Screening for physical conditions that may be comorbid

45. When using a rational choice model of policy-making, social workers make decisions based on:

A. Minimizing disruption
B. Maximizing benefit
C. Ensuring continuity
D. Maintaining social structures

46. What is the PRIMARY distinction between defense and coping mechanisms?

A. Defense mechanisms are discrete reactions to traumatic stressors while coping mechanisms are continuous unconscious actions taken to deal with everyday life events.
B. Defense mechanisms fluctuate depending upon situational and personality factors while coping mechanisms are stable and rigid over time.
C. Defense mechanisms are maladaptive methods of addressing threatening events while coping mechanisms are based on healthy decisions aimed toward self-preservation.
D. Defense mechanisms are unconscious while coping mechanisms involve deliberate cognitive and emotional modifications.

47. In an initial meeting with a man who has been mandated to receive counseling due to severely beating his young son, a social worker explains the terms outlined in the court order and what can be expected in treatment. The social worker ends by asking the client,

"What do you think about what we have talked about so far?" The purpose of this question is to:

A. Determine the level of resistance that can be expected from the client
B. Identify whether the client is aware of the legal mandates placed upon him
C. Convey to the client that treatment is a mutual and reciprocal process
D. Assess the presence of denial with regard to the incident in question

48. Which prevention strategy is associated with community mobilization?

A. Secondary
B. Primary
C. Tertiary
D. Short term

49. In an initial meeting with a man who is seeking assistance after several arrests, a social worker determines that his reasoning is significantly impaired as he admits to using drugs before the meeting. The social worker wants to obtain the man's consent to find out more about his arrests and begin providing services aimed at assisting him to meet his basic needs. However, the social worker questions his ability to understand what she is asking and understand the information provided on the agency's consent form. The social worker should:

A. Waive the informed consent procedures since the man is in need of services now
B. Ask the man to sign the consent form, which will be reviewed with him at a later time
C. Use verbal informed consent procedures in lieu of written forms given his impairment
D. Arrange to meet the man at a later time when informed consent can be obtained

50. During an assessment, a client reveals a long history of substance abuse, but states that she has not used drugs in the last 15 years. She reports that she was sexually abused as both an adult and child, engaging in prostitution for many years. The client states that she has a strained relationship with her three children who she did not raise. Recent health problems have resulted in loss of ambulation, requiring her to use a wheelchair when leaving the house. The client reports that she has become isolated and unable to meet her friends due to issues with transportation. Not seeing her friends has resulted in her feeling worthless and not important to anyone. The client feels that having dinner with her friends as she did in the past would help decrease her feelings of insignificance. What will be important in establishing the measureable target for this objective?

A. Finding out the frequency of contact in her premorbid functioning
B. Identifying available resources for accessible transportation
C. Determining the impact of the poor relationships with her children on her current feelings
D. Assessing the magnitude of her hopelessness and depression

51. When using problem-oriented recording, social workers should put the client problem list:

A. In a separate secure location than the client case record
B. On a separate page within the client case record
C. Integrated within the progress notes in the client case record
D. At the conclusion of the assessment narrative in the client case record

52. Which of the following is NOT associated with reductions in emotional distress due to caregiving?

A. Transition of the person requiring care into a nursing home
B. Death of the person requiring care
C. Improvement in activities of daily living of the person requiring care
D. Recovery from illness which impeded functioning of the person requiring care

53. In written reports, subjective opinions of social workers must be:

A. Omitted so that documents only contain factual information
B. Differentiated from objective data collected
C. Limited to positive strengths and resources of clients
D. Approved by clients prior to submission

54. Which is NOT a core function in social work advocacy?

A. Development
B. Representation
C. Mobilization
D. Empowerment

55. A client who is homosexual tells a social worker that he is very distressed over his sexual attractions toward other men. His shame has prevented him from disclosing his sexual orientation to others in his family. He has low self-esteem and appears distraught. The client feels that he will not be accepted by others. In assisting the client to formulate treatment goals, the social worker should:

A. Role model helpful methods to discuss his sexual orientation with family members and others
B. Complete a suicide risk assessment
C. Help the client understand the effects of internalized homophobia on his feelings
D. Explore the client's past relationship with his family to better understand his concerns

56. A social worker receives a counseling referral for a student who is getting a social work degree at a local university. The social worker teaches a course in the program, but has not had the student in class. In order to handle the situation ethically, the social worker should:

A. Determine how the student learned about the social worker in order to evaluate the appropriateness of the referral
B. Meet with the student to assess whether there are any problems which could interfere with the student's ability to appropriately practice in the field
C. Inform the student that services cannot be provided given the potential for a conflict of interest
D. Refer the student to a colleague who has experience treating mental health professionals who are impaired

57. Which attribute is NOT a negative symptom of Schizophrenia?

A. Diminished feelings of pleasure in everyday life
B. Experiencing sensory experiences in the absence of a stimulus

C. Difficulty beginning and sustaining activities
D. Reduced speaking

58. When a social worker is meeting with a court-ordered client for the first session, the client appears apprehensive about discussing mandated services. This behavior is MOST likely an indication of the client's:

A. Fear of having information shared with those in the criminal justice system
B. Unwillingness to change the behavior which caused the current problems
C. Resentment toward not being given a choice about service provision
D. Lack of understanding about the services which must be provided

59. A social worker has been asked by a city council to engage in social planning aimed at addressing youth violence. In order for the effort to be effective, the social worker must:

A. Review the outcomes of current policies and programs aimed to address the issue
B. Outline incremental steps to bring about change with clear objectives
C. Understand the causes of the problem as defined by the city council
D. Ensure that members of the community are decision makers in the process

60. A social worker who is treating a client with Binge Eating Disorder asks the client to engage in self-monitoring by writing down what is eaten and any triggers of excessive food intake. Which practice method is MOST likely being used by the social worker?

A. Task-centered treatment
B. Cognitive behavioral therapy
C. Narrative therapy
D. Crisis intervention

61. Hegemony within society is BEST defined as the:

A. Ability of diverse cultures to work toward common goals
B. Power of one group to lead and dominate other groups

C. Discrimination based on gender norms that promote masculine identities
D. Universal rejection of practices which do not value all people as equal

62. Which statement is TRUE about clients who have been diagnosed with Borderline Personality Disorder?

A. They are less likely than those without the disorder to be childhood neglect or abuse victims.
B. They are at greater risk of suicide as they get older.
C. They usually show little improvement in social and occupational functioning over time.
D. They frequently do not meet the full criteria for the disorder if assessed a decade after the first diagnosis.

63. A supervisor is reviewing a social worker's case records for a client who has been receiving services for a long time. The supervisor finds documentation related to the need for services, goals, and activities. The supervisor determines that the case recording is insufficient as it does not contain information on:

A. Diagnoses
B. Outcomes
C. Discharge plans
D. Demographic characteristics

64. According to the professional code of ethics, a social worker who is ordered to release information without a client's consent, and such disclosure would cause harm to a client, must do all of the following actions EXCEPT:

A. Request that the court withdraw the order
B. Minimize releasing harmful information by redacting sensitive material
C. Advocate to limit the court order as narrowly as possible
D. Promote that the records be maintained under seal

65. Which statement BEST supports the need for professional development of social workers?

A. Staying well-informed of social work issues and trends makes social workers more competitive in the job market.
B. Government reforms require social workers to be knowledgeable about changes in funding and reporting requirements.

C. New research provides social workers with information that can impact the use of interventions in practice.
D. Many licensing boards require social workers to take continuing education courses in order to obtain or maintain professional credentials.

66. What is the most significant contributor to cultural convergence?

A. Education
B. Globalization
C. Marriage
D. Advocacy

67. When completing intake paperwork, a client identifies as "Latinx." The social worker should consider use of this term to mean that the client:

A. Identifies with a demographic age cohort of people who were born in the mid-1960s
B. Rejects his or her ethnic heritage of origin
C. Values gender identities that are not strictly binary
D. Identifies with his or her Latin American origin or descent, but is not Spanish speaking

68. A social worker is terminating with an adolescent who has shown marked improvement in her anxiety. She received counseling for several months to address school absenteeism which resulted from her excessive nervousness. During the termination process, the social worker learns that the client will be going to a new school due to redistricting. In this situation, the social worker should:

A. Conduct an assessment to determine whether termination is still appropriate
B. Acknowledge progress that the client has made during treatment
C. Contact student services at the new school to see if follow-up services are available
D. Identify relaxation techniques which can be used to reduce her anxiety in the future

69. A social worker who wants to afford a client the greatest confidentiality protections should store psychotherapy notes:

A. In a section of the client's file so that they will not get disconnected from other key documents
B. Separate from the rest of the client's medical or clinical record with restricted access
C. At home as they are intended only for the social worker's use
D. According to agency policy so that administrative standards provide additional client protections

70. In therapeutic relationships, when should termination with clients be discussed?

A. Upon intake when initially meeting with clients
B. After goal attainment has occurred
C. During the last meetings with clients
D. Just prior to goal achievement when substantial progress is seen

71. A social worker receives a referral for a child with a Neurodevelopmental Disorder who is having trouble in school. The social worker's goal is to identify appropriate learning opportunities within the school setting that can help address areas of delay. In order to effectively work with this child, the social worker will need knowledge of:

A. Child growth
B. School policy
C. Past academic performance
D. Family supports

72. In a sociogram, the intensity of interpersonal relationships is indicated by:

A. Types of lines
B. Arrows which may point one or both ways
C. Shading of circles
D. Shapes of diagrams

73. A client who has a stable, well-paying job tells a social worker that she plans to quit in the coming weeks. The client states that she is miserable, but is not able to specify what she does not like about her current employment. The social worker feels that the client is making a poor decision which could have serious ramifications for her financial well-being. In order to handle this situation appropriately, the social worker must FIRST:

A. Acknowledge the client's right to make her own decisions about her life
B. Assess whether there have been changes in the client's life recently which are impacting on this decision
C. Warn the client about the potential consequences of her decision so she has all necessary information to make an informed choice
D. Assist the client with looking for another job quickly so she is able to meet her basic financial needs

74. A client with brain damage due to Korsakoff syndrome often tells stories based on false memories of events which never occurred. This disorder is known as:

A. Hallucinations
B. Denial
C. False memory syndrome
D. Confabulation

75. Current guidelines concerning social workers' duty to disclose confidential information without client consent to protect third parties from harm were initially established in:

A. Case law
B. Constitutional law
C. Regulatory law
D. Executive order

76. When a social worker experiences a value conflict with a client, the social worker must:

A. Refer the client to another social worker
B. Seek supervision to identify the reasons for the difference in beliefs
C. Respect the client's right to self-determination
D. Acknowledge the impact of this conflict on the problem-solving process

77. When working with involuntary clients, all of the following actions by social workers maximize client self-determination EXCEPT:

A. Setting goals and objectives established by clients in addition to mandated ones
B. Acknowledging clients' feelings related to loss of control and lack of choice
C. Allowing clients to choose methods and models of intervention to address identified problems
D. Advocating to change court orders for mandates which clients believe are inappropriate

78. Intersectionality is BEST defined as:

A. Psychological crises that result when cultural biases erode the self-image of those who are not in the majority
B. Widespread negative impacts in social, emotional, psychological, and economic life domains due to discrimination
C. Interdependent forms of privilege and oppression resulting from different social locations, power relations, and experiences
D. Conflicting ethnic and racial values which are rooted in differences in beliefs and customs that undermine cultural pluralism

79. A social worker receives a referral for a young woman who was recently arrested after assaulting someone on the street. At intake, she reports being surprised that she got into a fight, but admitted that she was drinking at the time of the incident. In describing her childhood, she uses a flat affect when mentioning severe physical and sexual abuse at the hands of her mother's boyfriend between ages 4 and 15. The client states that her abuse does not affect her life now, but she is unable to answer specific questions about the abuse due to being unable to remember much about the time period. The client is likely experiencing which of the following responses to trauma?

A. Excessive guilt
B. Intrusive thoughts and memories
C. Depression
D. Dissociation

80. A social worker employed in a senior center is contacted by an adult child of a client who is concerned about the client's decision not to move into an assisted living facility despite a doctor's recommendation. The adult child is worried about her parent's safety and would like the social worker to help facilitate the move. In this situation, the social worker should:

A. Encourage the client to move due to medical and safety concerns
B. Evaluate the client's competence to make decisions about life matters
C. Explain to the adult child that the social worker must support the client's decision
D. Contact the doctor to find out why the recommendation was made

81. Family-centered social work practice is preferred over individual counseling when:

A. Boundaries within the family structure are continually being violated.
B. A family member lacks commitment to address critical issues.
C. Violence is being perpetrated by one family member against another.
D. Stabilization is needed for a family member in crisis due to substance abuse and/or psychosis.

82. When clients sue social workers for malpractice, which statement BEST describes social workers' ability to release information?

A. No information can be released as the client is not a danger to self or others.
B. All client files can be released as the client has waived all rights to confidentiality.
C. Only records which the client reviews and approves can be released.
D. Client information relevant to the legal issues may be released to the court.

83. A social worker is conducting an assessment with a client who has been living with a chronic disease for many years. The client has been able to manage the symptoms of her illness successfully with no reported negative impact on her daily life. She has just learned that she will need to begin a complicated medication regimen in the coming weeks in order to slow the illness's progression. The client is very worried about ensuring that the drug administration does not adversely affect her current routine. The client's needs can BEST be met by the provision of:

A. Case management
B. Psychoeducation
C. Behavioral intervention
D. Psychotherapy

84. A social worker is hired by an agency to provide consultation aimed at reducing high client dropout rates. According to the funder, a greater proportion of this agency's clients leave services when compared with clients of similar providers. What is the source of the social worker's authority when making recommendations?

A. Agency employment
B. Funding mandates
C. Professional expertise
D. Organizational structure

85. A mother seeks treatment with a social worker due to her 9-year-old daughter's behavior. The child has refused to go to school due to unwillingness to be separated from her mother and is falling behind in her schoolwork. The situation has caused stress within the family and the woman reports that she will likely be fired due to being preoccupied with her daughter's problems while at work. The mother feels hopeless and frustrated. The social worker's MOST appropriate intervention is to:

A. Suggest that the woman explain the reasons for her recent behavior to her employer
B. Acknowledge that hopelessness and frustration are common in these situations
C. Teach the woman ways to cope while addressing the causes of her daughter's behavior
D. Recommend that the woman speak to the school about providing in-home instruction

86. Which of the following findings on social development is the BEST justification for mainstreaming of children with unique learning needs?

A. Peer interactions such as smiling, touching, and babbling occur at a very early age.
B. Peer relationships depend on inhibiting impulses and understanding cause–effect relationships.
C. Peer acceptance is affected by family support, parental interactions, and sibling relationships.
D. Peer friendships are protective factors from later psychological problems and better self-image.

87. Which of the following statements described the need for client consent for using electronic search engines to gather client information?

A. Client consent is never needed when using electronic search engines to gather client information.
B. Client consent is always needed except in emergency circumstances when searches may help protect clients or others at risk.
C. Client consent is always needed when using electronic search engines to gather client information.
D. Client consent is never needed as social workers should not use electronic search engines to gather client information.

88. A social worker is observing to determine if the frequency of a high-rate behavior has declined due to operant conditioning. What is the MOST significant concern about using this approach?

A. Observation is a very costly method of data collection.
B. The client is in the presence of the social worker for part of the day.
C. Some behaviors do not lend themselves to observational study.
D. There are ethical issues with the use of punishment to extinguish behaviors.

89. A social worker is meeting with a third-grade boy who is struggling in school. Despite his poor grades, his parents seem disinterested in assisting him with his schoolwork. He is frustrated by his academic performance, but does not know how to do better. What psychosocial problem is the boy MOST likely to experience if this situation is not addressed?

A. Mistrust
B. Isolation
C. Guilt
D. Inferiority

90. Which of the following consent procedures BEST informs clients of the nature and expectations of the social worker/client relationship, including confidentiality?

A. Discussing written policies throughout the problem-solving process
B. Providing clients with copies of all signed written consent and other forms
C. Asking clients to sign written consent forms prior to initial meetings
D. Ensuring that written policies are updated regularly and signed by clients

91. In object relations theory, what occurs when two contradictory thoughts or feelings cannot be tolerated simultaneously, causing only one to be recognized at a time?

A. Isolation
B. Resistance
C. Splitting
D. Rapprochement

92. A member whose behavior aims to draw attention away from addiction in the family unit is known as the:

A. Enabler
B. Mascot
C. Scapegoat
D. Lost child

93. The acknowledgment that various problems, needs, goals, and values of clients require different helping relationships and methods of intervention is known as:

A. Individualization
B. Self-determination

C. Mutuality
D. Reciprocity

94. A school social worker learns that the academic needs of a new student can be adequately met in either the regular classroom with additional supports or a separate resource room for students who require special assistance. The parents would like their child to remain with his friends in the classroom, but the guidance counselor feels strongly that the student would be better served in a resource room for at least part of the day. In this situation, the social worker should:

A. Meet with the child to determine whether there is a preference about the settings offered
B. Review the academic record to better understand the guidance counselor's recommendation
C. Suggest ways to maintain friendships while the child receives instruction in a resource room
D. Advocate for the child to receive any supports needed in the regular classroom

95. A hospital social worker is asked by his supervisor to serve on a task group with representatives from all departments. A decision is proposed which the social worker feels will limit the self-determination of clients. There is strong support for the decision so it will easily get the votes needed for approval. In this situation, the social worker should:

A. Voice support for the proposal since it represents the opinions of the group's majority
B. Refrain from voting to signify some concern over the proposed action
C. Speak to his supervisor about objections to the group's decision
D. Vote against the proposition after explaining the reason for the concern

96. A social worker in a hospital emergency department meets with an elderly client who demonstrates significant memory and cognitive loss. In order to differentiate whether these impairments are due to Major Neurocognitive Disorder or Delirium, the social worker should determine the:

A. Symptom progression from first onset
B. Severity of memory loss

C. Family history of neurologic or organic disorders
D. Impact on all areas of adaptive functioning

97. When completing a functional behavioral assessment, a social worker should FIRST:

A. Determine why an intervention is needed now
B. Identify antecedents which are hypothesized to cause the behavior
C. Define a problem behavior in measurable terms
D. Explain the limits of confidentiality which govern service delivery

98. Which is NOT a threat to social workers having shared power with clients?

A. Social workers often can see issues more objectively than clients.
B. Most services are delivered in agency-based settings.
C. Clients may want social workers to take responsibility for change processes.
D. Shared power challenges the claims of expert power.

99. A client is having trouble achieving a treatment goal, so the social worker breaks it down into small successive steps and rewards the client after achieving each one. This behavioral technique is known as:

A. Biofeedback
B. Modeling
C. Shaping
D. Flooding

100. During the stages of grief and mourning, hope is:

A. Only present during bargaining before depression and acceptance occur
B. Strong initially, but fades by the end of the process, leading to depression
C. Evident throughout the entire process
D. Absent initially, which explains the presence of denial and isolation

101. A social worker recently terminated with a client who made substantial progress in managing her anxiety. The former client has been asked by her church to facilitate a peer support group for others who have experienced similar problems. The former client is nervous about this request and asks the social worker to be a cofacilitator. The social worker feels that the former client would benefit from this peer interaction. In this situation, the social worker should:

A. Assist with helping prepare for, but not cofacilitate, the group
B. Help cofacilitate for several sessions until the former client feels more comfortable
C. Agree to cofacilitate as the experience will be beneficial to the former client
D. Encourage participation while declining the request to cofacilitate

102. A school social worker who is facilitating a group for adolescents notices that one member who recently immigrated with her family from Japan interacts very little during most of the sessions. In order to meet this client's needs, the social worker should:

A. Suggest that meeting individually may be more appropriate to facilitate expression of feelings
B. Determine class participation to see if this behavior occurs in other settings
C. Create ongoing varied opportunities for interaction by all group members
D. Ask for input in establishing rules which govern group participation

103. During an initial session, a client appears reluctant to speak and states, "I am not sure if this is going to work out." In this situation, it is BEST for the social worker to:

A. Ignore the comment as the feelings will likely subside over time
B. Clarify what can be expected, including the roles of the social worker and client
C. Use this comment as an opening to address any hesitancy as a therapeutic issue
D. Ask about other situations in which the client has felt this way

104. A young man who has a criminal history for violent acts later becomes an acclaimed boxer—which of the following defense mechanisms is the young man MOST likely using?

A. Introjection
B. Incorporation
C. Sublimation
D. Undoing

105. Conversion is BEST defined as a:

A. Therapeutic process aimed at turning negative thoughts directed at others into positive ones
B. Reaction to trauma which limits emotional growth and development throughout the life course
C. Defense mechanism in which a repressed urge is expressed by disturbance of a body function
D. Strategy used in family therapy to get consensus among those with divergent viewpoints

106. A social worker is seeing an elderly woman who has recently experienced declining health due to aging and loss due to the deaths of several close friends. She has missed several appointments due to illness and states that she is not participating in many of her prior community activities as she is too tired to do so. In order to determine if the client is in crisis, the social worker should:

A. Review her most recent physical evaluation to determine the severity of her health problems
B. Refer her for neuropsychiatric testing to identify mental disorders which may be present
C. Conduct an interview with her to gather subjective data on recent life events and changes
D. Obtain information from collaterals to get a more comprehensive understanding of her current functioning

107. A client who is recently divorced shares with a social worker that she has recently submitted information to an Internet dating site with the hopes of forming a new romantic relationship. After seeing her posting, the social worker is concerned about the dangers associated with some of the information disclosed. The social worker should:

A. Inform the client about the risks and possible consequences
B. Keep silent about the issue in order to respect the client's self-determination
C. Advise the client to avoid Internet dating sites as a way to meet suitable partners
D. Identify boundaries as a topic to discuss in treatment

108. Emotional or psychological trauma is MOST significantly associated with events that:

A. Occurred in adulthood
B. Happened unexpectedly without warning
C. Were anticipated due to existing antecedents
D. Could have been prevented

109. A family seeks counseling as their adolescent daughter recently ran away from home. During the first session, the daughter states her parents do not care about her well-being and are overly concerned with meeting their job demands. She feels that all interactions with them are contentious and end in arguments. The mother admits to feeling overwhelmed by daily life and disconnected from both her husband and her daughter at times. The father feels that the root of the problem is that the daughter has been given too much control in the household. Using a structural family therapy approach, the social worker should:

A. Gather information on how the childhoods of both parents influenced their parenting styles
B. Assess whether the current state of the mother requires immediate attention due to a risk of self-harm
C. Instruct the daughter to discuss with her parents a current concern that she has that she feels they are not addressing
D. Determine when each family member's concerns began in an attempt to determine the etiology of the problem

110. When social workers engage in peer supervision, the PRIMARY method for learning is:

A. Modeling
B. Summative evaluation

C. Positive reinforcement
D. Formative feedback

111. A social worker is developing a contract with a client who has been mandated for treatment. All of the following actions by the social worker aim to promote the client's self-determination EXCEPT:

A. Explaining directives contained in the court order to the client
B. Advocating for clinically appropriate modifications to mandates based on client wishes
C. Eliciting input from the client about the methods of intervention to be used
D. Setting goals that the client wants to pursue

112. At the conclusion of the sixth session, a client states that her attorney would like to speak to the social worker. When the social worker asks about the nature of the request, the client states that she does not know and the social worker will need to contact the attorney to find out. The social worker should:

A. Contact the attorney immediately with the assurance that all legal matters will be discussed with the client in future sessions
B. Decline the request until the social worker's role is clarified and the client's expectations are better understood
C. Explore with the client why she is not being forthcoming about the reasons for the attorney request
D. Arrange a time for the client to be present during the social worker–attorney conversation to ensure that the client is aware of what is disclosed

113. During the first session, a client blames the recent termination from his job for many of his other problems. He reports that his girlfriend ended their relationship as she was angry that he was fired. He also had to move in with a relative as he could no longer afford his rent. He reports feeling like a failure and does not know "how things got so bad." The social worker should respond by:

A. Assisting him to find another job as his self-worth appears closely tied to his unemployment
B. Identifying which problem is the top priority so it can be targeted for immediate assistance

C. Assuring him that many people lose their jobs and experience similar feelings
D. Exploring the reasons for his termination in order to get at the root cause of the problem

114. A social worker, who is counseling a couple, learns that the husband has been recently diagnosed with a rare medical condition that is being treated with medication. The wife reports that this medication causes dramatic mood changes, which she has witnessed. Due to a lack of knowledge about this medical condition and the medication prescribed, the social worker contacts a physician for consultation. The social worker's action is based on which of the following concepts?

A. Interdisciplinary collaboration
B. Coordinated service delivery
C. Team building
D. Standard of care

115. Which of the following statements is TRUE about the blending and braiding of resources in human service programs?

A. Federal categorical limitations make blending and braiding of resources difficult to administer.
B. Blending of resources is preferred by funders over braiding due to administrative efficiencies.
C. Braiding of resources is seen as advantageous by administrators due to ease of implementation.
D. Blending and braiding of resources allows collective reporting on how monies are spent overall.

116. A client reports that she is very upset by her 17-year-old daughter's behavior. She has not been completing her homework and is showing up late for her classes. The client reports that she recently took away her daughter's cell phone until her behavior changes. Which of the following behavioral techniques is the mother using?

A. Positive reinforcement
B. Negative reinforcement
C. Positive punishment
D. Negative punishment

117. When an agency receives a single disbursement for services provided by two or more providers during a single episode of care or over a specific period of time, the payment methodology is known as:

A. Capitation
B. Fee-for-service
C. Bundled payment
D. Shared savings

118. A client who is planning on ending her marriage comes from a culture in which divorce is strictly prohibited. The client has a poor self-image due to years of feeling a duty to stay married despite being unhappy. In order to be most effective, the social worker should:

A. Use universalization when speaking with the client about her situation
B. Ensure that the client understands the consequences of her actions
C. Help the client identify the steps needed for her to achieve her goal
D. Explore why the client wants to end her marriage now

119. A social worker whose client engages in heavy alcohol consumption notices that he has confusion, problems with muscle coordination, drowsiness, and memory loss which persist even when he has not been drinking. These symptoms, which are associated with his alcoholism, are BEST treated with:

A. Thiamine injections
B. Cognitive rehabilitation
C. Physical therapy
D. Antipsychotic medications

120. A social worker is providing counseling to a client who is having trouble in her workplace. The client feels isolated as she does not have any meaningful collegial relationships in her job. The client, who is lesbian, feels that her support system is limited to her partner with whom she has been living for the past 2 years. At the end of a session, the client gives the social worker a hug while thanking her for understanding the situation. The social worker, who has a policy not to have physical contact with her clients, hesitates, which causes the client to accuse her of being homophobic. In this situation, the social worker should:

A. Ask the client why the action is being viewed as homophobic
B. Explain the reasons for the rule about not touching clients
C. Continue to hug the client after apologizing for the hesitation
D. Provide assurance that the response was not meant to be homophobic

121. A social worker is reviewing referral information for a new client which identifies him as xenophobic. In order to address this fear, services should focus on:

A. Exploring the benefits of his interaction with those who are younger
B. Educating him about the importance of injections, especially for required vaccinations
C. Managing the anxiety which results from his physical contact with others
D. Understanding his aversion to those from other countries and their cultures

122. A social worker spends long hours at her job and is feeling fatigued. She is assigned a new project by her supervisor which requires acquisition of both new knowledge and skills. While feeling overwhelmed when first given the assignment, the social worker believes that she will be successful in completing the job competently. The social worker is demonstrating:

A. Self-regulation
B. Self-care
C. Self-efficacy
D. Self-determination

123. In the provision of mental health counseling, the primary purpose of social workers' case notes is to:

A. Serve as documentation by which supervisors can evaluate worker performance and skill
B. Provide evidence of service receipt for reimbursement by third-party insurers

C. Ensure continuity of care as well as means by which to evaluate client progress
D. Comply with agency and regulatory requirements which exist to ensure service quality

124. The goal of a client with terminal cancer is to receive hospice services at home. Her health has deteriorated rapidly, but the social worker is having difficulty finding an appropriate provider due to the complexity of the client's medical condition and her current living situation. In order to meet the needs of the client, which social work value is most critical when intervening?

A. Dignity and worth of the person
B. Competence
C. Integrity
D. Social justice

125. A social worker at an outpatient treatment program observes a court-mandated client who is being treated for Alcohol Use Disorder become outraged during a group session when leniency for those arrested for addiction-related offenses is discussed. The client states that severe punishment, as opposed to treatment options, must be required. This behavior surprises the social worker as the client has repeatedly expressed his appreciation for being offered treatment in lieu of imprisonment. Based on this behavior, the social worker feels that the client is MOST likely using which of the following defense mechanisms?

A. Denial
B. Projection
C. Displacement
D. Reaction formation

126. When evaluating the effectiveness of treatment, which technique statistically controls on a post-hoc basis for differences between nonequivalent groups on outcomes of interest?

A. Random sampling
B. Case-mix adjustment
C. Interrater reliability
D. Descriptive analyses

127. A social worker is working with a client who is attending an adult medical day program. Staff report that her hygiene has deteriorated and she is increasingly disoriented. She has a visiting nurse coming to her home to administer her medications on the evenings when her adult son, with whom she lives, works. After a stroke several months ago, she began getting home-delivered meals. The client requires constant supervision while in the day program and the social worker is concerned about her current safety. Which collateral source will be MOST helpful in making this assessment?

A. The client's adult son
B. The client herself
C. The agency staff who are providing direct care and ancillary services
D. The client's physician who is prescribing her medications

128. Fee splitting is unethical in social work practice because it:

A. Represents a conflict of interest, which can adversely impact client care
B. Establishes rates, which do not consider what clients can afford to pay
C. Creates prohibited dual relationships, which are boundary violations
D. Occurs without client consent, which is mandatory for all treatment decisions

129. A mother and her adult son with developmental disabilities meet with a social worker for assistance in helping the young man move into his own apartment. While both the mother and son would like this move to occur, they have concerns as he will need support to meet his daily living needs, as well as attend to ongoing medical issues. The social worker recommends a multidisciplinary team approach to service planning. The FIRST step in this process would be to:

A. Complete a biopsychosocial history so that team members have adequate background information for planning
B. Determine whether there are professionals known to the family who would be good team members

C. Develop a timeline for the problem-solving process to help structure the team's decision making
D. Identify areas of anticipated support to ensure that individuals with needed skills and perspectives are identified for the team

130. A former client contacts a social worker and requests a copy of her record. The social worker asks about the reason for the request, but no explanation is provided. While the social worker is not worried about the client seeing the information in the record, the social worker is concerned about the client sharing it with others as it contains sensitive information about the client's history. The social worker should:

A. Send a copy of the entire record to the client
B. Meet with the client to assess why she has not explained how the record will be used
C. Remove material that may be harmful to the client if shared and send the remaining information
D. Ask the client to put her request and the reason for it in writing prior to making a decision

131. Which approach focuses on well-being and happiness through cultivation of meaningful experiences?

A. Psychoanalysis
B. Positive psychology
C. Behaviorism
D. Psychoeducation

132. Which statement BEST describes the difference between values and ethics?

A. Values are unwritten personal belief systems while ethics are written rules or regulations that guide professional behavior.
B. Values are principles which guide behavior while ethics dictate whether this behavior is appropriate based on a moral code of conduct.
C. Values are customs that are considered desirable by individuals while ethics are collective practices embraced by larger groups or societies.
D. Values are individual standards of conduct which are stable over time while ethics vary based on cultural changes and advances.

133. Magical thinking is a characteristic of which cognitive developmental stage?

A. Concrete operations
B. Preoperational
C. Formal operations
D. Sensorimotor

134. Which criteria must be present for a social worker to diagnose a child with Gender Dysphoria?

A. Dislike of one's sexual anatomy
B. Sexual interest in those of the same gender
C. Desire to be the other gender or belief that one is the other gender
D. Preference for clothing and playmates of the other gender

135. Which of the following statements is TRUE about the inclusion of assessment and service provision descriptions in client discharge plans?

A. Reasons for admission should not be incorporated, but descriptions of treatment must be contained in client discharge plans.
B. Both reasons for admission and services provided must be included in client discharge plans.
C. Client discharge plans should include reasons for admission, but not descriptions of treatment provided.
D. Neither reasons for admission nor services provided should be included in client discharge plans.

136. Which nonverbal technique used in social work practice aims to primarily gain rapport at the unconscious level?

A. Questioning
B. Clarifying
C. Mirroring
D. Reframing

137. A counseling agency charges the same amount to all clients enrolled in its group treatment program. Given a recent bequest, the board of directors proposes providing a standard subsidy to all group therapy clients to reduce their fees by a set amount. A social worker in the agency advocates for these subsidies to be proportional, with clients having the lowest incomes receiving the highest subsidies. The social worker argues that some clients can afford to pay the actual cost while those who have lower incomes cannot and should receive the subsidies. The social worker's recommendation for resource allocation promotes:

A. Equity
B. Sustainability
C. Equality
D. Fidelity

138. A client expresses that she has romantic feelings toward a social worker who has been providing counseling for several months. To appropriately deal with the situation, the social worker should FIRST:

A. Ignore the client's comments as they are not relevant to treatment
B. Refer the client to another social worker to maintain appropriate boundaries
C. Explore underlying reasons for the feelings with the client
D. Inform the client that these feelings are common in helping relationships

139. A social worker is interested in determining the impact of culture and race on self-image using an ethnographic approach. The BEST method for this inquiry would be:

A. Statistical regression
B. Participant observation
C. Experimental design
D. Self-administered questionnaires

140. Unconditional positive regard is supported by the social work core value of:

A. Importance of human relationships
B. Self-determination
C. Dignity and worth of the person
D. Integrity

141. In helping relationships, who has the responsibility to ensure that integrity is maintained at all times?

A. Social workers exclusively
B. Social workers and clients equally
C. Clients exclusively
D. Primarily social workers with input by clients

142. At which age does object permanence typically develop?

A. 18 months
B. 8 months
C. 3 years
D. 5 years

143. A social worker is providing counseling to a couple who are experiencing communication problems in their marriage. During a session, the wife becomes angry as she states that she never gets to speak or express her opinions. The social worker calls attention to an observation that the wife has done almost all of the talking during the weekly sessions to date. The social worker is using which of the following interviewing techniques?

A. Confrontation
B. Interpretation
C. Universalization
D. Clarification

144. A client tells a social worker that he needs help managing his anxiety as it is interfering with both his professional and personal lives. He states that he has had problems with anxiety throughout his life, but it has become worse lately. The client reports being overwhelmed and wanting to change, but not knowing where to start. The social worker should FIRST:

A. Explore options for treatment including relaxation techniques to provide immediate relief
B. Examine what informal or formal treatments have been tried in the past to address the symptoms
C. Provide cognitive behavioral therapy to replace unhelpful thoughts occurring in fearful situations
D. Determine any risk for self-harm due to the report of being overwhelmed

145. A social worker has been working with an 8-year-old girl for over a year. The client's mother, who is going through a divorce, states that she is going to ask if the social worker can be appointed to supervise visits with the father. The need for supervised visitation has already been determined by the court. The mother feels strongly that the social worker is the best choice given the presence of a strong relationship with the child. The social worker should:

A. Inform the mother that this additional role would not be possible
B. Determine the child's feelings about the mother's request since the child is the client
C. Request to meet with the father to determine if he feels comfortable with the arrangement
D. Explore with the mother the impacts of the divorce on the child

146. When engaging in reflective listening, it is critical for social workers to:

A. Think about what should be said next to move clients through the therapeutic process
B. Reconstruct what clients are thinking and feeling through verbal and nonverbal methods
C. Direct discussion toward nonthreatening topics when clients become emotional
D. Help clients understand social workers' responsibilities in the problem-solving process

147. The primary goal of interdisciplinary service collaboration is to:

A. Reduce duplication in order to avoid wasting scarce resources
B. Address the holistic needs of clients across life domains
C. Develop innovative strategies for addressing social problems
D. Increase effectiveness of assistance provided to clients

148. A 22-year-old woman meets with a social worker due to her excessive fear of heights. During the assessment, the client states that she avoided climbing trees and other activities which raised her above the ground when she was a child. Recently, she has been unable to fly in planes and drive over bridges, causing her to be restricted in her travels. The client is very upset as she spends a great deal of time worrying about whether she will need to cross a bridge, causing her to sweat, breath heavily, and feel anxious throughout the day. During a recent visit with her physician, she was prescribed medication for this condition. Which medication was MOST likely recommended?

A. Mellaril
B. Ativan
C. Risperdal
D. Tegretol

149. A social worker formats client case records into distinct sections representing all relevant information, issues to be addressed, and activities that need to be undertaken, respectively. Which model of case recording is this social worker MOST likely using?

A. Narrative
B. SOAP
C. DAP
D. APIE

150. A social worker is approached by a group therapy client who is concerned about the confidentiality of information that he would like to share during the next session. The social worker should:

A. Inform the client that information disclosed during meetings will be kept private unless it involves danger to himself or others
B. Ask the client about the nature of the disclosure so that appropriate guidance can be given as to whether it should be shared
C. Advise the client not to disclose sensitive information as there may be repercussions associated with sharing it with others
D. Inform the client that confidentiality cannot be guaranteed as group members are not legally prohibited from disclosing information that is learned

151. A client has been approved for six sessions with a social worker by his insurance company. In formulating treatment goals, the client articulates changes which the social worker does not feel are achievable in the time frame approved. The social worker should:

A. Inform the client that more feasible goals must be developed
B. Advocate for the insurance company to authorize additional sessions

C. Respect the client's right to self-determination by working toward the client's desired changes
D. Identify other issues which may be of concern to the client

152. A social worker is working in a cultural community in which bartering is the accepted practice for obtaining goods and services. In order for the social worker to accept goods from clients for the provision of services, all of the following criteria have to be met EXCEPT:

A. Clients must demonstrate that these arrangements will not be detrimental.
B. Bartering must be essential for the provision of services.
C. Coercion must not be used in the negotiation of the arrangement.
D. Clients must initiate the request for bartering arrangements.

153. According to family systems theory, in what types of relationships does blame for the dynamics rest with specific individuals?

A. Parent–child
B. Polygamous
C. Abusive
D. Adulterous

154. A social worker who is seeing a client for the first time asks the client how she would like to be addressed. The social worker's action demonstrates:

A. Cultural sensitivity
B. Professional boundaries
C. Practitioner objectivity
D. Ethnocentrism

155. A social worker proposes a pilot program for youth with substance use problems in order to determine whether an intervention which has been highly effective with adults has similar results with children. The social worker wants to examine whether outcomes can be generalized to younger age groups before offering the service to all minors in the agency. The pilot program aims to address concerns about:

A. Measurement error
B. Internal validity

C. Reliability
D. External validity

156. Which of the following is MOST critical for successful engagement in interdisciplinary collaboration by social workers?

A. Developing conflict resolution skills which are not exclusionary
B. Leveraging individual resources to bring to the collaborative process
C. Remembering that collaboration is not needed for all decisions
D. Acknowledging that others may have different personal and professional values

157. A social worker is counseling a middle-age client who regrets spending most of his time during his adult life building a business. He blames this decision for preventing him from getting married and having children. The client would like to spend more time focused on hobbies that he abandoned due to his work schedule, but does not know how to make this change. This client appears to be struggling with which stage of psychosocial development?

A. Ego identity versus despair
B. Generativity versus stagnation
C. Industry versus inferiority
D. Initiative versus guilt

158. After social workers determine that ethical dilemmas exist, they should NEXT:

A. Seek supervision to determine which agency policies impact on the situation
B. Prioritize the ethical values which must be used to choose correct courses of action
C. Weigh the issues in light of key social work values and principles
D. Determine the root causes of the problems so that they can be eradicated

159. The most effective treatment for Alcohol Withdrawal is:

A. Psychopharmacology
B. Self-help group participation
C. Cognitive behavioral therapy
D. Family therapy

160. With regard to client privacy, privilege is BEST defined as the:

A. Legal rule that protects communications from compelled disclosure in court proceedings
B. Mandate to obtain written consent from clients when information is to be disclosed
C. Duty to report concerns of child abuse and neglect to appropriate authorities
D. Requirement to keep treatment information of minors confidential even from their parents

161. A purpose of a forensic interview with a child is to:

A. Identify emotional and psychological strengths to be used in successfully coping with abuse and trauma
B. Gather abuse or trauma histories when making sentencing recommendations for juvenile offenders
C. Determine the occurrence of abuse or trauma based on information that can be used for prosecution of perpetrators
D. Assess whether abuse or trauma has led to the perpetration of violent acts against others

162. Which of the following is NOT considered a deficiency need?

A. Self-actualization
B. Safety
C. Esteem
D. Physiological

163. Which of the following actions by a social worker is considered unethical according to the professional code of ethics?

A. Charging rates which are significantly higher than those of other colleagues for the same services based on professional experience and training
B. Bartering in limited circumstances when it is an accepted cultural practice and not detrimental to clients or professional relationships
C. Soliciting private fees for providing services which are available through the social worker's employer or agency
D. Terminating services to clients who are not paying overdue balances after financial contractual arrangements have been made clear

164. A social worker at an inpatient psychiatric unit is reviewing an intake assessment completed on a 21-year-old college student who was admitted the previous day due to bizarre behaviors. He was brought to the emergency department by the police who responded to student concerns about him yelling in an agitated voice, even though there was no one nearby. When asked about his actions, the client stated that he was being monitored by a deadly chip implanted in his brain by evil aliens. When contacted, his parents reported that they began to worry about him 8 months ago due to the presence of some unusual behaviors, but their concerns grew in the last 2 months when he stopped attending classes altogether. The social worker sees that the client was examined by the psychiatrist upon intake and medication was prescribed. Due to these symptoms, the client was MOST likely prescribed:

A. Paxil
B. Lithium
C. Prozac
D. Clozaril

165. A woman comes to see a social worker as she does not want to cause conflict in her marriage, but is very unhappy. She has a preschool child and would like to return to working outside her home. The client reports that she misses working in the company that she left shortly before giving birth. She states that her husband's family comes from a culture which strictly forbids such employment. The social worker should view the problem as a:

A. Role conflict
B. Family issue
C. Cultural bias
D. Social injustice

166. "Doorknob disclosures" are MOST commonly caused by:

A. Premature closure of inquiry by social workers when doing biopsychosocial assessments
B. Fear and embarrassment by clients about information provided
C. Lack of empathetic responding by social workers during treatment
D. Perceived power imbalance by clients within therapeutic relationships

167. A mother comes with her 4-year-old daughter to a social worker as her husband is receiving hospice and she is worried about the child's reaction to his death in the coming weeks. The mother has many questions about the child's ability to comprehend what will happen. Based on developmental theories, the child is likely to view death as a:

A. Comforting experience which should not be feared
B. Temporary state which can be reversed at any time
C. Permanent condition which is caused by accidents and factors which cannot be controlled
D. Final part of the life course which inevitably happens to everyone

168. According to the professional code of ethics, social workers who need to report suspected abuse should:

A. Inform clients about the need to report and potential actions which may result *before* any disclosures are made
B. Seek supervision to determine that agency policies about informing clients are appropriately followed
C. Inform clients about the need to report and potential actions which may result *after* any disclosures are made
D. Refrain from telling clients about the need to and reasons for reporting in order to protect the integrity of abuse investigations

169. A social worker employed in an agency setting receives a referral for a former girlfriend who he has not seen in 20 years. The client is Spanish speaking and the social worker is the only staff linguistically competent to provide clinical services in Spanish. In order to act ethically in this situation, the social worker should:

A. Speak to his supervisor to disclose the prior relationship before meeting with the client
B. Inform agency personnel that he cannot provide services to the client
C. Meet with the client to determine the severity of the need in order to weigh the ethical options
D. Schedule an intake given the time that has passed since the prior relationship

170. For which diagnoses is brief cognitive behavioral therapy MOST appropriate?

A. Substance use Disorders
B. Personality Disorders
C. Dissociative Disorders
D. Adjustment Disorders

Answer Key

1. A
2. C
3. D
4. C
5. B
6. A
7. D
8. C
9. B
10. D
11. D
12. C
13. C
14. D
15. D
16. C
17. C
18. D
19. D
20. B
21. A
22. D
23. A
24. B
25. B
26. D
27. B
28. C
29. D
30. B
31. D
32. C
33. C
34. A
35. C
36. B
37. B
38. C
39. D
40. C
41. D
42. D
43. C
44. B
45. B
46. D
47. C
48. B
49. D
50. A
51. B
52. A
53. B
54. A
55. C
56. C
57. B
58. C
59. D
60. B
61. B
62. D
63. B
64. B
65. C
66. B
67. C
68. A

69. B
70. A
71. A
72. A
73. A
74. D
75. A
76. D
77. B
78. C
79. D
80. B
81. A
82. D
83. B
84. C
85. C
86. D
87. B
88. B
89. D
90. A
91. C
92. C
93. A
94. D
95. D
96. A
97. C
98. A
99. C
100. C
101. D
102. C
103. B
104. C
105. C
106. C
107. A
108. B
109. C
110. D
111. A
112. B
113. C
114. D
115. A
116. D
117. C
118. A
119. A
120. B
121. D
122. C
123. C
124. A
125. D
126. B
127. A
128. A
129. D
130. A
131. B
132. B
133. B
134. C
135. B
136. C
137. A
138. D
139. B
140. C
141. A
142. B
143. A
144. B
145. A
146. B
147. B
148. B
149. C
150. D
151. A
152. A
153. C
154. A
155. D
156. D
157. B
158. C
159. A
160. A
161. C
162. A
163. C
164. D
165. A
166. B
167. B
168. A
169. B
170. D

Answers With Analytic Rationales

1. A

Rationale

A **flashback** is an **indicator of trauma** that is characterized as reexperiencing a previous traumatic experience as if it were actually happening in that moment. It includes reactions that often resemble the client's reactions during the trauma. Flashback experiences are very brief and typically last only a few seconds, but the emotional aftereffects linger for hours or longer. Flashbacks are commonly initiated by a trigger, but not necessarily. Sometimes they occur out of the blue. Other times, specific physical states increase vulnerability to reexperiencing a trauma (e.g., fatigue, high stress levels). Flashbacks can feel like a brief movie scene that intrudes on the client. For example, hearing a car backfire on a hot, sunny day may be enough to cause a veteran to respond as if he or she were back on military patrol. Other ways people reexperience trauma, besides flashbacks, are via nightmares and intrusive thoughts of the trauma.

During flashbacks, clients need to focus on what is happening in the here and now, which is accomplished using **grounding techniques**. Social workers should be prepared to help the client get regrounded so that he or she can distinguish between what is happening now versus what had happened in the past.

There are lots of grounding techniques, but the best are those that use the five senses (sound, touch, smell, taste, and sight) as they bring attention to the present moment; for example, turning on loud music (sound), feeling something cold or comforting (touch), sniffing a strong pleasant fragrance (smell), and so on.

Social workers should also offer education about the experience of triggers and flashbacks, and then normalize these events as common traumatic stress reactions. Afterward, some clients need to discuss the experience and understand why the flashback or trigger occurred. It is often helpful for a client to draw a connection between the trigger and the traumatic event(s). This can be a preventive strategy whereby the client can anticipate that a given situation places him or her at higher risk for retraumatization and requires use of coping strategies, including seeking support.

Test-Taking Strategies Applied

The question contains a qualifying word—primarily—even though it is not capitalized. While all of the answers are helpful for survivors of trauma, the aim of grounding techniques is immediate assistance to get clients back to the "here and now." The incorrect answers involve "talk" or psychotherapy by discussing, understanding, and teaching. Several of them also do not address that clients are "experiencing flashbacks of past traumatic events," but instead deal with the impacts of or responses to trauma more broadly. Only the correct response choice deals with orienting the client to the present, which is necessary when flashbacks occur.

Knowledge Area

Unit II—Intervention Processes and Techniques for Use Across Systems (Content Area); Biopsychosocial History and Collateral Data (Competency); The Indicators of Traumatic Stress and Violence (KSA)

2. C

Rationale

Each culture has its own traditions, rituals, and ways of expressing grief and mourning. The **effects of culture, race, and ethnicity on behaviors, attitudes, and identity** must be considered. Almost every religion or culture has its own traditions involving mourning. Grief is the thoughts and feelings associated with loss, while mourning is the outward behaviors that represent a person's grief. Every culture has its own traditions regarding mourning, and it is important for people to realize that everyone mourns differently and that there is no right way to mourn. While social workers cannot be expected to know the mourning ceremonies and traditions of each client's culture, understanding some basics about how different cultures may prepare for and respond to death is important. Though difficult to ask, there are crucial questions that need to be part of conversations between social workers and clients. For example:

- What are the cultural rituals for coping with dying, the deceased person's body, the final arrangements for the body, and honoring the death? What are the family's beliefs about what happens after death?
- What does the client consider to be the roles of each family member in handling the death?
- Are certain types of death less acceptable (e.g., suicide) or are certain types of death especially hard to handle for that culture (e.g., the death of a child—in countries with high infant mortality, there may be different attitudes about the loss of children)?

Clients should be viewed as a source of knowledge about their special/cultural needs and norms—but social workers sometimes are at a loss about what to ask under such trying circumstances. While there are many similarities across cultures, such as wearing black as a sign of mourning, there are always exceptions. The mix of cultural/religious attitudes and behaviors surrounding death and dying can become very complex indeed. And when a death actually occurs, some clients break with tradition entirely, often creating chaos within families.

Test-Taking Strategies Applied

The question contains a qualifying word—MOST. The client's behavior may be psychotic, placing her at risk for self-harm. It also may be typical given the client's cultural practices and religious beliefs. In order to best understand these actions, the social worker must ask the client about her mourning rituals. It will be important for the client to employ coping strategies to deal with her loss, but there is no indication that they are not already being utilized and such identification is not directly related to the behaviors described in the case scenario.

Knowledge Area

Unit I—Human Development, Diversity, and Behavior in the Environment (Content Area); Diversity, Discrimination, and Stereotypes (Competency); The Effect of Culture, Race, and Ethnicity on Behaviors, Attitudes, and Identity (KSA)

3. D

Rationale

Group therapy is a form of psychotherapy in which a small group of clients receives services together at the same time. While group therapy is sometimes used alone, it is more often used as part of a greater treatment plan that may include one-on-one therapy.

Group therapy is sometimes loosely used to indicate any group of individuals that are experiencing and discussing distress (support groups, for instance). Group therapy can be based on any theoretical approach, from cognitive-behavioral to humanistic. However, in the psychodynamic sense, it specifically indicates a situation where the group context and group process are explicitly utilized as mechanisms of change by developing, exploring, and examining interpersonal relationships within the group. In short, the interpersonal dynamics that play out in the group are reflections of what happens in real life.

Some critical therapeutic concepts in group dynamics are as follows.

Imitative behavior is a way for group members to expand their personal knowledge and skills through the observation of others' personal development.

Catharsis is a release of strong feelings about past or present experiences by group members.

Altruism is a boost to self-concept by group members through extending help to others.

Test-Taking Strategies Applied

This question contains a qualifying word—BEST. While the incorrect answers may be related to group dynamics, the correct one is the definition. If "universality" is unfamiliar as a group therapy term, it may be possible to identify the correct answer by remembering "universalization," an interview technique meaning to normalize thoughts, feelings, or actions. "Normalization" means to look at ideas or actions as typical in everyday life. Seeing that there are others with similar feelings, thoughts, and problems can reduce isolation or make ideas or actions more common than was thought, reducing stigma and loneliness.

Knowledge Area

Unit I—Human Development, Diversity, and Behavior in the Environment (Content Area); Functioning of Various Systems (Competency); Theories of Group Development and Functioning (KSA)

4. C

Rationale

Therapy requires recognizing a client as part of a family system. Additionally, it focuses on studying the role that a client has in a **family dynamic**. Sometimes client problems arise due to dysfunctional communication within the family. Disturbed communication in families resulted in enormous pressure being felt by one or more members of that family system.

A **double bind** is a dilemma in communication in which an individual (or group) receives two or more conflicting messages, with one message negating the other; this is a situation in which successfully responding to one message means failing with the other and vice versa, so that the person will automatically be put in the wrong regardless of response. And the person can neither comment on the conflict, nor resolve it, nor opt out of the situation. Contradictory messages result in the "victim" feeling powerless and trapped in a "damned if you do and damned if you don't" double bind.

A **paradoxical directive** involves prescribing the very symptom the client wants to resolve. It is often equated with reverse psychology. The underlying principle is that a client engages in a behavior for a reason, which is typically to meet a need (rebellion, attention, a cry for help, and so on). In prescribing the symptom, a social worker helps a client understand this need and determine how much control (if any) he or she has over the symptom. By choosing to manifest the symptom, a client may recognize that he or she can create it, and therefore has the power to stop or change it.

A **negative feedback loop** is information that flows back into the family system to minimize deviation and continue functioning within prescribed limits. It helps to maintain homeostasis or keep things stable or the same over time.

A **metacommunication** is an implicit, nonverbal message that accompanies verbal communication.

Test-Taking Strategies Applied

This is a recall question which relies on social workers understanding communication patterns within families so that they can assist in addressing them when they interfere with effective functioning. Often roles within family units can be identified through assessing both verbal and nonverbal communication. Much of social work intervention focuses on helping clients with enhancing their expressive and receptive communication skills.

Knowledge Area

Unit II—Intervention Processes and Techniques for Use Across Systems (Content Area); Intervention Planning and Implementation (Competency); Family Therapy Models, Interventions, and Approaches (KSA)

5. B

Rationale

When a client has experienced multiple, severe forms of trauma, the psychological results are often multiple and severe as well; this phenomenon is sometimes referred to as complex posttraumatic disturbance. **Complex trauma** can be defined as a combination of early and late-onset, multiple, and sometimes highly invasive traumatic events, usually of an ongoing, interpersonal nature. In most cases, such trauma includes exposure to repetitive childhood sexual, physical, and/or psychological abuse, often (although not always) in the context of concomitant emotional neglect and harmful social environments. Complex trauma has a dramatic impact on development and resulting emotional dysregulation and the loss of safety, direction, and the ability to detect or respond to danger cues—this often sets off a chain of events leading to subsequent or repeated trauma exposure in adolescence and adulthood.

The impact of complex trauma includes anxiety and depression; dissociation; relational, identity, and affect regulation disturbance; cognitive distortions; somatization; "externalizing" behaviors such as self-mutilation and violence; sexual disturbance; substance abuse; eating disorders; susceptibility to revictimization; and traumatic bereavement associated with loss of family members and other significant attachment figures.

Clients who have experienced complex trauma may be diagnosed with a range of disorders, and consequently treated with multiple medications and therapies that are ultimately ineffective because they fail to address the underlying problem and do not reflect a trauma-informed approach to assessment and treatment. It is essential that social workers perform comprehensive assessments that capture the broad range of reactions. Thorough assessments must also carefully date and track the various traumatic events so they can be linked with developmental derailments. Treatment approaches that are limited to a single modality (e.g., exposure therapy, cognitive therapy, or psychiatric medication) may be less helpful—especially if the intervention is not adapted to the specific psychological and cultural needs of a client.

Treatment should focus on:

- *Removal of and protection from the source of the trauma and/or abuse*
- *Acknowledgment that recovery from the trauma is not trivial and will require* ***significant time*** *and effort*
- *Separation of residual problems into those that clients can resolve (such as personal improvement goals) and those that clients cannot resolve (such as the behavior of disordered family members)*
- *Acknowledgment of the trauma as real, important, and undeserved*
- Acknowledgment that the trauma came from something that was stronger than clients and therefore could not be avoided
- Acknowledgment of the "complex" nature of trauma (trauma may have led to decisions that brought on additional, undeserved trauma)
- Mourning for what has been lost and cannot be recovered
- Identification of what has been lost and can be recovered
- Placement in a supportive environment where clients can discover they are not alone and can receive validation for their successes and support through their struggles

Test-Taking Strategies Applied

The question contains a qualifying word—NOT—that requires social workers to select the response choice which is not a goal of treatment. When NOT is used as a qualifying word, it is often helpful to remove it from the question and eliminate the three response choices which are goals. This approach will leave the one response choice which is NOT a reason for conducting a needs assessment.

While recovery from complex trauma is possible, it will require significant time and effort. Thus, the correct answer is NOT a goal of treatment as it inaccurately indicates that recovery can occur quickly.

Knowledge Area

Unit II—Intervention Processes and Techniques for Use Across Systems (Content Area); Intervention Planning and Implementation (Competency); Methods and Approaches to Trauma-Informed Care (KSA)

6. A

Rationale

When evaluating agency programs, it is necessary to understand different types of assessment and the terms used to describe them. The resources organizations devote to particular programs are called **inputs**. Those resources can be financial or the time of staff or volunteers. Expertise, such as a consultant or a partner organization, can be considered an input as well.

Outputs, outcomes, and impacts are often used interchangeably, but are not the same.

Outputs are what are produced by programs. For instance, a training program provides graduates. A homeless shelter creates filled beds. Outputs are usually described with numbers. For instance, "96% of available beds were filled" or "the training program graduated 96 individuals." Outputs are measurable and readily determined. It is tempting to stop with outputs because they are easy to produce as they reflect the number of people served or meals distributed.

Outcomes are the effects programs produce on the people served or issues addressed. For instance, the result of a training program might be the number of graduates who get a job and keep it for a particular period. An outcome is a change that occurred because of a program. It is measurable and time limited, although it may take a while to determine its full effect. Measuring outcomes requires a bigger commitment of time and resources.

Impacts are the **long-term or indirect effects** of outcomes. Impacts are hard to measure since they may or may not happen. They are what is hoped that efforts will accomplish. For instance, graduating from a training program may eventually lead to a better quality of life for the individual.

Test-Taking Strategies Applied

This is a recall question about evaluation methods. Social workers are required to know terms, as well as key concepts, related to each of the KSAs. This case scenario requires the ability to distinguish between an output and outcome, as input and impact are clearly the response choices which are more easily eliminated.

Knowledge Area

Unit III—Intervention Processes and Techniques for Use With Larger Systems (Content Area); Program Development and Research (Competency); Methods to Evaluate Agency Programs (e.g., Needs

Assessment, Formative/Summative Assessment, Cost-Effectiveness, Cost-Benefit Analysis, Outcome Assessment) (KSA)

7. D

Rationale

Benzodiazepines are psychotropic medications that help relieve nervousness, tension, and other symptoms by slowing the central nervous system. Benzodiazepines are a type of *antianxiety drug*. While anxiety is a normal response to stressful situations, some clients have unusually high levels of anxiety that can interfere with everyday life. For them, benzodiazepines can help bring their feelings under control. The medicine can also relieve troubling symptoms of anxiety, such as pounding heartbeat, breathing problems, irritability, nausea, and faintness. They are also sometimes prescribed for other conditions, such as muscle spasms, epilepsy and other seizure disorders, phobias, Panic Disorder, withdrawal from alcohol, and sleeping problems. The family of antianxiety drugs known as benzodiazepines includes alprazolam (Xanax), chlordiazepoxide (Librium), diazepam (Valium), and **lorazepam (Ativan)**. These medicines take effect fairly quickly, starting to work within an hour after they are taken. Benzodiazepines are available only with a prescription and are available in tablet, capsule, liquid, or injectable forms.

Prolixin is an *antipsychotic medication* used to treat hallucinations and delusions.

Lithium is a *mood stabilizer* used for the treatment of Bipolar Disorder.

Prozac is an *antidepressant medication* used to treat depression.

Test-Taking Strategies Applied

This is a recall question about benzodiazepines (commonly called tranquilizers) which are useful for treating anxiety. They are highly addictive, and their use is normally limited to a short-term, as-needed basis. They need to be carefully controlled by prescribing physicians.

The examination requires social workers to be aware of the four major types of psychotropic medications—antipsychotics, antidepressants, mood stabilizers, and antianxiety drugs—and be able to identify some common medications in each of these types. While it is possible to have no medication questions on the examination as other KSAs under assessment, diagnosis, and treatment planning are tested instead, it is important to have some knowledge about psychotropic drugs. For example, knowing which types of medications are commonly prescribed for various diagnoses can be helpful.

Knowledge Area

Unit II—Intervention Processes and Techniques for Use Across Systems (Content Area); Biopsychosocial History and Collateral Data (Competency); Common Psychotropic and Non-Psychotropic Prescriptions and Over-the-Counter Medications and Their Side Effects (KSA)

8. C

Rationale

Enmeshment is a psychological term that describes a blurring of boundaries, typically among family members. Enmeshment often contributes to dysfunction in families and may lead to a lack of autonomy and independence that can become problematic.

Typically, boundaries that help determine how close family members are to each other, as well as who participates in specific family matters, exist within a family system. When these boundaries blur or are not clearly defined, the result may be enmeshment, a situation in which family members are close to an extent that it becomes difficult for each member to establish the level of independence considered healthy by most mental health and family therapy experts.

While many families value closeness and intimacy, enmeshment goes beyond the bonds of a close family. Enmeshment may mean parents center their actions or emotions on the children and their successes or mistakes, attempt to know and direct all of the children's thoughts or feelings, and rely heavily on the children for emotional support.

Enmeshment can be problematic because it can prevent people from developing a sense of self, engaging in peer relationships, and learning to self-regulate emotions. Children of enmeshed families may also experience diminished distress tolerance and find it difficult to assert themselves later in life.

Because enmeshment typically involves a long-standing pattern within a family, family therapy may be a particularly useful way to address it, especially if all family members acknowledge the issue and agree to work in counseling to alter the pattern. Family systems therapy, for example, is considered a good approach for addressing enmeshment. *A social worker can help members of a family learn to set boundaries and appropriately express their thoughts and feelings to each other.*

Individual therapy may also be helpful for people seeking to understand how an enmeshed family has impacted them and/or for those who are working to address the effects of enmeshment on their lives.

Test-Taking Strategies Applied

The question contains a qualifying word—primary. Unlike other questions, the qualifying word in this question is not capitalized. Qualifying words may be capitalized or not, so it is important to read questions carefully.

While social workers may work on information exchange, appropriate emotional bonding, and/or communication, forming clear boundaries is the foundation of treating enmeshed families as it addresses the root cause of the problem. It is not possible to do any of the incorrect response choices without the establishment of clear boundaries. Thus, differentiation or starting to view members as separate beings with their own goals and ideas is the main focus of working with enmeshed families.

Knowledge Area

Unit I—Human Development, Diversity, and Behavior in the Environment (Content Area); Functioning of Various Systems (Competency); Family Dynamics and Functioning and the Effects on Individuals, Families, Groups, Organizations, and Communities (KSA)

9. B

Rationale

Competently conducting **evaluations of practice** requires skill and knowledge. There are also many ethical considerations. Social workers engaged in evaluation should obtain voluntary and written informed consent from participants, when appropriate, without any implied or actual deprivation or penalty for refusal to participate; without undue inducement to participate; and with due regard for participants' well-being, privacy, and dignity. Informed consent should include information about the nature, extent, and duration of the participation requested and disclosure of the risks and benefits of participation in the research.

When evaluation or research participants are incapable of giving informed consent (including due to being below the age of consent), social workers should provide an appropriate explanation to the participants, obtain the participants' assent to the extent they are able, and obtain written consent from those legally authorized to act on their behalf.

Test-Taking Strategies Applied

This is a recall question which relies on social workers being fully informed of ethical standards of evaluation and research. The correct answer is that which is required for "the social worker to ethically conduct the evaluation." When questions concern ethical behavior, the 2008 *NASW Code of Ethics* must be remembered. Written consent is necessary, but not sufficient, as the assent of the children is also needed. Assent is a willingness to participate even though a child is not legally able to provide authorization. Children are not able to provide written consent as consent indicates authority to make legal decisions, which those under the age of majority are not able to do unless emancipated. Lastly, separate informed consent procedures are needed for evaluation and research. Those given for service participation cannot be used to indicate that participation in evaluation and research are permissible. Written permission from the agency is not sufficient as it is not legally authorized to act on behalf of the children or their guardians.

Knowledge Area

Unit IV—Professional Relationships, Values, and Ethics (Content Area); Professional Values and Ethical Issues (Competency); Research Ethics (e.g., Institutional Review Boards, Use of Human Subjects, Informed Consent) (KSA)

10. D

Rationale

Social workers must handle issues surrounding the **discharge and termination of services** very carefully. Clients whose services are discharged or terminated unethically may not receive needed supports.

Once services are provided, social workers have legal and ethical responsibilities to continue these services or properly refer clients to alternative providers. While social workers do not have to work with all those in need or requesting services, services cannot terminate abruptly once therapeutic relationships have been established. Social workers must take reasonable steps to avoid abandoning clients who are still in need of services. Social workers should withdraw services precipitously only under unusual circumstances, giving careful consideration to all factors in the situation and taking care to minimize possible adverse effects. Social workers should assist in making appropriate arrangements for continuation of services when necessary (*NASW Code of Ethics, 2008—1.16 Termination of Services*). When it is necessary to terminate services, social workers should provide clients with names, addresses, and telephone numbers of at least three appropriate referrals. *When feasible, they should follow up with clients who have been terminated. If clients do not visit the referrals, clients should be contacted about the risks involved with the lack of follow.*

Clients who will be terminated should be given as much advance notice as possible. When clients announce their decision to terminate prematurely, social workers must explain the risks involved and provide suggestions for alternative care. All decisions and actions related to termination of services should be documented in letters and clients should be provided with clear written instructions to follow and telephone numbers to use in the event of an emergency. Clients should be asked to sign a copy of the documents, affirming that they received the instructions and that the instructions were explained to them.

In instances involving court-ordered clients, social workers should seek legal consultation and court approval before terminating services.

Test-Taking Strategies Applied

The correct answer involves direct action by the social worker to assist with the referral and discharge process. Seeking consultation to review what has already occurred may be helpful for professional development after the situation has been resolved but it will not directly help reengage the client. Additionally, sending a letter is very passive and there is no reason to believe that the client is not aware of the discharge plan and contact information of the new provider. This action should have been taken earlier in the referral process and will not be helpful now. Lastly, meeting with the client to discuss "new issues" is contraindicated as the social worker needs to discharge the client. The client should be discussing new problems with a provider who will be able to assist with assessing and treating them.

Contacting the client about not following through is an active response to address the situation in the case scenario. Central to this contact can be an assessment of why the benefits of continuing treatment have not compelled the client to make contact.

Knowledge Area

Unit II—Intervention Processes and Techniques for Use Across Systems (Content Area); Intervention Planning and Implementation (Competency); Discharge, Aftercare, and Follow-Up Planning (KSA)

11. D

Rationale

Social workers must be aware of **models of supervision and consultation**, including that provided via contract. In situations in which an agency may not have a clinical supervisor who meets the qualifications of a supervisor, a social work supervisee may contract for supervision services outside the agency. Supervisees should contact the regulatory board in their jurisdictions in advance of contracting to confirm if such a practice is permitted and confirm the documentation required from the supervisor. The time frame required for the supervision period should also be verified. Contracting for "outside supervision" can be problematic and place a supervisor at risk. If the supervisee is paying for the services, he or she can dismiss the supervisor, especially if disagreements or conflicts arise. In addition, the supervisor may encounter conflicts between the supervisee and the agency.

Development of a contractual agreement among the social worker, the supervisor, and the employing agency is essential in preventing problems in the supervisory relationship. The agreement should clearly delineate the agency's authority and *grant permission for the supervisor to provide clinical supervision*. Evaluation responsibilities, periodic written reports, and issues of confidentiality should also be included in the agreement. Supervisors and supervisees should also sign a written contract that outlines the parameters of the supervisory relationship. *Monthly written progress reports prepared by the supervisor should be required* and, if appropriate, meet the standards established by the state licensing board for supervision related to licensing.

Test-Taking Strategies Applied

The question contains a qualifying word—EXCEPT—that requires social workers to select the response choice which is not a requirement when supervision is contractual. While it is always good to understand the practice histories of supervisors, including actions taken by licensing boards against them, before hiring and entering into contractual relationships, it is not necessary. Social workers may still choose to be supervised by supervisors who have had licensing infractions. The other three response choices directly relate to the parameters of the contracted relationship and/or monitoring the actions of social workers through progress reporting in order to ensure that client services are not compromised by these arrangements.

Knowledge Area

Unit III—Intervention Processes and Techniques for Use With Larger Systems (Content Area); Supervision and Administration (Competency); Models of Supervision and Consultation (e.g., Individual, Peer, Group) (KSA)

12. C

Rationale

Clients with mental health disorders are more likely than clients without mental health disorders to experience an Alcohol or Substance Use Disorder. **Co-occurring disorders** can be difficult to diagnose due to the complexity of symptoms, as both may vary in severity. In many cases, clients may receive treatment for one disorder while the other disorder remains untreated. This may occur because both mental and Substance Use Disorders can have biological, psychological, and social components. Other reasons may be inadequate training or screening by service providers, an overlap of symptoms, or that other health issues need to be addressed first. In any case, the consequences of undiagnosed, untreated, or undertreated co-occurring disorders can lead to a higher likelihood of experiencing homelessness, incarceration, medical illnesses, suicide, or even early death.

Clients with co-occurring disorders are best served through integrated treatment. With integrated treatment, social workers can address mental and Substance Use Disorders at the same time, often lowering costs and creating better outcomes. Increasing awareness and building capacity in service systems are important in helping identify and treat co-occurring disorders. Early detection and treatment can improve treatment outcomes and the quality of life for those who need these services.

Prescribed medications play a key role in the treatment of co-occurring disorders. They can reduce symptoms and prevent relapses of a psychiatric disorder. Medications can also help clients minimize cravings and maintain abstinence from addictive substances.

In order to get the most out of medication, clients must make an informed choice about taking medications, and understand the potential benefits and costs associated with medication use. In addition, they must take the medication as prescribed.

Taking medication is not substance abuse. Clients in recovery for a Substance Use Disorder may think it is wrong to take any medications.

However, a medication that manages clients' moods is very different from a drug that alters clients' moods.

Test-Taking Strategies Applied

As co-occurring disorders are so prevalent, social workers must be versed in their treatment. While not all clients with psychiatric comorbidities need or receive psychotropic medications, the treatment of mental health symptoms with medications can be effective in reducing the severity of the symptomatology. Much research has been done in this area. Further, it might reduce the elevated risk of suicide attributed to each of the comorbid disorders and to their combined effect. Reducing risk of suicide is an important aim of treatment.

Psychotropic medications should only be prescribed after clients understand their side effects, but informed consent is not unique to only those with co-occurring mental health and Substance Use Disorders—which makes it an incorrect answer.

Knowledge Area

Unit II—Intervention Processes and Techniques for Use Across Systems (Content Area); Biopsychosocial History and Collateral Data (Competency); Co-occurring Disorders and Conditions (KSA)

13. C

Rationale

There are many **models of supervision** described in the literature, ranging from traditional, authoritarian models to more collaborative models. Different models of supervision place emphasis, in varying degrees, on the client, the supervisor, the supervisee, or the context in which the supervision takes place. Ideally, the supervisor and the supervisee use a collaborative process when a supervision model is selected; however, *it is ultimately the responsibility of supervisors to select the model that works best for the professional development of supervisees.*

Supervision encompasses several interrelated functions and responsibilities. Each of these interrelated functions contributes to a larger responsibility or outcome that ensures clients are protected and that clients receive competent and ethical services. As a result, supervision services received by the client are evaluated and adjusted, as needed, to increase benefits. It is supervisors' responsibilities to ensure that supervisees provide competent, appropriate, and ethical services.

Test-Taking Strategies Applied

Social workers must be knowledgeable about supervision models. This question requires social workers to remember that supervisors are responsible for the quality of services delivered by supervisees and their ultimate benefit to clients. Ruling out administrators and funders leaves supervisees and supervisors as possible correct answers. As the question asks about "ultimate responsibility," supervisors are distinguished from the supervisees as they have authority in supervisory relationships. While administrators and funders have influence on service delivery, they are not direct parties in supervisory relationships and their directives should never be honored over those of supervisors.

Knowledge Area

Unit III—Intervention Processes and Techniques for Use With Larger Systems (Content Area); Supervision and Administration (Competency); Models of Supervision and Consultation (e.g., Individual, Peer, Group) (KSA)

14. D

Rationale

Many programs use the ability to perform **activities of daily living** (ADLs) and **instrumental activities of daily living** (IADLs) as eligibility criteria to determine eligibility and/or **level of care**. Whether or not clients are capable of performing these activities on their own or if they rely on family caregivers to perform the ADLs can serve as a comparative measure of their independence. Assessments can help with determining assistance needed.

Measuring a client's ability to perform the ADLs and IADLs is important not just in determining the level of assistance required, but as a metric for a variety of services and programs related to caring for older adults and for those with disabilities.

Many state-funded, non-Medicaid programs use an inability to perform two or three ADLs as one of the eligibility criteria for participation in their assistance programs.

Medicaid often requires older adults to be qualified for nursing home care, and nursing home care qualification can be determined by how much assistance one requires with ADLs. Long-term care insurance often uses an inability to perform the ADLs as a trigger for paying out on a policy. Social Security Disability Insurance (SSDI) also considers ADLs as a qualification factor.

ADLs are activities in which clients engage on a day-to-day basis. These are everyday *personal care* activities that are fundamental to caring for oneself and maintaining independence.

There are many variations on the definition of the ADLs, but most organizations agree there are five basic categories.

- Personal hygiene—bathing, grooming, and oral care
- Dressing—the ability to make appropriate clothing decisions and physically dress oneself
- Eating—the ability to feed oneself though not necessarily to prepare food
- Maintaining continence—both the mental and physical ability to use a restroom
- Transferring—moving oneself from seated to standing and getting in and out of bed

IADLs are activities related to *independent living*. The instrumental activities are more subtle than ADLs. They can help determine with greater detail the level of assistance required. The IADLs include:

- Basic communication skills—such as using a regular phone, mobile phone, email, or the Internet
- Transportation—either by driving oneself, arranging rides, or the ability to use public transportation
- Meal preparation—meal planning, preparation, storage, and the ability to safely use kitchen equipment
- Shopping—the ability to make appropriate food and clothing purchase decisions
- Housework—doing laundry, cleaning dishes, and maintaining a hygienic place of residence
- Managing medications—taking accurate dosages at the appropriate times, managing refills, and avoiding conflicts
- Managing personal finances—operating within a budget, writing checks, paying bills, and avoiding scams

Test-Taking Strategies Applied

The question contains a qualifying word—MOST. While it may be useful to assess all areas listed, level of care is primarily determined by the amount of help that the client needs to complete necessary personal assistance and independent living tasks.

Adapting to life changes may be important to the client's ability to adjust to his or her new home, but will not directly relate to "making a determination of the needed level of care." Managing medical problems may also need to be addressed. However, such assistance can be done by care management in any setting. Lastly, while cognition is related to self-care abilities, performing the tasks is also based on mobility or the ability to move upper or lower extremities in order to complete them. Thus, assessing cognitive tasks will not give a complete picture of assistance needed.

Knowledge Area

Unit II—Intervention Processes and Techniques for Use Across Systems (Content Area); Assessment Methods and Techniques (Competency); Placement Options Based on Assessed Level of Care (KSA)

15. D

Rationale

Clients engaged in **enmeshed interpersonal relationships** are nearly always the last to know. Often social workers work with adult children who are recovering from the pain and confusion caused by enmeshed relationships with parents.

There are many signs of enmeshed relationships including:

- Neglecting other relationships because of an obsession or concern about one relationship
- Happiness contingent upon a relationship
- Self-esteem contingent upon a relationship
- Excessive anxiety, fear, or a compulsion to fix the problem whenever there is a disagreement in a relationship
- Feeling of loneliness that overwhelms when not with the other person—often creating irrational desires to reconnect
- Symbiotic emotional connections which result in becoming angry, upset, or depressed when another person is angry, upset, or depressed
- Strong desire to fix another person's situation and change his or her state of mind

When relationships are enmeshed, they are no longer able to grow. Social workers must work to establish healthy boundaries and respect for autonomous choices. This process can be painful for clients.

Test-Taking Strategies Applied

In order to select the correct answer, social workers must first diagnose the problem. The feelings and behaviors of the couple are indicative of enmeshment. Once the cause of the problem is known, the question can be simplified to picking out the treatment focus when working with enmeshed relationships. The wife is not the client as the couple sought treatment, so focusing on the wife's self-worth will not address the problem. Finding out more about past intimate relationships is an assessment—not a treatment—task. Understanding each other's feelings will not help each person develop boundaries and differentiate from one another, which is the root of the issue.

Knowledge Area

Unit I—Human Development, Diversity, and Behavior in the Environment (Content Area); Effects of the Environment on Systems' Behavior (Competency); The Dynamics of Interpersonal Relationships (KSA).

16. C

Rationale

Case notes may be subject to a range of legislative processes and requirements during and following the conclusion of professional relationships. The nature of these requirements may differ greatly according to the state or nature/context of practice. Social workers should use care to make sure that case notes are impartial, accurate, and complete. Information may need to be added to client records to ensure that they are not misleading and are comprehensive. Care should be taken at all times to avoid errors or omissions. If a change must be made to correct an error or omission, the change must be recorded as a new and separate case note. In addition to outlining the error or omission as part of new case notes, it is advisable to provide explanations for earlier absences or inaccuracies.

An existing case note should never be amended or changed in light of additional information obtained at a later date. This should always constitute a new case note.

Test-Taking Strategies Applied

This case scenario requires knowledge about documentation and the management of practice records.

Careful and diligent documentation enhances the quality of services provided to clients. Social workers should take reasonable steps to ensure that documentation in records is accurate and reflects the services provided. In addition, social workers should include sufficient and timely documentation in records to facilitate the delivery of services and to ensure continuity of services provided to clients in the future. Comprehensive records are necessary to assess clients' circumstances, as well as plan and deliver services.

Social workers should know the professional protocol for adding or making changes to client records, so asking for supervisory input is not needed, making the first answer incorrect. Material should never be added to existing case notes as they need to accurately reflect documentation of "the facts" that were known at the times of these entries. Thus, the second answer is not correct. Lastly, client records should be complete, so not recording information in client files is also unethical, eliminating the last response choice listed.

Knowledge Area

Unit III—Intervention Processes and Techniques for Use With Larger Systems (Content Area); Record-Keeping and Reporting (Competency); The Principles of Case Recording, Documentation, and Management of Practice Records (KSA)

17. C

Rationale

Interviewing skills are essential to ensuring that clients feel understood, problems are assessed, and effective treatment is delivered. A comprehensive social work interview includes conducting a multiple biopsychosocial–spiritual–cultural assessment in order to better understand the presenting problem. Questions asked and techniques used may promote or inhibit information gathering and other aspects of the problem-solving process. Skills and questioning techniques used include active listening, empathy, rapport building, open- and closed-ended inquiries, silence, and so on.

When interviewing clients, social workers should avoid "Why" questions in order to prevent clients from feeling as though they need to defend their choices and actions. Although it may be necessary to learn the reasoning behind clients' choices and actions, the wording used may impact responses. For example, if a social worker needs to know why a client is missing doses of medication, instead of asking "Why haven't you been able to take your medication as prescribed?" it is better to ask "What are some of the reasons for skipping your medication?" The difference may be subtle, but it can affect the way a client perceives the question. With the "Why" method, a client may be defensive, whereas the "What" method allows a client to reflect on action without feeling judged.

Test-Taking Strategies Applied

The correct answer is the BEST question for the social worker to ask as part of the assessment. The use of the qualifying word, which is capitalized, indicates that other response choices may be appropriate, but are not as essential to identifying causes for the presenting problem, the primary aim of assessment. In the case scenario, the social worker must find out the reasons for the medication noncompliance. There is no indication that the client is not taking the medication to become hospitalized. It is also premature to see how the social worker can assist as the reasons for missing the doses is not known.

The correct "What" question is preferred to the inaccurate "Why" question to avoid having the client feel judged. The "Why" response choice also implies that the client's actions are in direct violation of the doctor's orders as she has not been able to take her medication "as prescribed." Pointing out that she has done something other than what the doctor stated can cause defensiveness or shame.

Knowledge Area

Unit II—Intervention Processes and Techniques for Use Across Systems (Content Area); Intervention Planning and Implementation (Competency); The Principles and Techniques of Interviewing (e.g., Supporting, Clarifying, Focusing, Confronting, Validating, Feedback, Reflecting, Language Differences, Use of Interpreters, Redirecting) (KSA)

18. D

Rationale

Family therapy is based on the idea that a family is a system of different parts. A change in any part of the system will trigger changes in all the other parts, so when one member of a family is affected by a **Substance Use Disorder**, everyone is affected. As a result, family dynamics can change in unhealthy ways. Some family members may take on too much responsibility, other family members may act out, and some may just shut down. Often a family remains stuck in unhealthy patterns even after the family member with the behavioral health disorder moves into recovery. Even in the best circumstances, families can find it hard to adjust to the person in their midst who is recovering, who is behaving differently than before, and who needs support. *Family therapy can help the family as a whole recover and heal.*

Family therapy is typically introduced after the individual in treatment for addiction has made progress in recovery. This could be a few months after treatment starts, or a year or more later. Timing is important because people new to recovery have a lot to do. They are working to remain stable in their new patterns of behavior and ways of thinking. They are just beginning to face the many changes they must make to stay mentally healthy, as well as remain clean or sober. They are learning such things as how to deal with urges to fall into old patterns, how to resist triggers and cravings, and how to avoid temptations to rationalize and make excuses. For them to explore family issues at the same time can be too much. It can potentially contribute to relapse. *Family therapy tends to be most helpful once the person in treatment is fully committed to the recovery process and is ready to make more changes.*

Test-Taking Strategies Applied

Social workers must understand family roles in addiction and codependency. Addiction is a "family affair"; therapy with the entire family involves understanding the roles that members assume which are dysfunctional and support the addictive behavior. However, it is important that clients have made progress in their recovery before taking on additional stress, which comes with understanding family roles in families impacted by addiction. Clients' acknowledgement of their addictions and family dysfunction, as well as detoxification—if needed—would come prior to the onset of family therapy. Clients may not yet be stable in their new patterns of behavior.

This question contains a qualifying word—best—even though it is not capitalized. There may be reasons for engaging in family therapy earlier or later in the recovery process, but it is most beneficial after individual progress has been made by clients. Only the correct answer describes this progress.

Knowledge Area

Unit I—Human Development, Diversity, and Behavior in the Environment (Content Area); Human Growth and Development (Competency); Addiction Theories and Concepts (KSA)

19. D

Rationale

Ethical and legal issues regarding mandatory reporting are very clear when victims are minors. There is both a legal and ethical obligation to report all child abuse to protective services. However, when the victim is a client who is now an adult, the required action becomes less clear. Laws vary by state and it is important for social workers to be aware of their legal duties.

Social workers face ethical dilemmas in these situations as they may want perpetrators to be accountable for their actions. However, if clients disclose such abuse in strict confidence and do not want it reported, there is a need to respect their privacy. This abuse does not meet any of the exceptions for disclosure: consent by clients, clear and immediate danger, and other requirements by law (such as duty to warn).

In these instances, social workers may provide clients with information and other support so they can consider their options more fully. For instance, they may not be familiar with what happens during abuse investigations, fearing that reports may lead to immediate notoriety and broad publication. Legal and procedural protections afforded to survivors of sex-related crimes may also not be known.

However, even with such information and support, adult clients may resist wanting their abuse reported. Thus, social workers must respect their right to self-determination and should avoid imposing their own beliefs on clients.

Test-Taking Strategies Applied

As the 2008 *NASW Code of Ethics* does not explicitly address the situation in the case scenario, it is necessary to consider the ethical principles of beneficence (doing good), nonmaleficence (avoiding doing harm), justice, and respect. While reporting the abuse may help protect other minors from being abused, it may be experienced as harm by the client as she is not emotionally ready to confront her father about the abuse. Reporting the abuse also may have a negative impact on the social worker/client relationship as the client may feel betrayed by the disclosure. From a justice perspective, reporting the abuse may be a method of bringing the alleged perpetrator to justice, but justice could entail prioritizing the client's emotional well-being. Finally, respect involves honoring the client's rights to privacy and self-determination.

The case scenario stated that the state did not legally require social workers to report past abuse when the survivor is no longer a minor. If it were required, the correct response may have been different. The case scenario also indicates that the father is not a danger to other children given his physical and/or mental status.

Meeting with the father is not appropriate as he is not the client and it is not the social worker's role to assess his risk. In addition, while supervision is always useful, the social worker should not be "passing the buck" and relying on the supervisor to make the decision. The social worker must be knowledgeable about the laws and issues regarding mandatory reporting.

Knowledge Area

Unit IV—Professional Relationships, Values, and Ethics (Content Area); Confidentiality (Competency); Ethical and/or Legal Issues Regarding Mandatory Reporting (e.g., Abuse, Threat of Harm, Impaired Professionals, etc.) (KSA)

20. B

Rationale

In using **feedback** during the beginning phase of treatment, a social worker encourages clients to comment about service purpose, social worker–client roles, ethical factors, or any other aspect of the introductory sessions. An important part of communicating effectively involves checking whether clients have understood the messages being conveyed. Seeking feedback serves this function. Seeking feedback early in the problem-solving process is part of the informed consent process. Clients are forced to identify areas that are unclear, share thoughts that have occurred to them, or express disagreements. The use of feedback sends the message that treatment is a mutual and reciprocal process and that social workers are interested in what clients have to say. It sets the expectation that clients will continue to be active participants throughout the helping process.

Test-Taking Strategies Applied

The question contains a qualifying word—EXCEPT—that requires social workers to select the response choice which is not a reason for seeking feedback. The question specifically asks about "the beginning phase of treatment." During the beginning phase, social workers introduce and identify themselves and seek introductions from clients. Following the exchange of introductions, social workers describe the initial purposes for meetings, identify professional roles that social workers might undertake, orient clients to the process, and identify relevant policy and ethical factors that might apply. Three of the response choices directly relate to this initial orientation and educating clients about the reciprocal nature of the work, as well as engaging them by showing interest. *The correct answer is important when actually intervening with clients, but is not appropriate for the beginning phase as the delivery of treatment occurs later in the process.*

Knowledge Area

Unit II—Intervention Processes and Techniques for Use Across Systems (Content Area); Intervention Planning and Implementation (Competency); Methods to Obtain and Provide Feedback (KSA)

21. A

Rationale

Social stratification refers to a system by which a society ranks categories of people in a hierarchy. By examining policies, procedures, regulations, and laws—as well as practices—it is perfectly clear that some groups have greater status, power, and wealth than other groups. Social stratification is based on four major principles:

1. Social stratification is a trait of society, not simply a reflection of individual differences.
2. Social stratification persists over generations.
3. Social stratification is universal, but takes different forms across different societies.
4. Social stratification involves both inequality and beliefs, as inequality is rooted in a society's philosophy.

Test-Taking Strategies Applied

This question requires social workers to understand the effects that policies, procedures, regulations, and laws have on practice, including perpetuating social stratification.

Racial inequality results from institutional discrimination in which policies and procedures do not treat all racial groups equally. While people of color often do not have the same opportunities, the question is broader, seeking the term which relates to differences in social status. These differences can also result from other attributes, such as gender.

Institutional malfeasance refers to wrongdoing by an organization or corporation.

Cultural difference involves the integrated and maintained system of socially acquired values, beliefs, and rules of conduct which impact the range of accepted behaviors distinguishable from one societal group to another. Cultural difference is not negative in nature, like social stratification.

Knowledge Area

Unit I—Human Development, Diversity, and Behavior in the Environment (Content Area); Diversity, Discrimination, and Stereotypes (Competency); Systemic (Institutionalized) Discrimination (e.g., Racism, Sexism, Ageism) (KSA)

22. D

Rationale

Supervision is an essential and integral part of training and continuing education required for the skillful development of professional social workers. The knowledge base of the social work profession has expanded and the population it serves has become more complex. Supervision protects clients, supports practitioners, and ensures that professional standards and quality services are delivered by competent social workers. It is important to the profession to have assurance that all social workers are equipped with the necessary skills to deliver competent and ethical social work services. Equally important to the profession is the responsibility to protect clients.

Documentation is an important legal tool that verifies that services, including supervision, occurred. Supervisors should assist supervisees in learning how to properly document client services performed, regularly review their documentation, and hold them to high standards. When appropriate, supervisors should train the supervisees to document for reimbursement and claim submissions.

Each supervisory session should be documented separately by supervisors and supervisees. Documentation for supervised sessions should be available to both parties and provided to supervisees within a reasonable time after each session. Social work regulatory boards may request some form of supervision documentation when supervisees apply for licensure. Records should be safeguarded and kept confidential.

Test-Taking Strategies Applied

The question contains a qualifying word—MOST. Supervisors are responsible for the actions of supervisees, but records should not only be kept by them. Failure to keep any documentation of supervision sessions is ill advised as information used to make critical treatment decisions will not be recorded. It is true that licensing entities may require supervision notes, but the correct answer describes the "MOST appropriate" documentation practice, namely that both supervisees and supervisors should maintain separate records.

Knowledge Area

Unit III—Intervention Processes and Techniques for Use With Larger Systems (Content Area); Supervision and Administration (Competency); Case Recording for Practice Evaluation or Supervision (KSA)

23. A

Rationale

Social workers employed in agency settings may find that they are required to have **multiple supervisors**. In circumstances in which a social worker is being supervised simultaneously by more than one person, it is best practice to have a contractual agreement or memorandum of understanding delineating the role of each supervisor, including parameters of the relationships, information sharing, priorities, and how conflicts will be resolved. If no agreement exists, the immediate employment supervisor may have the final say. If the setting permits, a separate third party may be brought in to help resolve the conflict.

Test-Taking Strategies Applied

Only the correct answer results in *a written agreement* delineating the role of each supervisor. Written parameters are superior to meeting together, reviewing professional standards, or understanding personal values. When a social worker must answer to more than one supervisor, the likelihood of conflict is enhanced; therefore, guidelines which outline the agreed upon flow of information and how conflicts should be resolved is essential.

Knowledge Area

Unit III—Intervention Processes and Techniques for Use With Larger Systems (Content Area); Supervision and Administration (Competency); Models of Supervision and Consultation (e.g., Individual, Peer, Group) (KSA)

24. B

Rationale

Social workers who do forensic work wrestle with professional ethical issues that emerge in determining **client mental fitness** to face prosecution. The process of evaluating whether a client is competent to stand trial involves two major areas. First, clients must understand the legal proceedings against them, what they have been charged with, what the roles of the different court personnel are, the difference between pleading guilty and not guilty, and what accepting a plea bargain means.

The second factor is the clients' ability to assist in their own defense or their ability to work with their attorneys and take an active part in their own defense.

If a client's mental status is in question, the social worker tells the defense attorney, who then brings the issue to the judge. Alternately, the state's attorney, or the judge could raise the issue. The judge then issues a court order mandating a formal evaluation of client **competency to stand trial**.

A formal evaluation may be done by a psychiatrist working alone or a team of mental health professionals, including a psychiatrist, psychologist, and/or forensic social worker.

After the formal evaluation of competence to stand trial, the next phase is often "restoration," in which clients are sent to a particular setting, most often a hospital, where they are "restored to competence." Clients are usually in the hospital for 60 to 90 days for the initial restoration, during which time they not only undergo a full evaluation by psychologists, psychiatrists, and social workers but also attend class to learn about the court process so they face their charges as competent defendants.

Competency restoration is a psychoeducational intervention in which clients who have been found incapable of proceeding in legal trials due to any combination of limited understanding, communication deficits, or impaired ability to conform their behaviors to the demands of the courtroom are rendered capable. It is generally a part of a multifaceted treatment strategy that may include anger management skills, relaxation training, and cognitive behavioral therapy (CBT) as adjunct interventions to education regarding general legal processes and specific aspects of the defendant's case. At the conclusion, clients should be able to discuss cases with their attorneys, differentially weigh the risks and possible benefits of the different pleadings, strategize the case in consideration of testimonials and evidence, testify, and conduct themselves in a manner suitable to the courtroom. Clients should understand the roles of the court officers, understand the responsibilities and limitations of judges and juries, and that their attorneys have their best interests in mind.

Test-Taking Strategies Applied

The question contains a qualifying word—primary—even though it is not capitalized. Competency restoration processes occur before sentencing or restitution decisions. Social workers evaluate and deliver services focused on developing or regaining clients' abilities to participate in legal proceedings. It is not the clients' responsibility to identify legal standards that may apply to their conduct, which eliminates the last response choice.

Knowledge Area

Unit IV—Professional Relationships, Values, and Ethics (Content Area); Professional Values and Ethical Issues (Competency); Client/Client System Competence and Self-Determination (e.g., Financial Decisions, Treatment Decisions, Emancipation, Age of Consent, Permanency Planning) (KSA)

25. B

Rationale

The right of **privileged communication**—which assumes that a professional cannot disclose confidential information without the client's consent—originated in British common law. The attorney–client privilege was the first professional relationship to gain the right of privileged communication. Over time, other groups of professionals have sought this right.

Social workers should understand the distinction between confidentiality and privileged communication. Confidentiality refers to the professional norm that information offered by or pertaining to clients will not be shared with third parties. Privilege refers to the disclosure of confidential information in court or during other legal proceedings.

Courts commonly cite the following four conditions that must be met for information to be considered privileged:

- The harm caused by disclosure of the confidential information would outweigh the benefits of disclosure during legal proceedings.
- The parties involved in the conversation assumed that it was confidential.
- Confidentiality is an important element in the relationship.
- The broader community recognizes the importance of this relationship.

A significant court decision for social workers concerning privileged communications was the landmark case of *Jaffe v. Redmond* (1996) in which the U.S. Supreme Court ruled that the clients of clinical social workers have the right to privileged communication in federal courts. Many states, though not all, now extend the right of privileged communication to clinical social workers' clients.

Test-Taking Strategies Applied

The question contains a qualifying word—NOT—that requires social workers to select the condition which does not need to be met in order for information to be considered privileged. When NOT is used as a qualifying word, it is often helpful to remove it from the question and eliminate the three response choices which are legal effects. This approach will leave the one response choice which is NOT a decision-making variable.

While documentation is important in the provision of social work services, confidentiality and privilege does not only apply to written materials.

Knowledge Area

Unit IV—Professional Relationships, Values, and Ethics (Content Area); Confidentiality (Competency); Legal and/or Ethical Issues Regarding Confidentiality, Including Electronic Information Security (KSA)

26. D

Rationale

There are four major **parenting styles** which reflect the skills and capabilities of clients.

Permissive parenting, sometimes referred to as indulgent parenting, has very few demands placed on children. Permissive parents rarely discipline their children because they have relatively low expectations of maturity and self-control. They are often nontraditional and lenient, not requiring mature behavior, allowing considerable self-regulation, and avoiding confrontation. Permissive parents are generally nurturing and communicative with their children, often taking on the status of a friend more than that of a parent.

Authoritative parenting establishes rules and guidelines that children are expected to follow. However, this parenting style is democratic. Authoritative parents are responsive to their children and willing to listen to questions. When children fail to meet the expectations, these parents are nurturing and forgiving rather than punishing. These parents monitor and impart clear standards for their children's conduct. They are assertive, but not intrusive and restrictive. Their disciplinary methods are supportive, rather than punitive. They want their children to be assertive as well as socially responsible, and self-regulated as well as cooperative.

In **authoritarian parenting**, children are expected to follow the strict rules established by the parents. Failure to follow such rules usually results in punishment. Authoritarian parents do not explain the reasoning behind these rules. If asked to explain, the parent might simply reply, "Because I said so." These parents have high demands but are not responsive to their children. These parents are obedience- and status-oriented, and expect their orders to be obeyed without explanation.

An **uninvolved parenting** style is characterized by few demands, low responsiveness, and little communication. While these parents fulfill the child's basic needs, they are generally detached from their child's life. In extreme cases, these parents may even reject or neglect the needs of their children.

Test-Taking Strategies Applied

This is a recall question on parenting styles. Social workers should be knowledgeable about the impact that parenting styles have on child development outcomes. Authoritarian parenting styles generally lead to children who are obedient and proficient, but they rank lower in happiness, social competence, and self-esteem. Authoritative parenting styles tend to result in children who are happy, capable, and successful. Permissive parenting often results in children who rank low in happiness and self-regulation. These children are more likely to experience problems with authority and tend to perform poorly in school. Uninvolved parenting styles rank lowest across all life domains. These children tend to lack self-control, have low self-esteem, and are less competent than their peers.

Knowledge Area

Unit I—Human Development, Diversity, and Behavior in the Environment (Content Area); Human Growth and Development (Competency); Parenting Skills and Capacities (KSA)

27. B

Rationale

Dysfunctional family dynamics are traits or behaviors that characterize unhealthy interactions between members. In dysfunctional families, members tend to communicate poorly and not listen to each other. **Triangulation** is a family therapy concept discussed most famously by multigenerational family systems theorist Murray Bowen. Bowen described dyads as being inherently unstable under stress, much like a two-legged stool. When in balance, the dyad is capable of functioning well and meeting the needs of both people in it. However, when thrown out of balance by conflict, stress, or transitions, the dyad will often pull in a third person, or "leg" of the stool, to help them stabilize the relationship.

According to Bowen, some triangulation is normal and even healthy in the course of family interactions. Because dyads are inherently unstable, the involvement of a third party can assist a two-person relationship in overcoming impasses, meeting needs, and coping through stressful times. This kind of triangulation occurs because both people in a dyad are looking for healthy and effective mediation. When the triangulated person gives input, it is accepted into the dyad and processed together in a way that moves the original dyad forward in their relationship. Healthy triangulation can also occur in the context of parents (or other family caregivers) who come together to meet the needs of a third member, such as a child.

Triangulation can become unhealthy in families when it causes undue stress on the third party and/or when it prevents, rather than invites, resolution of the dyad's conflict. In the case scenario, the triangulation is being sought by only one of the spouses. Furthermore, the input provided is not being brought back into the marriage for joint processing by both spouses. It is being withheld by the husband for his own individual purposes. The husband's conversations with his mother are essentially taking the place of the emotional process that needs to be occurring within the marriage itself in order to return the marriage to healthy functioning.

Role reversal is a situation in which two people have chosen or been forced to exchange their duties and responsibilities, so that each is now doing what the other used to do. This case scenario is not a role reversal as the mother has taken on being an emotional confidant, a function usually assumed by a spouse. However, the wife has not taken on the mother's duties or responsibilities.

Entropy, based in systems theory, is characteristic of randomness and disintegration within a structure.

The **Oedipal complex**, also known as the Oedipus complex, is a term used by Sigmund Freud in his theory of psychosexual stages of development to describe a boy's feelings of desire for his mother and jealousy and anger toward his father. This answer is not correct given the age of the man. It also does not address the "family dynamic" which includes the wife.

Test-Taking Strategies Applied

This is a recall question related to family systems. Even when the names of theories are not mentioned, social workers are often asked about their key terms and concepts. When proper names are listed as answers, it is useful to look at them first, before reading the question. Often a response choice will look correct after reading the question simply due to the words used. However, the one that looks the best is often not correct. Defining the terms in your head first helps you remember them without distraction or having the question's wording inappropriately influence your answer.

Knowledge Area

Unit II—Intervention Processes and Techniques for Use Across Systems (Content Area); Intervention Planning and Implementation (Competency); Family Therapy Models, Interventions, and Approaches (KSA)

28. C

Rationale

Delusions are false beliefs which clients hold with a strong amount of conviction. These beliefs are not typical of their culture or religion, and clients adhere to the erroneous beliefs despite evidence and proof which totally contradict them. **Delusions of reference** are perceptions that stimuli in the environment are directed toward clients themselves and referencing them specifically even though they are not. It is the belief that simple coincidences are relevant and specific to clients even though they are not connected to them in any way; for example, clients thinking people they do not know are talking about them or thinking that newscasters are speaking directly to them.

Clients with delusions of reference may think that things written in newspapers or stated in newscasts, passages found in a book, or the words in a song are about them directly. Thus, neutral events are believed to have special and personal meaning; for example, clients might believe billboards or celebrities are sending messages meant specifically for them.

These ideas and connections are delusions as they are thought to be true, though they are not. This can be a sign of mental illness such as Schizophrenia Spectrum and Other Psychotic Disorders.

Test-Taking Strategies Applied

The question requires knowledge about basic terminology associated with psychopathology or the study of mental illness or the manifestation of behaviors that may be indicative of mental illness or psychological impairment. There are also common delusions such as delusions of grandeur, control, guilt, persecution, jealousy, or paranoia. Social workers must be aware of the presence of delusional thoughts by clients and the diagnostic methods/tools that can be used to identify them.

The first response choice provides an accurate statement about delusions generally; for example, they are false, fixed beliefs despite evidence to the contrary, but it is incorrect as it does not provide information specifically about delusions of reference. The qualifying word—BEST—indicates that more than one listed answer may apply, but the most suitable definition is the one that illustrates the key attributes of this delusional type. Thus, the correct response choice is the one which indicates that neutral events are believed to have special and personal meaning.

Knowledge Area

Unit II—Intervention Processes and Techniques for Use Across Systems (Content Area); Biopsychosocial History and Collateral Data (Competency); The Indicators of Mental and Emotional Illness Throughout the Lifespan (KSA)

29. D

Rationale

The developmental model of **couples development** is based on the work of Margaret Mahler, who outlined the stages of early childhood development. It incorporates her concept of differentiation as well as certain aspects of attachment theory. Like other developmental models, this theory assumes a predictable sequence of developmental milestones exists.

Couples' relationships are likely to proceed through the following stages:

- **Bonding:** Bonding is the initial honeymoon period during which couples seek closeness, uncover their similarities, and begin falling in love.
- **Differentiation:** During this stage, couples begin to acknowledge and address their differences. A central task of this developmental stage is finding ways to resolve conflict.
- **Practicing:** During this period, couples explore their independence, nurture outside friendships, and spend time

developing their self-esteem and competence in areas separate from the relationship.

- **Rapprochement:** Rapprochement is a stage during which couples move away from and then return to one another. Often, a couple's sex life will deepen during this phase.
- **Synergy:** This stage of development embraces true intimacy, recognizing a couple can come together and be stronger together than each member is alone.

The following conditions apply to this developmental model of couples' development.

1. There is an invariable order to the stages of development.
2. No stage can be skipped.
3. Each stage is more complex than the preceding one, representing a transformation of what existed previously into a new form.
4. Each stage is based on the preceding one and prepares for the succeeding one.

Childhood experiences can enhance or inhibit an individual's ability to progress through the normal stages of growth that characterize adult relationships. However, stages cannot be skipped in order for couples' relationships to achieve true intimacy.

Test-Taking Strategies Applied

The question contains a qualifying word—NOT—that requires social workers to select the response choice which is not true about couples' relationships using a developmental model. When NOT is used as a qualifying word, it is often helpful to remove it from the question and eliminate the three response choices which are true. This approach will leave the one response choice which is NOT accurate. Remembering developmental models to explain individual human development will be helpful as the answers apply to them as well. Individuals must also go through all sequential stages; none can be skipped, as each is needed for progressive growth.

Knowledge Area

Unit I—Human Development, Diversity, and Behavior in the Environment (Content Area); Functioning of Various Systems (Competency); Theories of Couples Development (KSA)

30. B

Rationale

Social workers must be knowledgeable about **legal documents** related to confidentiality of client information. **Confidentiality of mandated clients** is particularly tricky as documents may be subject to release without client consent.

Social workers have a duty to claim privilege on behalf of their clients when asked to release any information without client permission. **Privilege** is a right owned by clients to prevent their confidential information from being used in legal proceedings. The *NASW Code of Ethics* requires social workers to wait until *ordered by the court before disclosing information* in legal proceedings, absent client consent or an imminent threat of harm. A **subpoena** is a mandate to provide evidence or testimony—but is not a final ruling or order by a court on the legal requirement to provide information or admissibility of the evidence. A subpoena is not a **court order**. Most subpoenas are issued by attorneys.

The NASW Code of Ethics *provides that when a court-ordered disclosure could cause harm to the client, the social worker should request that the court withdraw or limit the order or keep the records under seal.* It is not clear how a social worker can meaningfully implement this provision. The social worker could refuse to obey a court's order as a matter of conscience, but this should be done only if she is prepared to be found in contempt of court and face time in jail, a fine, or both.

The need to be aware of court or legal mandates is the cost of doing business in a profession where clients can be involved in legal disputes or matters.

Test-Taking Strategies Applied

Clients who are mandated to receive services may also be referred to as involuntary or court-ordered clients. All of these terms indicate that clients did not voluntarily choose or consent to receipt of services. There is legal authorization to mandate the receipt of treatment. Thus, there may also be a similar mandate to get access to documentation related to the receipt of services. The extent of what will need to be disclosed can vary and social workers are advised to be aware of these limits before the onset of treatment and review them with clients in their initial meetings.

In the case scenario, it is the social worker's responsibility to understand the extent to which documentation is privileged, so there is no need to have the client see a lawyer. The social worker should be aware of any specific limits to confidentiality before the onset of services, so seeking supervision and/or consultation to understand them is problematic. Documentation associated with treatment needs to be generated according to practice standards. It would not be appropriate to forgo keeping notes which are essential to continuity of care just because they may be released. Also, promising the client that he or she will be able to consent to information release when mandated by the court can be misleading.

The court order and any relevant legal documents should be obtained by the social worker and consulted whenever there are questions related to the service provision and/or reporting. Social workers have legal mandates to comply with court orders once they are appointed to be providers of services and agree to the terms. If there is concern about mandates in court orders, social workers should try to get them changed or be removed as treating professionals by the appointing courts.

Knowledge Area

Unit IV—Professional Relationships, Values, and Ethics (Content Area); Confidentiality (Competency); Legal and/or Ethical Issues Regarding Confidentiality, Including Electronic Information Security (KSA)

31. D

Rationale

When **addiction and substance abuse** occur during pregnancy, it can have effects not only on the pregnant mother, but also on the unborn child. **Opioid use** in pregnancy is associated with an increased risk of adverse outcomes. *The current standard of care for pregnant women with opioid dependence is referral for opioid-assisted therapy with methadone.* Medically supervised tapered doses of opioids during pregnancy often result in relapse to former use. Abrupt discontinuation of opioids in an opioid-dependent pregnant woman can result in preterm labor, fetal distress, or fetal demise. After birth, special considerations are needed for women who are opioid-dependent to ensure appropriate pain management, to prevent postpartum relapse and a risk of overdose, and to ensure adequate contraception to prevent unintended pregnancies. Stabilization with opioid-assisted therapy is compatible with breastfeeding. Neonatal abstinence syndrome is an expected and treatable condition that follows prenatal exposure to opioid agonists.

The rationale for opioid-assisted therapy during pregnancy is to prevent complications of illicit opioid use and narcotic withdrawal, encourage prenatal care and drug treatment, reduce criminal activity, and avoid risks to a client of associating with a drug culture. Methadone maintenance, as prescribed and dispensed on a daily basis by a registered substance abuse treatment program, is part of a comprehensive package of prenatal care, chemical dependency counseling, family therapy, nutritional education, and other medical and psychosocial services as indicated for pregnant women with opioid dependence.

Test-Taking Strategies Applied

This is a recall question which assesses social workers' awareness of the effects of addiction and appropriate treatment protocols. Medically supervised withdrawal from opioids in opioid-dependent women is not recommended during pregnancy because the withdrawal is associated with high relapse rates. During pregnancy, chronic untreated heroin use is associated with an increased risk of fetal growth restriction, fetal death, preterm labor, and other adverse outcomes. Additionally, the lifestyle issues associated with illicit drug use put the pregnant woman at risk of engaging in activities, such as prostitution, theft, and violence, to support herself or her addiction.

Methadone is an opioid used to treat pain and as maintenance therapy or to help with tapering in clients with opioid dependence. Thus, discontinuation of all opioids is an incorrect answer. Intensive therapy and social support are beneficial, but not sufficient for treating heroin. Best practice includes medication-assisted treatment for all clients, including pregnant women.

Knowledge Area

Unit II—Intervention Processes and Techniques for Use Across Systems (Content Area); Biopsychosocial History and Collateral Data (Competency); The Effects of Addiction and Substance Abuse on Individuals, Families, Groups, Organizations, and Communities (KSA)

32. C

Rationale

Older adulthood is a time of continued growth. Clients in the later stages of life contribute significantly to their families, communities, and society. At the same time, clients face multiple biopsychosocial–spiritual–cultural challenges as they age: changes in health and physical abilities; difficulty in accessing comprehensive, affordable, and high-quality health and behavioral health care; decreased economic security; increased vulnerability to abuse and exploitation; and loss of meaningful social roles and opportunities to remain engaged in society. Social workers must understand the needs of older adults and issues that may be facing them.

Sundowning is a term used to refer to behavioral changes that often occur in the late afternoon or evening in people with Alzheimer's disease and similar conditions. The behavioral changes may take the form of aggression, agitation, delusions, hallucinations, paranoia, increased disorientation, or wandering and pacing about. Sundowning is not a disease, but a group of symptoms that occur at a specific time of the day that may affect people with dementia. The exact cause of this behavior is unknown. Factors that may aggravate late-day confusion include fatigue, low lighting, increased shadows, disruption of the body's "internal clock," and/or difficulty separating reality from dreams. Reducing sundowning can be assisted by maintaining a predictable routine for bedtime, waking, meals and activities, and limiting daytime napping.

When sundowning occurs in a nursing home, it may be related to the flurry of activity during staff shift changes or the lack of structured activities in the late afternoon and evening. Staff arriving and leaving may cue clients with Alzheimer's to want to go home or to check on their children—or other behaviors that were appropriate in the late afternoon in their past. It may help to occupy their time with another activity during that period.

Folie à deux, or shared psychosis, is when symptoms of a delusional belief and hallucinations are transmitted from one individual to another. While not listed in the *DSM-5*, recent psychiatric classifications refer to the syndrome as shared psychotic disorder.

Dementia is a chronic or persistent disorder of the mental processes caused by brain disease or injury and marked by memory disorders, personality changes, and impaired reasoning.

Neurodegeneration is an umbrella term for the progressive loss of structure or function of neurons. Many neurodegenerative diseases including amyotrophic lateral sclerosis, Parkinson's, Alzheimer's, and Huntington's occur as a result of neurodegenerative processes. Such diseases are incurable.

Test-Taking Strategies Applied

This is a recall question which relies on social workers being able to recognize and understand terms associated with neurogenerative diseases, such as Alzheimer's. Such diseases cause changes in client behavior. One of the response choices, folie à deux, is used to describe shared psychosis which is not associated with neurogenerative disease. Social workers must be well versed in actions associated with typical human development, as well as those which indicate the presence of disease or disturbance.

Knowledge Area

Unit II—Intervention Processes and Techniques for Use Across Systems (Content Area); Biopsychosocial History and Collateral Data (Competency); Symptoms of Neurologic and Organic Disorders (KSA)

33. C

Rationale

There is tremendous importance placed on social relationships. Thus, social workers often rely on the **use of collaterals to obtain relevant information** to assist clients. Unfortunately, while the 2008 *NASW Code of Ethics* advises social workers of their ethical obligations to clients, it is silent on what obligations, if any, social workers owe to clients' family members, friends, and other collaterals who may be brought into the helping process. Thus, social workers must adhere to broad professional values when interacting with collaterals regardless of whether a particular situation is explicitly covered by the *Code of Ethics*.

In the absence of ethical standards, it is helpful for social workers to have agency policies and contracts that fill these gaps. For instance, before meeting with collaterals, there should be an agreement regarding the meeting's purpose, what information will be shared, and how that information may be used. Although contracts have traditionally been used with clients, they can also be used with collaterals to clarify expectations, to preempt conflicts, and to provide clients, collaterals, and social workers with legal safeguards. Service contracts with collaterals could include, but not be limited to, explaining the roles of social workers, their primary commitments to clients, any commitments to collaterals, the roles of collaterals, the nature of collateral involvement, benefits and risks to collaterals, and/or confidentiality issues.

Test-Taking Strategies Applied

The case scenario relates to the client's request to have his daughter come to the next session. Using other family members or friends as collaterals may be helpful, but does not address the suggestion at hand. Confidentiality is a client right, so a social worker can share information with others when requested by the client. It is allowed and appropriate to discuss client information with collaterals as long as the social worker ensures that the sharing is done at the client's wishes and there is a clear understanding about what will be discussed. Including his daughter in discussions about the extent of the client's current problems was suggested by the client. Thus, it is not appropriate for the social worker to identify them without addressing the desire to use her as a collateral informant to obtain relevant information.

The correct response choice ensures that there is a mutual understanding about key ethical issues which may arise when using the daughter as a collateral informant.

Knowledge Area

Unit II—Intervention Processes and Techniques for Use Across Systems (Content Area); Assessment Methods and Techniques (Competency); Methods of Involving Clients/Client Systems in Problem Identification (e.g., Gathering Collateral Information) (KSA)

34. A

Rationale

With the increasing focus on **interdisciplinary practice** in recent years, social workers may be supervised by a professional of a different discipline. Although this may be appropriate within the team or unit context, social workers should seek supervision or consultation from another social worker with regard to specific social work practices and issues. Similarly, a social worker providing supervision to a member of another discipline should refer that supervisee to a member of his or her own profession for practice-specific supervision or consultation.

Test-Taking Strategies Applied

While a qualifying word is not used in the case scenario, a social worker should review the response choices and select the one that best assists in resolving a social work practice issue. It is unlikely that another supervisor will be assigned, and requesting one will not necessarily mean that a new supervisor will be familiar with social work practice. Self-help resources may be helpful, but should have already been consulted. The social work profession has a unique set of values and practice standards, so it is essential that the social worker seek supervision or consultation from another social worker. The hospital supervisor should be aware that such supervision is being sought and involved clients must be informed of the need for "outside" supervision or consultation if applicable.

Knowledge Area

Unit III—Intervention Processes and Techniques for Use With Larger Systems (Content Area); Supervision and Administration (Competency); The Process of Interdisciplinary and Intradisciplinary Team Collaboration (KSA)

35. C

Rationale

Performance monitoring is used to provide information on (a) key aspects of how programs are operating; (b) whether, and to what extent, program objectives are being attained (e.g., numbers of clients served compared to target goals, reductions in target behaviors); and (c) identification of failures to produce program outputs, for use in managing or redesigning program operations. Performance indicators can also be developed to (d) monitor service quality by collecting data on the satisfaction of those served and (e) report on program efficiency, effectiveness, and productivity by assessing the relationship between the resources used (program inputs) and the outcome indicators.

If conducted frequently enough and in a timely way, performance monitoring can provide social workers with regular feedback that will allow them to identify problems, take timely action, and subsequently assess whether their actions have led to the improvements sought.

Performance monitoring involves identification and collection of specific data on program outputs, outcomes, and accomplishments. Although they may measure subjective factors such as client satisfaction, data is often numeric, consisting of frequency counts, statistical averages, ratios, or percentages.

Test-Taking Strategies Applied

The question contains a qualifying word—NOT—that requires social workers to select the response choice which is not an aim of performance monitoring. When NOT is used as a qualifying word, it is often helpful to remove it from the question and eliminate the three response choices which are aims. This approach will leave the one response choice which is NOT a reason for doing performance monitoring.

Justification of the need for a service is not the aim of performance monitoring. Performance monitoring occurs during implementation of services while identification of needs happens before they are designed or planned. Needs assessments are conducted to determine the scope and severity of problems. Performance monitoring should not be approached as a perfunctory task to justify ongoing operations or delivery or it will not lead to quality evaluations of what is working and what is not.

Knowledge Area

Unit III—Intervention Processes and Techniques for Use With Larger Systems (Content Area); Supervision and Administration (Competency); Quality Assurance, Including Program Reviews and Audits by External Sources (KSA)

36. B

Rationale

Clients who suffer from severe depression may be at **risk of suicide**. Although suicide cannot be predicted or prevented with certainty, knowing the warning signs can help recognize when clients are at risk. The most effective way to try to prevent suicide is to recognize the warning signs, respond immediately, and treat underlying causes of suicide such as depression.

Some warning signs of suicide include the following behaviors:

- Talking about suicide or death
- Feeling hopeless, helpless, or worthless and saying things like, "It would be better if I wasn't here" or "I want out"
- Exhibiting deep sadness, loss of interest in pleasurable activities, trouble sleeping and eating
- *Having abrupt change of mood, from extreme sadness to happiness or calm*
- Engaging in risk-taking behavior such as driving too fast and recklessly
- Calling or visiting people to say goodbye
- Putting affairs in order such as making changes to a will

Along with these behaviors, clients who are depressed have a higher risk of attempting suicide if they have ever previously made attempts, have chronic or terminal illnesses, are separated or divorced, are underemployed or unemployed, or have family histories of suicide.

Test-Taking Strategies Applied

The question contains a qualifying word—FIRST. There may be more than one appropriate response choice, but the order in which they are to occur is critical. In this situation, the social worker must immediately find out more information about the reasons for the change in mood.

Improvement in depressive symptoms can be an indication of upcoming suicide attempts. Clients who have put plans in place to end their lives often appear to be calmer or happier. The knowledge that they will be ending their lives soon appears to bring with it peace or happiness for clients plagued by depression.

Asking about changes which have recently taken place in the client's life is too vague and does not contain the questions needed to do a proper suicide risk assessment. Documentation and praise will not assist the social worker in understanding the client's current mental status. The need for a suicide risk assessment is most immediate when warning signs are present, such as those described in the case scenario.

Knowledge Area

Unit II—Intervention Processes and Techniques for Use Across Systems (Content Area); Biopsychosocial History and Collateral Data (Competency); The Indicators and Risk Factors of the Client's/Client System's Danger to Self and Others (KSA)

37. B

Rationale

Roles describe sets of expected behaviors and obligations based on position in life and relative to others. People have multiple responsibilities and roles are blueprints to guide behavior. Role theory posits that a large proportion of day-to-day social behavior and interaction is defined by people carrying out their roles.

Role theory can predict behavior; if the expectations for a particular role are understood, a large portion of the behavior in those roles can be predicted. Roles not only guide behavior, they also influence beliefs as the theory holds that people will change their attitudes to be in line with their roles. Role theory also posits that changing behavior requires changing roles.

In some instances, different roles are not compatible; as a result, conflict occurs. When the roles have two different statuses, the result is called **status strain**. When conflicting roles both have the same status, **role strain** results. Role strain happens when a person who needs to fulfill a certain role is strained because of obligations or extensive demands on energy, time, or resources caused by multiple roles.

A woman who has a professional career experiences **role conflict** when expectations for what it means to be a "good wife" or "good mother"—both external and internal—conflict with the goals and responsibilities she may have in her professional life.

Other terms related to role theory are as follows.

Role complementarity: When roles are complementary, partners in a relationship identify self and others correctly, accurately assume expected roles, and perform appropriately.

Role reciprocity: Reciprocity involves the typical and expected pairing of role positions, such as husband/wife, mother/child, and worker/client. Both roles must be present to complete the function.

Test-Taking Strategies Applied

Social workers must be familiar with role theory as it helps one to understand, explain, and predict client behavior. There are many terms used to explain role functioning. This is a recall question which includes some of these terms. Even if not familiar with these terms, it may be possible to identify the correct answer. In the case scenario, there is no exchange between the roles described, which is associated with reciprocity. Complementarity sounds as if the roles fit together easily, which they clearly do not from the client's perspective. Lastly, the client is not confused about what is expected in each of her roles—there is just a struggle to fulfill both of them, which is a conflict.

Knowledge Area

Unit I—Human Development, Diversity, and Behavior in the Environment (Content Area); Effects of the Environment on Systems' Behavior (Competency); Role Theories (KSA)

38. C

Rationale

Preparing a **case presentation** can be a daunting task for a social worker. While there is no standard format, there are key sections which should be included. Sections include:

- **Demographics:** Age, gender, ethnicity, living situation, social work involvement, etc.
- **Background:** Relevant history
- **Presenting Problem/Key Findings:** Details of the presenting problem and current situation—signs and symptoms of illness, environmental factors that impinge on the situation, and actual or potential resources

- **Formulation:** Understanding of why things are as they are—including one or more theoretical perspectives and any uncertainty or ambivalence about the situation
- **Interventions and Plans:** What has been done and what plans exist to address the situation
- **Reason for Presentation:** Explanation of why this situation is being discussed—unique challenges? unusual problems?

More detailed case presentations may include additional sections including legal/ethical, crisis/safety, diversity, and so on.

Test-Taking Strategies Applied

The supervisor is used in this question to determine if all the necessary elements of a case presentation were included. The goal of supervision is to ensure that clients receive the most effective and efficient services possible. Thus, the supervisor will appear in many questions throughout the examination to provide quality assurance, ensuring that a social worker is meeting acceptable standards.

The case presentation described only contains some of the required elements. Even a brief case presentation must contain information on the presenting problem. The presenting problem was not mentioned, making the case presentation incomplete.

Knowledge Area

Unit III—Intervention Processes and Techniques for Use With Larger Systems (Content Area); Supervision and Administration (Competency); The Elements of a Case Presentation (KSA)

39. D

Rationale

Economic justice is a component of social justice. It is a set of moral principles for building economic institutions, the ultimate goal of which is to create an opportunity for each person to have adequate resources to have a dignified, productive, and creative life. It promotes policies which open the doors of access and opportunity for everyone, particularly those in greatest need. For example, implementing policies that reflect the goal of economic justice might involve eliminating discriminatory hiring practices and permitting people to work freely where their business skills are required.

An example of an economic justice institution is **progressive taxation**—a system of taxation where tax percentage increases as the base amount increases. The goal of progressive taxation is to remedy income inequality and to provide funds for social services, public infrastructure, and education. Earned income credit, affordable housing, and need-based federal financial aid for college students are other examples of programs to promote economic justice.

Other tax structures include:

Proportional tax: Otherwise known as a **flat tax**, a flat tax rate is applied to all earned income regardless of amount.

Regressive tax: In a regressive tax system, families who are poor pay a higher percentage of their incomes or tax rate.

Test-Taking Strategies Applied

The criterion for selecting the correct answer must be based on promoting economic justice. It is important to understand the basis of economic justice, which is that policies should ensure that those who earn less are able to have resources which enable them to have dignified, creative, and productive lives. Thus, those who earn more should pay more in taxes in an effort to distribute resources fairly. Understanding the differences in taxation structures is also necessary when selecting the correct response. Often, having general knowledge, as well as recalling key terms, is needed in order to answer correctly.

Knowledge Area

Unit I—Human Development, Diversity, and Behavior in the Environment (Content Area); Effects of the Environment on Systems' Behavior (Competency); Social and Economic Justice (KSA)

40. C

Rationale

Attending is a term frequently used to describe the process of nonverbally communicating to clients that social workers are open, nonjudgmental, accepting of them as people, and interested in what they say. The purpose of attending is to encourage clients to express themselves as fully and freely as possible. During the beginning of the problem-solving process, especially, nonverbal presentation is equally important to verbal communication as clients are usually doing most of the talking.

Many of the guidelines available may be useful, but they tend to reflect nonverbal characteristics of majority-member, middle- and upper-class adults. Good attending behavior is usually described as follows.

- **Eye Contact:** Looking at clients is one way of showing interest. However, social workers can make clients feel uncomfortable if they stare at them too intensely. The best way of showing that social workers are listening is by looking at clients naturally.
- **Posture:** This is a natural response of interest. It is best to lean slightly toward clients in a relaxed manner. Relaxation is important, since social workers want to shift focus from themselves so they are better able to listen to clients.
- **Gesture:** Social workers communicate a great deal with body movements. If hands are flailed, arms are crossed, or chest/ shoulders are hunched, then messages, whether intentional or unintentional, will be communicated.
- **Facial Expressions:** Facial expressions, such as smiling, eyebrow raising, and frowning, indicate responsiveness.

Test-Taking Strategies Applied

Social workers must be aware of verbal and nonverbal communication techniques. This question requires recall of the name of a nonverbal technique. Determining the scope and severity of client problems, as well as the barriers which impede progress, are assessing tasks. Identifying alternatives which will result in change is a planning or intervening action. Attending behavior is heavily used in engaging, though it continues throughout the problem-solving process. The correct answer is much broader than the other response choices and is the aim of attending behavior.

Knowledge Area

Unit II—Intervention Processes and Techniques for Use Across Systems (Content Area); Intervention Planning and Implementation (Competency); Verbal and Nonverbal Communication Techniques (KSA)

41. D

Rationale

Effective interventions depend on using the most appropriate theory and practice strategies for a given problem or situation. *Different theories/ interventions are best suited for different problems*. Evidence-based practices (EBPs) are treatments that have been proven effective (to some degree) through outcome evaluations. EBPs are interventions that have strong scientific proof that they produce positive outcomes for certain types of disorders. *Clearly defining problems will help rationalize the implementation of EBPs and help inform the selection process.*

Other interventions—sometimes labeled promising practices—may also produce good outcomes, but research has not been conducted at a level to say that there is strong evidence for those practices. As such, EBPs are treatments that are likely to be effective in changing target behaviors if implemented with integrity.

The selection of an EBP depends on client problems, the outcomes desired, and treatment preferences. For example, both antidepressant medications and psychotherapy interventions are effective in the treatment of depression in older adults. The choice of one of these interventions over the other may vary with respect to the nature and severity of depression, the presence of other health conditions or medications, tolerability of side effects or required effort, and the preferences and personal values of older adults regarding these treatment characteristics.

Test-Taking Strategies Applied

The question contains a qualifying word—MOST—that indicates that all response choices may be considered, but the correct answer is the factor which must drive this decision. Treatment modalities differ depending upon presenting problems. Social workers should not limit available options to clients based on available resources, past history, and/or setting. EBPs which have demonstrated that they are effective for problems at hand must be used. Social workers can advocate for additional resources or refer clients to settings which provide the appropriate treatment if it is not available in the current setting. In addition, treatment decisions should not be based predominantly on what has been done in the past. Interventions can be very effective to address some problems and useless in helping others. Thus, matching EBPs/interventions to presenting problems is vital to ensuring that change will occur.

Knowledge Area

Unit II—Intervention Processes and Techniques for Use Across Systems (Content Area); Intervention Planning and Implementation (Competency); The Criteria Used in the Selection of Intervention/ Treatment Modalities (e.g., Client/Client System Abilities, Culture, Life Stage) (KSA)

42. D

Rationale

The 2008 *NASW Code of Ethics* provides standards with regard to **confidentiality**, including the process for disclosing information as a result of **mandatory reporting**. Social workers should respect clients' right to privacy. Social workers should not solicit private information from clients unless it is essential to providing services or conducting social work evaluation or research. Once private information is shared, standards of confidentiality apply. Social workers may disclose confidential information when appropriate with valid consent from a client or a person legally authorized to consent on behalf of a client. Social workers should protect the confidentiality of all information obtained in the course of professional service, except for compelling professional reasons. The general expectation that social workers will keep information confidential does not apply when disclosure is necessary to prevent serious, foreseeable, and imminent harm to a client or other identifiable person. In all instances, social workers should disclose the least amount of confidential information necessary to achieve the desired purpose; only information that is directly relevant to the purpose for which the disclosure is made should be revealed. *Social workers should inform clients, to the extent possible, about the disclosure of confidential information and the potential consequences, when feasible before the disclosure is made. This applies whether social workers disclose confidential information on the basis of a legal requirement or client consent.*

Test-Taking Strategies Applied

The case scenario calls for reporting the suspicions to the child protection agency (referred to as the authorities in this question). The social worker does not need to prove that the abuse is occurring or identify the perpetrator. The child protection agency is responsible for doing the investigation. While two answers include reporting the suspicions, only the correct one involves informing the clients about the disclosure and the information which needs to be legally released without the clients' consent. Informing clients—or even involving them in the process—is required, when feasible, according to the 2008 *NASW Code of Ethics*.

Knowledge Area

Unit IV—Professional Relationships, Values, and Ethics (Content Area); Confidentiality (Competency);Ethical and/or Legal Issues Regarding Mandatory Reporting (e.g., Abuse, Threat of Harm, Impaired Professionals, etc.) (KSA)

43. C

Rationale

A social worker's own **values and beliefs** can greatly influence the social worker–client relationship. Culture, race, and ethnicity are strongly linked to values. *Social workers must have self-awareness about their own attitudes, values, and beliefs and a willingness to acknowledge that they may be different than those served.* Differences in values and beliefs are very common when working with diverse populations. A social worker is responsible for bringing up and addressing issues of cultural difference with a client and is also ethically responsible for being culturally competent by obtaining the appropriate knowledge, skills, and experience.

Social workers should:

1. Move from being culturally unaware to aware of one's own heritage and the heritage of others
2. Value and celebrate differences of others rather than maintaining an ethnocentric stance
3. Have an awareness of personal values and biases and how they may influence relationships with clients
4. Demonstrate comfort with racial and cultural differences between themselves and clients
5. Have an awareness of personal and professional limitations
6. Acknowledge their own attitudes, beliefs, and feelings

Test-Taking Strategies Applied

The question acknowledges that "both school officials and the social worker feel that the student is making a mistake." Thus, it is critical for the social worker to acknowledge the differences in values between the professionals involved and the student as she is choosing family responsibilities over pursuit of her education. This choice is based on the personal principles and tenets that are important to her.

The incorrect answers may be useful, but the correct one is essential for the formation of a social worker–client relationship built on the core values of the profession, including the student's right to self-determination. Despite the extent of the existing responsibilities, her career goals, and/or the supports available, the student may value the needs of her family over furthering her own education.

Knowledge Area

Unit IV—Professional Relationships, Values, and Ethics (Content Area); Professional Development and Use of Self (Competency); The Influence of the Social Worker's Own Values and Beliefs on the Social Worker–Client/Client System Relationship (KSA)

44. B

Rationale

Many believe that **Gender Identity Disorder, Gender Incongruence**, and **Gender Dysphoria** should be viewed and approached from the perspective of a **medical model** rather than that of a **mental health model**. Many anatomical inconsistencies can now be corrected surgically or chemically to align with the experienced true self. A medical diagnosis for individuals who are transgender, whose self-experienced gender does not match the sex assigned at birth, and who require medical services to align the body with the experienced self is considered more appropriate and consistent with research and best practices.

Those with the aforementioned diagnoses already are stigmatized by society due to myths and misunderstandings, and victimized by intolerance and prejudice. The effects of this stigma are profound and longstanding, resulting in increased risks for negative health, mental health, educational, professional, and social outcomes. Continuing to include these diagnoses in the *DSM* contributes to sustained oppression of those who receive them.

Labeling individuals with Gender Identity Disorder, Gender Incongruence, and Gender Dysphoria views these conditions as aberrant and is harmful. Considering medical diagnoses instead is more appropriate and addresses intolerance, discrimination, and oppression related to considering these diagnoses as psychological problems needing to be fixed.

Test-Taking Strategies Applied

This question requires knowledge about "using a medical model." A **medical model** is based on the assumption that abnormal behavior is the result of physical problems and should be treated medically. Providing therapy as mentioned in the first response choice implies that a mental health model is being used. Also, treatment may involve corrective surgery—not just medication. Exploring the mind–body connection and screening for physical conditions may help in considering biological or medical issues, but are not directly related to gender identity. The question contains a qualifying word—BEST—that requires selecting a response choice that is essential if these diagnoses are viewed using a medical model or resulting from physical problems—not psychological ones.

Knowledge Area

Unit I—Human Development, Diversity, and Behavior in the Environment (Content Area); Diversity, Discrimination, and Stereotypes (Competency); Gender and Gender Identity Concepts (KSA)

45. B

Rationale

Rational choice theory is a theory in social science that argues human behavior, and social life in general, can be explained in terms of rational choices of individuals. Social interaction, including political interaction, is considered to be a type of exchange where individuals will interact with each other if the expected gains outweigh the expected costs arising from the interaction.

In this approach, public policy is seen as that which achieves maximum social gain for expended costs. Policy alternatives are evaluated according to this criterion. A rational choice model assumes that the preferences of society as a whole can be known and weighted.

Incrementalism is based on fear of unintended consequences and sees policies as variations of what has been done in the past.

Institutionalism sees policy as a product of the government with individuals having little power.

Elite theory posits that policies are enacted that maintain the status quo or preserve the positions of those who currently have power.

Test-Taking Strategies Applied

The question relies on social workers having knowledge about various theoretical approaches to policy development and analysis. Recall questions are intermixed with problem-solving questions on the examination. There are few strategies that can be used in recall questions. However, answers are always those which focus on increasing benefits to clients or delivering the most effective services possible. Viewing answers with this aim in mind may assist as "maximizing benefits" is the only response choice that speaks to positive impacts for clients.

Knowledge Area

Unit III—Intervention Processes and Techniques for Use With Larger Systems (Content Area); Methods for Social Change (Competency); Concepts of Social Policy Development and Analysis (KSA)

46. D

Rationale

Defense mechanisms are *unconscious* mechanisms which are activated in times of anxiety, stress, and distress without any choice or conscious intentionality. They are a necessary tool of protection and in moderate use contribute to successful adaptation. Defense mechanisms are a part of normal functioning, but they can be considered as pathological in some instances.

Coping, on the other hand, includes *conscious* strategies that enable clients to attain realistic goals by using available resources and past experiences while acting within society's rules of conduct. While defense mechanisms are unconscious processes whereas coping methods are conscious, in reality, sometimes clients exhibit rational coping simultaneously with unconscious defenses.

Coping mechanisms are often confused and interchanged with defense mechanisms due to their similarities. Both processes are activated in times of adversity. Defense mechanisms and coping strategies reduce arousal of negative emotions. Furthermore, both processes aim at achieving adaptation; only the means to the end differ. Defenses help the individual by distorting reality and coping strategies attempt to solve the problem, thus changing the reality. Coping behaviors involve conscious modification of cognitive and emotional appraisals, which eventually modify the reactions to the stressful event rather than distort the perception of the event. Clients have full control of coping strategies used. They can choose to stop certain coping styles and choose others.

Defense mechanisms, on the other hand, operate outside consciousness and awareness. Clients cannot intentionally choose to use other defense mechanisms.

Coping involves flexibility, and defenses are more rigid. The choice of coping mechanism is perceived more as dependent on timing, situation, and personality factors. Different situations lead to different coping strategies. Defense mechanisms are more stable and habitual.

The idea regarding whether defense mechanisms produce adaptive and functional behaviors is still controversial. In the long term, defense mechanisms do contribute to the development of severe pathology, yet the fact that they seem to help individuals to cope in the short term should not be ignored or dismissed. Defenses are efficient mechanisms that help deal with threatening and, at times, traumatic stressors. Pathology probably does not originate from the actual use of defense mechanisms; it is caused by a continuous reliance on defenses, instead of actually attempting to solve the core problems that cause their necessity in the first place.

Test-Taking Strategies Applied

The question contains a qualifying word—PRIMARY—that indicates that there may be more than one distinction between defense and coping mechanisms. However, the correct response choice is the one which contains the most fundamental or important difference. Defense mechanisms and coping strategies describe distinct psychological processes, namely those which are unconscious and unintentional versus those which are not.

In addition, the first three response choices are not accurate statements. Coping mechanisms are not "unconscious actions" as stated in the first answer. Additionally, defense mechanisms are rigid and do not fluctuate like coping skills, contrary to what is stated in the second response choice. Lastly, defense mechanisms can be adaptive and functional ways to deal with stress, making the third answer incorrect as well.

Knowledge Area

Unit I—Human Development, Diversity, and Behavior in the Environment (Content Area); Effects of the Environment on Systems' Behavior (Competency); Psychological Defense Mechanisms and Their Effects on Behavior and Relationships (KSA)

47. C

Rationale

Feedback during engagement in the problem-solving process encourages clients to comment about treatment purpose, social worker/client roles, policy or ethical factors, and so on. An important part of communicating effectively involves checking to see whether clients have understood social workers' messages. Seeking feedback serves this function. In addition, seeking feedback is essential for informed consent by inviting clients to identify areas that are unclear, share thoughts that have occurred to them, introduce new topics, or express disagreement. *By seeking feedback, social workers effectively send messages that treatment is a mutual and reciprocal process. Social workers convey that they are genuinely interested in what clients have to say and there is a desire to have them actively participate in the process.*

Social workers routinely seek feedback throughout the problem-solving process by asking, "How does that sound to you?" Other feedback can be elicited by inquiring, "What do you think about what we have talked about so far?" It is also good to find out about client questions or comments.

Test-Taking Strategies Applied

When provided with a case scenario, it is necessary to determine when it is taking place within the problem-solving process. In this question, the social worker is "in an initial meeting with a man," indicating that engagement is occurring. During engagement, a social worker must begin to form a working alliance with a client. A client must feel respected and understand that a social worker can be a valuable resource toward making change, but cannot solve a client's problems and is not there to tell him or her what to do.

In this case scenario, the social worker's question demonstrates to the client that his opinions about treatment matter despite the involuntary nature of the service. It aims to get the client talking about his feelings, which is the first step in forming a therapeutic relationship. While the client may reveal some resistance when answering, the question is not aimed to do so. It also does not seek to determine if denial is present or identify whether the client is aware of his legal mandates. All of these are assessment tasks which will occur later. Assessment follows engagement in the problem-solving process. In addition, a social worker should not make assumptions about the presence of resistance or denial just because a client is mandated into services.

Universal among involuntary clients is that other entities have the power to influence terms of their treatment, which may make them feel that they have less control in the process. Social workers can address this issue by eliciting their feedback, sending the message that their input is essential.

Knowledge Area

Unit II—Intervention Processes and Techniques for Use Across Systems (Content Area); Intervention Planning and Implementation (Competency); Methods to Obtain and Provide Feedback (KSA)

48. B

Rationale

Community mobilization is based on the simple premise that human beings are by nature social creatures whose behaviors, attitudes, and beliefs are profoundly affected by the norms of the communities in which they live. It is the process of engaging communities to change the norms within their own communities. *By its very nature, it tends to be primary prevention*. Its goal is to engage the community in activities that can prevent social problems. Its purpose is not to educate communities, although communities will learn throughout the process. Its purpose is not to provide services to communities, although communities may develop strategies that include providing support. The purpose of community mobilization is to empower communities to recognize and change the existing norms.

Community mobilization is essentially a process for reaching out to different sectors of a community and creating partnerships in order to focus on, and ultimately address, a pressing issue. For example, community mobilization supports teen pregnancy prevention efforts by empowering community members and groups to take action to facilitate change. This includes mobilizing necessary resources, disseminating information, generating support, and fostering cooperation across public and private sectors in the community.

Primary prevention aims to prevent a problem while **secondary prevention** focuses on reducing the impact by detecting it as early as possible. **Tertiary prevention** is directed at helping manage a problem that has lasting effects.

Test-Taking Strategies Applied

Social workers need to be familiar with both community mobilization and prevention strategies in order to get this question correct. Both are aimed at social change, which is an important social work competency. Community mobilization is long-term and complex—trying to change norms, which is not easily done. Often questions require the integration of knowledge related to multiple KSAs.

Knowledge Area

Unit III—Intervention Processes and Techniques for Use With Larger Systems (Content Area); Methods for Social Change (Competency); Techniques for Mobilizing Community Participation (KSA)

49. D

Rationale

Social workers' commitment to **informed consent** is based on clients' right to self-determination. The informed consent process is one of the clearest expressions of social workers' respect for clients' dignity and worth as individuals to make choices which are best suited to meet their needs.

A client must have the right to refuse or withdraw consent. Social workers should be prepared for the possibility that clients will exercise these rights. Social workers should inform clients of their rights and help clients make thoughtful and informed decisions based on all available facts and information about potential benefits and risks.

Social workers must be familiar with informed consent requirements concerning clients' right to consent, especially when working with those who are incarcerated, children, individuals with cognitive impairments, and so on.

While state and federal laws and regulations vary in interpretations and applications of informed consent standards, there are essential standards in all processes which are needed for their validity.

First, coercion and undue influence must not have played a role in clients' decisions. As social workers often maintain control over approving benefits, admission into programs, and the termination of services, they must ensure that clients do not feel pressured to grant consent based upon this control.

Second, social workers must not present clients with general, broadly-worded consent forms that may violate clients' right to be informed and may be considered invalid if challenged in a court of law. The use of broad or blank consent forms cannot possibly constitute informed consent. Social workers should include details that refer to specific activities, information to be released, or interventions. Typical elements include details of the nature and purpose of a service or disclosure of information; advantages and disadvantages of an intervention; substantial or possible risks to clients, if any; potential effects on clients' families, jobs, social activities, and other important aspects of their lives; alternatives to the proposed intervention or disclosure; and anticipated costs for clients. This information should be presented to clients in clear, understandable language. Consent forms should be dated and include a reasonable expiration date.

Third, clients must be mentally capable of providing legal consent. Clearly, clients with significant permanent cognitive deficits may be unable to comprehend the consent procedure. Social workers should assess clients' ability to reason and make informed choices, comprehend relevant facts and retain this information, appreciate current circumstances, and communicate wishes. *Some clients may be only temporarily unable to consent, such as individuals who are under the influence of alcohol or other drugs or are experiencing transient cognitive symptoms at the time consent is sought. Clients who are unable to consent at a given moment may be able to consent in the future if the incapacity is temporary.*

Test-Taking Strategies Applied

The case scenario described a man who is using drugs which interfered with his ability to give informed consent. It is not appropriate to waive consent procedures or have the man sign a form which he does not understand. Verbal consent procedures are also problematic as "the social worker questions his ability to understand what she is asking." Thus, he cannot give consent if he is unable to understand parameters of the information to be gathered or the services to be delivered (the nature and purpose of the service; the advantages and disadvantages of an intervention; substantial or possible risks; anticipated costs; and so on).

His impairment may be temporary as he admits to using drugs which interfered with his reasoning prior to the meeting.

Arranging to meet him at a later time may result in him being in a mental state in which he can make informed choices and comprehend relevant facts, which are necessary elements for informed consent.

Knowledge Area

Unit IV—Professional Relationships, Values, and Ethics (Content Area); Confidentiality (Competency); The Principles and Processes of Obtaining Informed Consent (KSA)

50. A

Rationale

Developing goals, objectives, and interventions is critical to alleviating client problems. The document that contains the problem statement, goals, objectives, and methods is the **intervention, treatment, or service plan** (contract). It is a road map that outlines the journey from problems that are identified through assessment to life when those issues have been successfully addressed.

The first step in any helping process is to identify the solvable problem and why a client is seeking help now. Once the problem is identified, goals and objectives can be specified that will help toward a solution. *Goals are long-term, general, and often the opposite of the problem.* The most basic goal should be for a client to be able to function at the level of functioning before the current problem started. This baseline is referred to as premorbid functioning.

The specific steps taken to achieve the goal are called objectives. *Objectives are short-term and specify who does the action, for how long, and how often to achieve the desired outcome (who will do what by when).* Because the goals and objectives derive from the assessment, the frequency of the desired outcome should not be made up out of thin air. Using the frequency before the problem starts and working backwards is helpful. Being realistic and precise in targets will assist in achieving success. Considering premorbid functioning ensures that goals and objectives are not set too high.

Strategies are the means by which treatment goals are achieved. Each objective can have more than one intervention. Interventions are typically specific to varying theoretical approaches.

Test-Taking Strategies Applied

In the case scenario, since the client is feeling worthless—specifically that she is not important to anyone—the goal or solution is to help her see that she is important to someone. This is obviously not the only problem in her life, but it is the one identified to be worked on. The identified objective was to meet friends, which is not happening now. If she met friends weekly in the past, prior to her feelings of worthlessness, the objective would be to engage in that behavior again. The objective has a baseline (zero times a week) as well as a target (once a week). It will also need a time frame for achievement.

The incorrect response choices do not relate to the stated objective of seeing her friends or are a method needed to achieve the objective (such as identifying accessible transportation) of establishing "the measurable target."

Knowledge Area

Unit III—Intervention Processes and Techniques for Use With Larger Systems (Content Area); Program Development and Research (Competency); Methods to Develop and Evaluate Measurable Objectives for Client/Client System Intervention, Treatment, and/or Service Plans (KSA)

51. B

Rationale

Problem-oriented recording (POR) is a method of **record-keeping** that often has been used in hospitals and medical programs and is now used by many social agencies, as well. POR has a number of advantages as it permits the worker, agency supervisor, outside consultants, or researchers to review the way in which a particular problem was approached; displays the interrelatedness of problems experienced by a client, yet permits focused attention on each specific problem; provides continuity of professional attention on specific problems, even when there is personnel turnover in the agency; and provides a mechanism for follow-up and the monitoring of progress toward problem resolution.

POR consists of four components, which are related to the basic steps of the problem-solving process: (a) establishment of a database; (b) listing of specific problems, each of which is assigned an identifying number; (c) development of an action plan to address each problem; and (d) implementation of the plan.

The database consists primarily of the information collected during the intake phase and includes a description of the problem that brought clients to the agency. All problems become part of the problem list. Each problem is assigned a number and described in behavioral language. Diagnostic labels are avoided, if possible. The problem list serves to focus case planning and intervention. What a social worker does should be logically related to a specific problem in the list. As problems are resolved, they are removed from the list. However, the resolved problem's number is not reassigned; each number is used only once. Thus, the intervention and progress on a specific problem can be traced throughout the case record. In a sense, the numbering system serves as an audit trail. *It is important that the problem list be on a separate page in the case record; this makes it easy to find the list and provides a ready reference point for a review of progress and planning.*

Using a master problem list also facilitates program evaluation and research on the types of problems brought to the agency and the types of services provided. POR requires some type of response to each item on a client's problem list. Basically, three actions are possible: (a) to intervene, (b) to secure additional information in order to more fully understand the problem, or (c) to do nothing except monitor the situation and wait for further developments.

If an identified problem requires an intervention (i.e., planned change), it is helpful to use a SOAP or other format to describe the proposed action and its rationale. The acronym SOAP represents information collected related to subjective reports, objective indicators, assessment, and planning.

Test-Taking Strategies Applied

This is a recall question about POR. There are many formats for recording; social workers should be familiar with their use as they provide concise methods to ensure that needed client information is documented in a manner that is readable, usable, and easy to access.

Given that POR focuses on problem identification and tracking, it seems likely that problems would be distinguished from other elements, such as the assessment and progress notes, in the case file. It is never advisable to store service information in a separate location than the client case record.

Knowledge Area

Unit III—Intervention Processes and Techniques for Use With Larger Systems (Content Area); Record-Keeping and Reporting (Competency); The Principles of Case Recording, Documentation, and Management of Practice Records (KSA)

52. A

Rationale

Understanding **the impact of caregiving** includes understanding transitions into and out of caregiving.

There is much evidence on the health effects of caregiving. Providing assistance with basic ADLs has resulted in increased depression and psychological distress, impaired self-care, and poorer self-reported health.

Also studied are the effects of making the transition out of the caregiving role because individuals improve, enter institutions, or die. Improved functioning of care recipients is associated with reductions in caregiver distress. The death of the care recipient has been found to reduce caregiver depression, and caregivers are often able to return to normal levels of functioning within a year. However, the effects of a transition to a nursing home are less positive, with caregivers continuing to exhibit the same level of psychiatric morbidity after placement.

Test-Taking Strategies Applied

The question contains a qualifying word—NOT—that requires social workers to select the response choice which is not associated with reduced emotional distress due to caregiving. When NOT is used as a qualifying word, it is often helpful to remove it from the question and eliminate the three response choices which do result in reduced distress for caregivers. This approach will leave the one response choice which does not alleviate some of the caregiving stress.

The incorrect response choices, even the death of the person requiring care, alleviate responsibilities associated with care. While nursing home placements may reduce the strain associated with physical assistance, family members often still have responsibilities associated with caregiving, including the added financial burden of paying for out-of-home care and/or losing complete control over the delivery of services.

Knowledge Area

Unit II—Intervention Processes and Techniques for Use Across Systems (Content Area); Biopsychosocial History and Collateral Data (Competency); The Impact of Caregiving on Families (KSA)

53. B

Rationale

The integrity of **client/client system reports** is critical as they are used to make decisions about clients' lives. Poorly written reports can adversely impact clients. Reports need to be clear and well-written to have credibility—that is, influence and impact. Documentation is central to social work practice.

With report writing, the structure of the text is particularly important. The structure needs to help the reader see how the information provided supports the recommendations being made. Use of headings, subheadings, and bullets can assist to highlight areas of emphasis.

It is important to explicitly differentiate between fact, analysis, and opinion, and to show how any opinions expressed are supported by evidence. As reports are used for important decisions often beyond their original intent, it is important that they are measured and modest in their content. They become part of clients' records and have lives lasting well beyond the times in which they were written. Lastly, they should be dated and the names/credentials of authors must be listed.

Test-Taking Strategies Applied

Reports generated by social workers can contain professional recommendations or opinions as long as these subjective assertions are evidence-informed and limited to social workers' knowledge and expertise. Social workers should not be opining about areas which are outside their scope of practice and competence. Reports may include professional opinions, which are not limited to client strengths. For example, social workers may make child custody or visitation recommendations which suggest limited or supervised contact due to client problems. Social workers should include strengths and resources in any assessment, but reports can also contain less positive information. Lastly, it is best practice that all reports generated by social workers are shown to clients prior to submission and clients authorize their release. However, at times, social workers prepare reports which are court-ordered; these are submitted regardless of whether clients approve of the statements made by social workers in these documents.

Knowledge Area

Unit III—Intervention Processes and Techniques for Use With Larger Systems (Content Area); Record-Keeping and Reporting (Competency); The Elements of Client/Client System Reports (KSA)

54. A

Rationale Social work advocacy is the exclusive and mutual representation of a client(s) or a cause in a forum, attempting to systematically influence decision making in an unjust or unresponsive system(s). Advocacy can be defined as the practical use of knowledge for purposes of social changes These changes can be directed to government policies, laws, procedures, or sometimes to ourselves. Advocacy is an act of supporting an issue and persuading the decision makers on how to act in order to support that issue.

Advocacy is about motivating and mobilizing the community. It starts with a small group of people who share concerns about a specific problem and are willing to devote time, their expertise, and their resources to reach the desired change. Empowerment of those who may not otherwise be heard or are disenfranchised is at the heart of advocacy.

Advocacy can be divided in three primary activities:

1. Representation: to speak in public
2. Mobilization: to encourage others to become involved
3. Empowerment: to help those who are not otherwise heard make change

Representation

When representing others, it is important that they are sharing information with advocates, advocates are presenting the information received, and advocates are contacting those who are the focus of advocacy efforts.

Mobilization

Mobilization means the inclusion of others in activities and actions toward fulfillment of common goals. The number of people who advocate is important, especially if all the people are advocating for a common goal.

Empowerment

By encouraging participation and playing an important role in policy and practice, there is a sense of ownership over changes achieved. People are encouraged through this process to experience change about their place in the community and recognize that they have rights that can be actively used. Advocacy encourages people to challenge the traditional roles of government and society and convinces them that they have both responsibility and rights in the society.

Test-Taking Strategies Applied

The question contains a qualifying word—NOT—that requires social workers to select the function which is not "core" or an essential task in advocacy. While advocacy may result in the development of resources or services, it does not focus on activities related to growth or expansion. Advocacy may be focused on eliminating a policy or program—not developing one. Representation, mobilization, and empowerment are all basic advocacy duties, which means that they should be eliminated as this question is looking for a duty which is not (or less) important.

Knowledge Area

Unit III—Intervention Processes and Techniques for Use With Larger Systems (Content Area); Methods for Social Change (Competency); Theories and Methods of Advocacy for Policies, Services, and Resources to Meet Clients'/Client Systems' Needs (KSA)

55. C

Rationale

Despite advances in human rights and acceptance, stigma, both internal and external, continues to be the greatest problem facing **sexual and gender minorities**. Internally, many people who are lesbian, gay, bisexual, transgender, queer, or intersex (LQBTQI) develop an internalized homophobia that can contribute to problems with self-acceptance, anxiety, depression, difficulty forming intimate relationships, and being open about what sexual orientation or gender identity one actually has. Externally, stigma may be exhibited by the surrounding society and even from within the LGBTQI community. For example, some people who are gay or lesbian may have difficulty accepting those who are bisexual. People who are transgender also have historically been excluded from some gay organizations.

In addition, most people who are LGBTQI are not raised by people who identify as LGBTQI. Accordingly, they might not have the ability to seek support from parents or peers who may understand these struggles.

Lastly, those who are LGBTQI struggle with higher rates of anxiety, depression, and Substance Use Disorders. Many have struggled with stigma and the self-acceptance process. Alarmingly, those who are LGBTQI have higher rates of suicide or suicidal behavior.

They are also at greater risk for discrimination, verbal abuse, physical assaults and violence, and so on. Though legal protections have been increasing, fear of potential discrimination contributes to not seeking needed help.

Appropriately, in 1973, the American Psychiatric Association (APA) voted to remove "Homosexuality" from the second edition of the *DSM* (*DSM-II*), which meant that homosexuality was officially no longer considered a disorder. However, the diagnosis of homosexuality was immediately replaced by "Sexual Orientation Disturbance," renamed "Ego-Dystonic Homosexuality" in *DSM-III*, which was released in 1980. **Ego-Dystonic Homosexuality** was specifically aimed at clients who expressed ongoing distress or sadness about their sexual orientation, even if homosexuality could no longer be considered a mental illness. Many used the diagnosis of Ego-Dystonic Homosexuality as an excuse to legitimize reparative therapy. Although the diagnosis was removed from the *DSM* in 1987, it remains today as "Ego-Dystonic Sexual Orientation" in the tenth edition of the World Health Organization's *International Classification of Diseases*. The diagnosis of "Gender Dysphoria" in the *DSM-5*, released in May 2013, also bears a strong resemblance, framing the distress commonly associated with gender variance as an individual rather than social problem.

Test-Taking Strategies Applied

In the case scenario, the distress experienced by the client is an issue which can result from oppression and discrimination. It is critical for the client to understand that his lack of self-worth comes from societal problems and should not be associated with his sexual feelings or preferences. Treatment is directed toward decreasing shame over the homosexual orientation and integrating the client's social role and personal identity.

The case scenario also asks about appropriate actions "in assisting the client to formulate treatment goals," which is part of the problem-solving process. While those who are LGBTQI are at higher suicide risk, there are no immediate risk factors mentioned; being distraught does not mean suicidal. In addition, the question is asking about treatment goals. Suicide risk would have been assessed earlier, and nothing in the case scenario indicates the presence of new signs or feelings. Exploring familial relationships is an assessment task which would have happened prior to planning. Lastly, role modeling can be effective, but it does not help address the feelings which are the basis of the client's concerns.

Knowledge Area

Unit I—Human Development, Diversity, and Behavior in the Environment (Content Area); Diversity, Discrimination, and Stereotypes (Competency); The Influence of Sexual Orientation on Behaviors, Attitudes, and Identity (KSA)

56. C

Rationale

Many ethical standards speak to the **professional boundaries** that social workers should maintain with clients. Social workers must ensure that they do not engage in dual or multiple relationships that may impact on the treatment of clients. Social workers should be alert to and avoid conflicts of interest that interfere with the exercise of professional discretion and impartial judgment. Social workers should avoid potential or real conflicts of interest. Dual relationships can be simultaneous or consecutive.

Test-Taking Strategies Applied

In this case scenario, the social worker cannot commence a relationship with the student given the presence of a dual relationship. The student may not be able to be honest with the social worker if therapy were to begin, given a belief that what would be disclosed may impact his or her standing in the social work program. Contrarily, the social worker may receive information that would otherwise not be known by a faculty member, calling into question the ability of the student to competently practice. Even though the social worker did not have the student in class, there is a conflict of interest as the social worker is a faculty member in the program.

The means by which the student learned about the social worker does not impact the decision to treat the student. Meeting with the student is inappropriate given the presence of an existing relationship. Lastly, referring the student is also inappropriate. Social workers should refer clients to other professionals when the other professionals' specialized knowledge or expertise is needed to serve clients fully or when social workers believe that they are not being effective or making reasonable progress with clients and additional service is required. *When making a referral, it is critical that a social worker refers to a competent provider, someone with expertise in the problem that a client is experiencing*. In the case scenario, the social worker is unaware of the student's problem, so it is impossible to ensure that the provider is competent in this issue. In addition, the student may feel pressured to go to this provider as he or she was selected by a social worker who is a faculty member in his or her program. "Inform the student that services cannot be provided given the potential for a conflict of interest" is the correct method "in order to handle the situation ethically."

Knowledge Area

Unit IV—Professional Relationships, Values, and Ethics (Content Area); Professional Values and Ethical Issues (Competency); Ethical Issues Related to Dual Relationships (KSA)

57. B

Rationale

Schizophrenia is a brain disorder that affects how clients think, feel, and perceive. The hallmark symptom of Schizophrenia is psychosis, such as experiencing auditory hallucinations (voices) and delusions (fixed false beliefs).

Clients with the disorder may hear voices or see things that are not there. They may believe other people are reading their minds, controlling their thoughts, or plotting to harm them. This can be scary and upsetting to clients with the illness and make them withdrawn or extremely agitated. It can also be scary and upsetting to others around them.

Clients with Schizophrenia may sometimes talk about strange or unusual ideas, which can make it difficult to carry on a conversation. They may sit for hours without moving or talking. Sometimes clients with Schizophrenia seem perfectly fine until they talk about what they are really thinking.

The symptoms of Schizophrenia fall into three broad categories: positive, negative, and cognitive symptoms.

Positive symptoms are psychotic behaviors not generally seen in healthy people. Clients with positive symptoms may "lose touch" with some aspects of reality. For some, these symptoms come and go. For others, they stay stable over time. Sometimes they are severe, and at other times they are hardly noticeable. The severity of positive symptoms may depend on whether a client is receiving treatment. Positive symptoms include the following:

Hallucinations are sensory experiences that occur in the absence of a stimulus. These can occur in any of the five senses (vision, hearing, smell, taste, or touch). "Voices" (auditory hallucinations) are the most common type of hallucination in Schizophrenia. Many clients with the disorder hear voices. The voices can either be internal, seeming to come from within one's own mind, or they can be external, in which case they can seem to be as real as another person speaking. Sometimes clients with Schizophrenia talk to the voices that they hear. Clients with Schizophrenia may hear voices for a long time before family and friends notice the problem.

Other types of hallucinations include seeing people or objects that are not there, smelling odors that no one else detects, and feeling things like invisible fingers touching their bodies when no one is near.

Delusions are strongly held false beliefs that are not consistent with a client's culture. Delusions persist even when there is evidence that the beliefs are not true or logical. Clients with Schizophrenia can have delusions that seem bizarre, such as believing that neighbors can control their behavior with magnetic waves. They may also believe that people on television are directing special messages to them, or that radio stations are broadcasting their thoughts aloud to others.

Thought disorders are unusual or dysfunctional ways of thinking. One form is called "disorganized thinking." This is when a client has trouble organizing his or her thoughts or connecting them logically. He or she may talk in a garbled way that is hard to understand.

Movement disorders may appear as agitated body movements. A client with a movement disorder may repeat certain motions over and over. In the other extreme, a client may become catatonic. Catatonia is a state in which a client does not move and does not respond to others.

Negative symptoms are associated with disruptions to normal emotions and behaviors. These symptoms are harder to recognize as part of the disorder and can be mistaken for depression or other conditions. These symptoms include the following:

- "Flat affect" (reduced expression of emotions via facial expression or voice tone)
- *Diminished feelings of pleasure in everyday life*
- *Difficulty beginning and sustaining activities*
- *Reduced speaking*

Clients with negative symptoms may need help with everyday tasks. They may neglect basic personal hygiene. This may make them seem lazy or unwilling to help themselves, but the problems are symptoms caused by Schizophrenia.

For some, the **cognitive symptoms** of Schizophrenia are subtle, but for others, they are more severe; clients may notice changes in their memory or other aspects of thinking. Similar to negative symptoms, cognitive symptoms may be difficult to recognize as part of the disorder. Often, they are detected only when specific tests are performed. Cognitive symptoms include the following:

- Poor "executive functioning" (the ability to understand information and use it to make decisions)
- Trouble focusing or paying attention
- Problems with "working memory" (the ability to use information immediately after learning it)

Poor cognition is related to worse employment and social outcomes and can be distressing to clients with Schizophrenia.

Test-Taking Strategies Applied

The question contains a qualifying word—NOT—that requires social workers to select the response choice that does not contain a negative symptom of Schizophrenia. When NOT is used as a qualifying word, it is often helpful to remove it from the question and eliminate the three response choices which are negative symptoms. This approach will leave the one response choice which is NOT a negative symptom.

This question is particularly tricky as all the response choices are, in fact, symptoms of Schizophrenia. However, the correct answer is a *positive* symptom—not a negative one. It is necessary to know the difference between negative, positive, and cognitive symptoms of Schizophrenia in order to answer correctly. Experiencing sensory experiences in the absence of a stimulus is referred to as hallucinating and is classified as positive as it is "added on" to a client's experience as a result of having the illness.

Knowledge Area

Unit II—Intervention Processes and Techniques for Use Across Systems (Content Area); Assessment Methods and Techniques (Competency); The Use of the Diagnostic and Statistical Manual of the American Psychiatric Association (KSA)

58. C

Rationale

Engagement with mandated clients takes skill and patience. Most therapeutic models are based on the assumption that the process of therapy will be a voluntary endeavor in which both clients and social workers will engage in therapeutic relationships through mutual consent. While clients often seek mental health services because they feel the need to, many may also be referred involuntarily to mental health professionals for treatment. Mandated clients are individuals who are sent or brought by someone else for treatment, including courts, protective service agencies, employment assistance programs, schools, and so on. Clients mandated for therapy may indicate the insistence of others as their reasons for coming to therapy, present themselves as not needing help, or demonstrate little willingness to establish a relationship with social workers. The involuntary nature of the relationship could present hurdles early on in the therapeutic process, making it exasperating both for social workers and their involuntary clients. *Clients mandated into therapy may view the process of therapy as* *being forced upon them, with social workers representing yet another part of the legal system*. On the other hand, social workers may anticipate certain attitudes in mandated clients and label them as resistant, unmotivated, uncooperative, involuntary, defiant, reluctant, difficult, or noncompliant.

Test-Taking Strategies Applied

The question contains a qualifying word—MOST. While the apprehension by the client to speak to the social worker in the case scenario may be an indication of more than one of the response choices listed, it is likely related to the involuntary nature of the relationship. Only two answers are directly related to being court-ordered to receive services—the correct one and an incorrect response choice which attributes the apprehension to fear of having the information shared. The client would be correct in realizing that not all shared information is confidential. However, it is unlikely that the client would be providing information in the first session that would be highly sensitive. The question also states that the client is apprehensive to discuss mandated services—not current problems. The discussion of mandated services would not likely be personal in nature.

The first session focuses on engagement and the formation of a therapeutic alliance. It is likely that the client will be upset about being told that he or she has to see the social worker, regardless of a willingness to make changes. The assumption that legally mandated clients will not contemplate change and voluntary clients are open to modifying behavior is not supported by research. Those who are court-ordered into treatment often have made decisions that changes are needed. However, they must learn to trust social workers who they did not choose to see. Acknowledging clients' lack of choice during the first meeting can often be common ground upon which to build relationships in the future.

Knowledge Area

Unit II—Intervention Processes and Techniques for Use Across Systems (Content Area); Intervention Planning and Implementation (Competency); Methods to Engage and Work With Involuntary Clients/Client Systems (KSA)

59. D

Rationale

Social planning is the process by which community problems are solved or conditions in the community are improved. It aims to devise and implement policies which take the form of laws, regulations, incentives, programs or services, and so on. Traditionally, social planning has meant that policy-makers decided what they thought was good for a community or a population, and imposed policy that was meant to bring about the results desired. These efforts have often not been successful as social planning should not take a top-down approach. Many social programs now carry requirements for community participation in planning and implementing programs and initiatives due to the acknowledgement that social initiatives work better, and generate better policy, when those affected by them are involved in creating them.

Community participation makes it more likely that policy will be effective. Without the knowledge of the history and social structure of the community that community members can contribute, there is a risk of serious error. Attempting to repeat something that did not work in the past, or assuming that particular groups will work together when actually they have been at odds for years, can undermine a community development effort before it starts.

Community participation leads to community ownership and support of whatever initiatives come out of a social planning effort. When people have a hand in planning and decision making, they feel that whatever plan is implemented is theirs, and therefore they will strive to make it work. The same is rarely, if ever, true about plans that are imposed on a community from outside.

Community participation can create community relationships and partnerships among diverse groups who can then work together. By involving all sectors of the community, it can bring together groups and individuals who would normally not have—or might not want—contact with one another, and help them understand common interests.

Community participation contributes to institutionalizing the changes brought about by changes in policy. Community members are far more likely to buy into policy that has been created with the participation of all sectors of the community. Their support over time will lead to permanent change.

Test-Taking Strategies Applied

While the incorrect answers may be helpful, they are not essential for the effectiveness of the social planning effort. It is good to know what policies and programs are already in place, but new initiatives may be effective by deviating significantly from what has been done previously. Such reviews are helpful, but not necessary. Radical change may be needed rather than incremental steps, depending on the problem. Lastly, understanding the problem as defined by the city council is important, but more critical is understanding the problem as seen by community members. Their views will help shape the policy changes needed and increase residents' commitment to follow them as they are based on their ideas and not the views of others about their lives.

Knowledge Area

Unit III—Intervention Processes and Techniques for Use With Larger Systems (Content Area); Methods for Social Change (Competency); Community Organizing and Social Planning Methods (KSA)

60. B

Rationale

Self-monitoring is a key feature of cognitive behavioral therapy (CBT) for Feeding and Eating Disorders. It provides a detailed measure of eating problems and the circumstances under which they occur. It indexes the progress of treatment and helps guide the focus of each therapy session. Food diaries are self-monitoring tools.

One of the reasons self-monitoring is so helpful is that it can be very difficult to recall thoughts, feelings, or behaviors after some time has passed. In the moment, self-monitoring makes it possible to get an accurate picture of what is really going on with eating behavior. This can be an important tool when clients are working to change behaviors or problems.

CBT focuses on the relationship between thoughts, feelings, and behaviors. Social workers assist clients in identifying patterns of irrational and self-destructive thoughts and behaviors that influence emotions.

Task-centered practice is a short-term treatment where clients establish specific, measurable goals. Social workers and clients collaborate together and create specific strategies and steps to begin reaching those goals.

Narrative therapy externalizes a person's problem by examining the story of the person's life. In the story, the client is not defined by the problem, and the problem exists as a separate entity. Instead of focusing on a client's depression, in this social work practice model, a client would be encouraged to fight against the depression by looking at the skills and abilities that may have previously been taken for granted.

Crisis intervention is used when someone is dealing with an acute crisis. The model includes seven stages: assess safety and lethality, rapport building, problem identification, address feelings, generate alternatives, develop an action plan, and follow up. This social work practice model is commonly used with clients who are expressing suicidal ideation.

Test-Taking Strategies Applied

The question contains a qualifying word—MOST. While self-monitoring may be used in various social work practice models, it is a common cognitive behavioral technique with Socratic questioning, homework, behavioral experiments, systematic desensitization, and so on. CBT is also effectively used with Feeding and Eating Disorders, which may be an additional clue as to the correct answer.

Knowledge Area

Unit II—Intervention Processes and Techniques for Use Across Systems (Content Area); Intervention Planning and Implementation (Competency); Client/Client System Self-Monitoring Techniques (KSA)

61. B

Rationale

Hegemony refers to the leadership, dominance, or great influence that one entity or group of people has over others. Historically, this term often referred to a city-state or country that exerted power over other city-states or countries indirectly rather than through military force. Modern uses often refer to a group in a society having power over others within that society. For example, the wealthy class might be said to have hegemony over the poor because of its ability to use its money to influence many aspects of society and government. Wealthy individuals can contribute the most money to the campaigns of certain political candidates, political parties, or causes. To ensure reelection or continued contributions, government officials who use those funds might then pass laws or create policies that favor those who contributed to the campaigns. People who don't have the money to contribute, however, are unable to influence the government in the same way.

This word is derived from the Greek verb *hegeisthai*, which translates as "to lead." Early leaders who were able to exert control and influence over a group of people might be referred to as hegemons. A hegemon had to have the support from at least one dominant class of people to keep the population as a whole from rebelling against the leadership. A single country might also be considered to be hegemonical if it has enough power to influence the way that other countries behave.

Test-Taking Strategies Applied

The question contains a qualifying word—BEST. While all of the answers relate to diversity among groups and/or its impact on values, only the correct response choice speaks to the power to "lead" or dominate which is the essence of hegemony. Social workers must be familiar with key concepts and terms related to the KSAs, including those related to morals and beliefs that are consistent with and antithetical to the social work profession.

Knowledge Area

Unit I—Human Development, Diversity, and Behavior in the Environment (Content Area); Diversity, Discrimination, and Stereotypes (Competency); Systemic (Institutionalized) Discrimination (e.g., Racism, Sexism, Ageism) (KSA)

62. D

Rationale

Borderline Personality Disorder (BPD) is characterized by emotional instability, distress, and neurosis. Clients with this disorder tend to experience difficulty in forming stable relationships. A paranoid fear of being abandoned haunts these clients, and this fear frequently becomes a self-fulfilling prophecy. Angry outbursts are common. Clients with BPD tend to view people in black and white, idealizing someone one day and devaluing that person the next.

Clients with BPD have an increased incidence of childhood neglect and abuse. They are also at greater risk of suicide, but the risk is greatest in early adulthood and decreases with age. Many clients who have been diagnosed with BPD are told that their chronic disorder is not treatable. However, BPD can have a good prognosis if properly treated. Specialized psychotherapy can significantly improve the lives of individuals with this debilitating disorder. A majority of clients with BPD attain greater stability in their relationships and vocational functioning in their 30s and 40s.

Major research has been conducted on the prognosis of clients with BPD, namely two long-term studies called the Collaborative Longitudinal Personality Disorders Study (CLPS) and the McLean Study of Adult Development (MSAD). These studies examined the course of BPD in those seeking treatment for the disorder.

One major finding was that the remission rate went from about 30% to 50% by the second year follow-up, and up to about 80% by the 10th year. Thus, remission of symptoms is more frequent than what researchers and clinicians previously believed.

Test-Taking Strategies Applied

The question contains a qualifying word—TRUE. It is even capitalized to assist with identifying the distinguishing factor of the correct response from the rest. Each statement must be read carefully and evaluated as to its accuracy. The correct answer is identified through the process of elimination, with each false assertion being excluded.

Knowledge Area

Unit II—Intervention Processes and Techniques for Use Across Systems (Content Area); Assessment Methods and Techniques (Competency); The Use of the Diagnostic and Statistical Manual of the American Psychiatric Association (KSA)

63. B

Rationale

Case recording is integrally related to social work practice. It is a task that consumes a significant proportion of social workers' time, with many viewing it as their most difficult task.

In the simplest terms, case records document who did what and why they did it. Records ensure that clients receive adequate and appropriate services, assure service continuity, and provide a means for administrative monitoring. They are tools for diagnosis, assessment, treatment planning, ongoing monitoring of services to clients, and, in some states, are considered legal documents. They may be used for teaching and supervision, for interprofessional communication, and to improve practice skills. Case records also provide agency administrators with information necessary for management and resource planning.

The record provides clinical, legal, and ethical accountability to the client, the organization, and the profession. It documents that the agency and the worker met expected standards of care. Records are used to plan, implement, and evaluate services to clients. Decisions about granting or withholding benefits are based on case records.

The content of case records has changed over time. Traditional narrative-style records focused on understanding clients and documented the worker's diagnostic thinking and the development of the client's self-knowledge and social competence. Today's records concentrate more narrowly on the definition and remediation of a specific problem or need. *They focus primarily on four components: need for service/diagnosis; service goals and plans; service activities/treatment; and service impact/outcome.*

Test-Taking Strategies Applied

In the case scenario, there is no documentation of service impact or outcomes. Social workers must always use methods to evaluate services delivered as per the problem-solving process. The client may not have a mental disorder and, therefore, a *DSM* diagnosis. There is already information in the record about the need for services or the presenting problem. Identifying the issue(s) is diagnosing in a general sense as diagnosis means identification of the difficulty—not assigning a label from the *DSM*.

There is no indication that the client is ready for discharge despite his long service receipt. However, outcomes should have been seen during this extensive period. Lastly, demographic information is usually contained in case records, but is not an essential component as it does not help with goal setting, service continuity, accountability, and the other reasons which necessitate proper case recording.

Knowledge Area

Unit III—Intervention Processes and Techniques for Use With Larger Systems (Content Area); Record-Keeping and Reporting (Competency); The Principles of Case Recording, Documentation, and Management of Practice Records (KSA)

64. B

Rationale

Resisting disclosure of privileged information is required to protect the **confidentiality of clients**. Social workers must employ varying methods to protect the confidentiality of clients during legal proceedings to the extent permitted by law. *When a court of law or other legally authorized body orders social workers to disclose confidential or privileged information without a client's consent and such disclosure could cause harm to the client, social workers should request that the court withdraw the order or limit the order as narrowly as possible or maintain the records under seal, unavailable for public inspection.*

Social workers can use several additional strategies to protect clients' confidentiality during legal proceedings. If social workers believe a subpoena is unwarranted or without merit, they can arrange for a lawyer to file a motion asking the court to rule that the request is inappropriate. In addition, social workers may request that a judge review clinical notes and records in chambers to protect confidentiality and then rule on whether the information should be revealed in open court and made a matter of public record. A judge may issue a protective order explicitly limiting the disclosure of specific privileged information to certain portions of a social worker's clinical notes or certain aspects of his or her interpersonal communications.

Social workers are instinctively inclined to protect clients' confidentiality. Clients' legal right to privileged communication strengthens social workers' ability to protect clients. To fulfill their ethical duty, social workers should be familiar with the concept of privileged communication, practical steps they can take to protect clients, and exceptions to clients' right to privileged information.

Test-Taking Strategies Applied

The question contains a qualifying word—EXCEPT—that requires social workers to select the response choice which is not specified in the 2008 *NASW Code of Ethics*. When EXCEPT is used as a qualifying word, it is often helpful to remove it from the question and eliminate the three response choices which must be done as per ethical standards. This approach will leave the one response choice which is not required.

Redacting information is not recommended when a social worker receives a court order which mandates release of information which can be harmful without client consent. This action is probably prohibited by law as the court has requested the information in its entirety. In addition, if a social worker is successful in getting the court to withdraw an order, it would be better to not submit any documentation even if the most sensitive parts have been redacted.

Knowledge Area

Unit IV—Professional Relationships, Values, and Ethics (Content Area); Confidentiality (Competency); Legal and/or Ethical Issues Regarding Confidentiality, Including Electronic Information Security (KSA)

65. C

Rationale

Professional development ensures that social workers continue to strengthen their skills and learn throughout their career. The most effective professional development engages social workers to focus on meeting the needs of their clients. Social workers learn new skills and competencies to ensure clients receive the most effective and efficient services possible.

Professional development refers to many types of educational experiences. Social workers participate in professional development to learn and apply new knowledge and skills that will improve service delivery.

Effective professional development enables social workers to develop the knowledge and skills they need to address complex client problems. To be effective, professional development requires thoughtful planning followed by careful implementation with feedback to ensure it responds to social workers' needs. Social workers who participate in professional development then must put their new knowledge and skills to work. Professional development is not effective unless it causes social workers to learn new theory and techniques aimed at helping clients reach their goals.

Test-Taking Strategies Applied

This question contains a qualifying word—BEST. While the incorrect answers may be reasons that social workers engage in professional development, the correct one focuses on its benefits for improved practice. Correct answers on the examination are always ones that focus on the delivery of effective services and place client needs above agency policy, regulatory requirements, and employment considerations.

Knowledge Area

Unit III—Intervention Processes and Techniques for Use With Larger Systems (Content Area); Supervision and Administration (Competency); Professional Development Activities to Improve Practice and Maintain Current Professional Knowledge (e.g., In-Service Training, Licensing Requirements, Reviews of Literature, Workshops) (KSA)

66. B

Rationale

Interaction of people, organizations, and governments is the process of **globalization**. The process is determined by trade between the nations, investments in their businesses, and data gathered through information technology, and has some effects on the cultural, environmental, political, and economic development of the countries. Globalization can have both negative and positive effects on quality of life.

Cultural convergence means bringing together different cultural groups, which results in these cultures becoming more alike in terms of technology, sports, language, and even politics.

Globalization and culture are interdependent. Globalization lies at the heart of modern culture; culture practices lie at the heart of globalization. Their relationship is reciprocal.

History shows that contact between different cultures leads to trade of products between them or globalization. Travelers and merchants from one culture to another culture bring products with them which make people know about the other culture and its products. Technology has made nations know about other nations and even adopt their customs if they like them.

Globalization is resulting in greater homogeneity around the globe, but it is also said that globalization is demolishing local cultures and traditions. Thus, there are positive and negative impacts of globalization.

Test-Taking Strategies Applied

The question contains a qualifying word—most—even though it is not capitalized. Though some of the incorrect responses can lead to cultural convergence, globalization is the greatest or most significant contributor. Globalization causes the greatest interaction between people, which results in cultural convergence. Social workers must be familiar with how human behavior changes as a result of the interactions of those from different societies and parts of the world.

Knowledge Area

Unit I—Human Development, Diversity, and Behavior in the Environment (Content Area); Effects of the Environment on Systems' Behavior (Competency); The Impact of Globalization on Clients/Client Systems (e.g., Interrelatedness of Systems, International Integration, Technology, Environmental or Financial Crises, Epidemics) (KSA)

67. C

Rationale

Gender identity is an individual sense of femaleness or maleness or neither. It is also, to some degree, a social construction that categorizes certain behaviors into primarily binary, male and female, roles. Gender identity conflicts can stem from gender identity not matching an individual's biological sex, gender identity being neither completely male nor female, or biological sex not being uniquely male or female. The use of Latinx began more than a decade ago and is the gender-neutral alternative to Latino or Latina. The use of Latinx is gaining popularity as part of an effort to move beyond gender binary and be inclusive of the intersecting identities of Latin American descendants.

Latinx makes room for people who are trans, queer, agender, nonbinary, gender nonconforming, or gender fluid. In Spanish, the masculinized version of words is considered gender neutral, but that does not work for some who think it is inappropriate to assign masculinity as gender neutral. The use of "x" is a way of rejecting the gendering of words and recognition that language changes in order to accommodate the times in which it is used.

Though people may not identify as Latinx for various reasons, it is important to respect others who do and who want to be referred to as such. Latinx is a way to be more inclusive of identities that go beyond gender norms that are rapidly shifting and being redefined in today's culture. It is seen by some as vital to expressing who they are and being able to explain it to others.

Test-Taking Strategies Applied

This question requires knowledge of a specific term related to gender identity. There are always several questions on every version of the examination which include very unique and specific knowledge. While this term may be unfamiliar, it is possible to use reasoning to get to the correct answer with some familiarity that most nouns (not all) are assigned a gender—masculine or feminine—in the Spanish language. The endings of words often indicate whether they are masculine or feminine. As "Latinx" does not end in the traditional "a" or "o" for this word, it may be possible to reason that the substitution concerns the assignment of gender.

When a question asks about a term that is unknown, it is best to use any information or reasoning available and select the answer that appears to be most logical (even if it is just a guess). Failing the exam will not occur just because there are a handful of unfamiliar names or concepts.

Knowledge Area

Unit I—Human Development, Diversity, and Behavior in the Environment (Content Area); Diversity, Discrimination, and Stereotypes (Competency); Gender and Gender Identity Concepts (KSA)

68. A

Rationale

Termination is an important part of the problem-solving process as there is a beginning, middle, and end to all clinical relationships. Most social work focuses on engaging clients in services, followed by helping them obtain stability. Too often, references to the inevitable end of client–social worker relationships are absent during all steps in the treatment process. Yet, clinical relationships have an end point. Some have clearly defined time limits, while others use assessment of clinical outcomes to determine when clients are ready for discharge. Even long-term programs serving chronic populations such as those with mental illness, persons with developmental disabilities, or persons with chronic medical conditions still experience staff turnover requiring termination issues to be broached.

The final stages of treatment with clients can be met with a range of emotion from jubilation to deep sorrow. Nevertheless, if work has been done during the initial and maintenance phases of treatment, transition and termination discussion should not be a surprise and should actually be expected.

During termination, greater independence should be encouraged. As it is important that clients not feel cast aside or abandoned, in-depth conversation about clients' reactions to the end of their clinical relationships should take place in order to let them voice their fears. In addition, progress must be reviewed and appropriate actions if problems reappear should be identified.

Test-Taking Strategies Applied

In the case scenario, the social worker is in the last step in the problem-solving process, termination. However, new information about the client's situation has been revealed. This information appears to be directly related to the problem which originally brought her into treatment. While her anxiety has improved in recent months, a change in her environment, such as going to a new school, may serve as a stressor. Thus, termination may be premature as the client could require additional support. *Assessment is an ongoing activity which can take place during any step in the problem-solving process*. Thus, the social worker should determine whether termination is still appropriate through a thorough assessment.

Acknowledging progress made during treatment and identifying needed follow-up services are standard activities which occur during termination. However, they are incorrect answers as they do not consider the third sentence in the case scenario, which presents the social worker with new information about the client's situation. Identifying relaxation techniques appears to be an intervention which should have been done prior to termination, making it incorrect.

Knowledge Area

Unit II—Intervention Processes and Techniques for Use Across Systems (Content Area); Intervention Planning and Implementation (Competency); The Indicators of Client/Client System Readiness for Termination (KSA)

69. B

Rationale

The Health Insurance Portability and Accessibility Act of 1996 Medical Privacy Regulations (known as the HIPAA Privacy Rule) has important implications for the **confidentiality of psychotherapy notes**. The HIPAA

Privacy Rule recognizes the unique characteristics of "psychotherapy notes" and defines them as notes that are:

- Recorded (in any medium) by a mental health professional documenting or analyzing the contents of conversation during a private counseling session or a group, joint, or family counseling session; and
- Separated from the rest of the individual's medical or clinical record.

Thus, any additional privacy protection that may be available to clients' psychotherapy notes depends on whether the notes are maintained separately from the rest of the clinical file. This has been interpreted to mean in a separate file (paper or electronic), rather than a subsection of a file. The underlying rationale is that the notes are intended primarily for use by social workers. Access to the notes should be limited to primary clinicians.

Under the Privacy Rule, the definition of "psychotherapy notes" does not include session start and stop times, modalities and frequency of treatment, medication monitoring, clinical tests, or summaries of diagnosis, prognosis, treatment plan, or progress.

If a social work practice decides to maintain separate psychotherapy notes, all of the previously listed excluded material would be maintained in the primary client file or "medical record," while the psychotherapy notes would be kept elsewhere. Thus, the primary client chart would include, as applicable:

- Medication prescription and monitoring
- Counseling sessions, start and stop times
- The modalities and frequencies of treatment furnished
- Results of clinical tests
- Any summary of diagnosis, functional status, treatment plan, symptoms, prognosis, and progress to date
- Intake information
- Billing information
- Formal evaluations
- Notes of collateral contacts
- Records obtained from other providers

The previous information would be considered the "medical record" for HIPAA purposes and subject to disclosure with a general consent or authorization to release information, as required by the 2008 *NASW Code of Ethics* 2008.

Under the Privacy Rule, in order for separately maintained psychotherapy notes to be released, the client must sign a separate authorization form. This means clients will be more aware as to when such a specific request has been made, and clinicians can provide clients an opportunity to consider whether or not they wish to sign a separate authorization for release of psychotherapy notes. Thus, if a clinician receives a request for "all records" or the "complete medical record," along with a signed authorization, this is not sufficient to release separately maintained psychotherapy notes. A separate signed authorization, specific to the psychotherapy notes, is required. This provides additional protection from routine disclosure of the notes to third parties, such as insurers.

Test-Taking Strategies Applied

This is a recall question which relies on social workers understanding confidentiality standards concerning psychotherapy notes.

Storing them in a section of a client's file does not afford them "the greatest confidentiality protections" under HIPAA. Social workers should never take client information home where there is a greater likelihood of confidentiality breaches. Additionally, such actions violate trust as clients are unlikely to think that their personal information is leaving the security of professional offices. Lastly, agency policy will not provide additional protections if separate files are not maintained for psychotherapy notes.

Knowledge Area

Unit IV—Professional Relationships, Values, and Ethics (Content Area); Confidentiality (Competency); Legal and/or Ethical Issues Regarding Confidentiality, Including Electronic Information Security (KSA)

70. A

Rationale

Social workers' **therapeutic relationships** with their clients eventually come to an end. However, the way they end and how the social worker handles terminations is critically important. *Preparation for termination should occur at the beginning of the problem-solving process.*

Termination should be discussed early so both social workers and clients understand the parameters of relationships and that they are time-limited.

Termination is the conclusion of the social worker–client intervention process, a systematic procedure for disengaging the working relationship. It occurs when goals are reached, when the specified time for working has ended, or when the client is no longer interested in continuing. Termination often includes evaluating the progress toward goal achievement, working through resistance, denial, and flight into illness. The termination phase also includes discussions about how to anticipate and resolve future problems and how to find additional resources to call on as future needs indicate.

While the act of termination usually occurs after reasons for services have been resolved, it is critical to discuss it early in the process as it provides a framework for outlining responsibilities of social workers and clients in helping relationships.

Test-Taking Strategies Applied

This is a recall question which relies on social workers knowing that termination with clients begins in initial meetings. Social workers must outline the parameters of the therapeutic relationship from the onset of services. These parameters include that the social worker–client relationship is time-limited and social workers are only acting as resources during times of need.

Knowledge Area

Unit IV—Professional Relationships, Values, and Ethics (Content Area); Professional Development and Use of Self (Competency); Methods to Clarify the Roles and Responsibilities of the Social Worker and Client/Client System in the Intervention Process (KSA)

71. A

Rationale

The **Neurodevelopmental Disorders** are a group of conditions with onset in the developmental period. The disorders typically manifest early in development, often before the child enters grade school, and are characterized by developmental deficits that produce impairments of personal, social, academic, or occupational functioning. Diagnosing them involves understanding strong knowledge of **child development** and its milestones.

The range of developmental deficits varies from very specific limitations of learning or control of executive functions to global impairments of social skills or intelligence. The Neurodevelopmental

Disorders frequently co-occur with individuals with Autism Spectrum Disorder often having Intellectual Disability (Intellectual Developmental Disorder), and many children with Attention-Deficit/Hyperactivity Disorder also having a Specific Learning Disorder. For some disorders, the clinical presentation includes symptoms of excess as well as deficits and delays in achieving expected milestones.

Test-Taking Strategies Applied

The case scenario requires that the correct answer be one that is needed "to effectively work with this child." The first sentence is critical as it indicates that the child has a Neurodevelopmental Disorder characterized by deficits in typical functioning. As the social worker is charged with developing learning opportunities to address these delays, it is essential that these activities be developmentally appropriate and targeted at areas needing growth.

While the case scenario does not contain a qualifying word, there is a need to pick out the most salient or relevant answer. School policy and family supports may be useful when developing an intervention plan, but they do not directly speak to the child's area of need, addressing areas of delay. Past academic performance will not be needed to effectively work with the child as it is likely poor, hence the reason for the current referral.

Knowledge Area

Unit II—Intervention Processes and Techniques for Use Across Systems (Content Area); Assessment Methods and Techniques (Competency); The Use of the Diagnostic and Statistical Manual of the American Psychiatric Association (KSA)

72. A

Rationale

A **sociogram** is a graphic representation which serves to reveal and analyze the relationships of a person with his or her family or social circle, or to visualize the relationships within the family or of certain members of the family with their external environment such as health and education services, leisure time activities, work, friends, or place in the extended family.

A **genogram** gives information about the composition of families and the interactions and influences between generations, but it does not show the nature of the relationships within a family nor those with the exterior environment, which may be very useful in certain situations. Sociograms are used to illustrate human resources and networks that can be mobilized to support clients.

A client is born within a family, with parents who protect him, a family circle, and a specific environment. This is known as the **belonging group**, with which, in one way or another, a client maintains a lifelong tie. A human group, whatever its nature, always presents a particular character, with specific values, distinct cultural tastes, a dynamic, and an ideology which make it unique. The persons, groups, or organizations which serve as role models for a client's moral, religious, or political conduct is the **reference group**. The sociogram can target either one or the other of these groups.

In this graphic representation, as in the genogram, the **intensity of the ties is indicated by a code of lines**: a dotted line indicates a weak relationship, and as the dots get weaker, the relationship is weaker.

Arrows pointing one or both ways show whether a relationship is reciprocal or only one-way, where one person is providing and the other person is not allowed/able to give back.

Circles with names inside, big or small, represent the different members of a family based on the importance they have in the family.

The shading of circles or shapes of diagrams do not have any intrinsic meaning.

Test-Taking Strategies Applied

This is a recall question which relies on social workers understanding techniques and instruments used in assessment. While knowledge about sociograms may not be as robust as that about genograms, many of the features are the same. Usually relationships are depicted as lines. Intensity does not directly relate to direction, so arrows can be eliminated. Shapes and shading do not also intuitively have to do with connections, which are the essence of relationships. Often the correct answer in recall questions happens through the process of elimination.

Knowledge Area

Unit II—Intervention Processes and Techniques for Use Across Systems (Content Area); Assessment Methods and Techniques (Competency); Techniques and Instruments Used to Assess Clients/Client Systems (KSA)

73. A

Rationale

Social workers respect and promote the right of clients to **self-determination** and assist clients in their efforts to identify and clarify their goals. Social workers may only limit clients' right to self-determination when, in the social workers' professional judgment, clients' actions or potential actions pose a serious, foreseeable, and imminent risk to themselves or others. Limitation should not be made when social workers feel that clients are simply making poor choices or the actions could have negative ramifications for their well-being, but these consequences are not serious, foreseeable, and imminent.

Test-Taking Strategies Applied

The question contains a qualifying word—FIRST. There may be more than one appropriate action by the social worker to the case scenario, but each must be done after recognition that this decision is ultimately to be made by the client. Despite the social worker's belief that the decision is a poor one, the client must not be judged and instead must be supported throughout the process.

The decision by the client to leave her employment does not meet the threshold of causing serious, foreseeable, and imminent harm. The social worker may assess whether changes in the client's life have influenced this decision, help the client to understand the consequences of her decision, and assist the client with locating new employment. However, these actions should occur after the right of the client to make such a choice is acknowledged.

Knowledge Area

Unit IV—Professional Relationships, Values, and Ethics (Content Area); Professional Values and Ethical Issues (Competency); Client/Client System Competence and Self-Determination (e.g., Financial Decisions, Treatment Decisions, Emancipation, Age of Consent, Permanency Planning) (KSA)

74. D

Rationale

The **effects of substance abuse and/or dependence** can be detrimental to client functioning. **Wernicke's encephalopathy** and **Korsakoff syndrome** are different conditions that often occur together. Both are due to *brain damage* caused by a lack of vitamin B_1. Korsakoff syndrome is most commonly caused by alcohol misuse, but can also be associated with certain other conditions. Korsakoff syndrome is often, but not always, preceded by an episode of Wernicke's encephalopathy, which is an acute brain reaction to severe lack of thiamine. Wernicke's encephalopathy is a medical emergency that causes confusion, staggering and stumbling, lack of coordination, and abnormal involuntary eye movements. Symptoms of Korsakoff syndrome include inability to form new memories, loss of memory, making up stories (confabulation), and seeing or hearing things that are not really there (hallucinations).

Confabulation is defined as the spontaneous production of false memories: either memories for events which never occurred, or memories of actual events which are displaced in space or time. These memories may be elaborate and detailed. The exact causes of confabulation are unknown, but basal forebrain damage may lead to memory impairments, while frontal damage may lead to problems in self-awareness. Thus, a client may have a memory deficit, but be unaware of this deficit.

Confabulators are not lying. They are not deliberately trying to mislead. In fact, clients are generally quite unaware that their memories are inaccurate, and they may argue strenuously that they have been telling the truth.

Test-Taking Strategies Applied

The correct answer must be the name of a disorder which is characterized by telling stories based on false memories due to brain damage. Hallucinations are hearing, seeing, smelling, or touching things that are not there. While **hallucinations** can be associated with Korsakoff syndrome, the creation of false memories is not characteristic of hallucinations. **Denial** is the refusal to accept reality—not creating false memories. Lastly, confabulation should not be confused with **false memory syndrome**, the phenomenon whereby otherwise typical clients suddenly "remember" repressed incidents of childhood abuse or other trauma. Confabulation is a clinical syndrome resulting from injury to the brain, whereas false memory syndrome is not.

Knowledge Area

Unit I—Human Development, Diversity, and Behavior in the Environment (Content Area); Human Growth and Development (Competency); Addiction Theories and Concepts (KSA)

75. A

Rationale

Many **ethical issues in social work**—although certainly not all—require some **legal knowledge**. In addition, the 2008 *NASW Code of Ethics* requires social workers to consult laws that are relevant to ethical decisions. In the United States, three branches of government create laws: legislative, executive, and judicial. Statutory laws, regulatory laws, case laws, the U.S. Constitution, and executive orders often have profound implications when social workers make ethical decisions.

Statutory law is enacted by Congress (federal) and legislatures (state). Statutes govern social workers' obligation to report suspected abuse and neglect of children, elders, and other vulnerable people; minors' right to consent to mental health counseling and to drug and alcohol abuse treatment; protection of school social workers' confidential records; and federal Health Insurance Portability and Accountability Act of 1996 (HIPAA) laws.

Regulatory law is promulgated by federal and state government agencies, such as the U.S. Department of Health and Human Services and state human service, child welfare, and mental health agencies. Under the U.S. system of law, federal and state agencies have the authority to establish enforceable regulations. Public agencies must follow strict procedures when they create regulations (e.g., providing public notice and opportunity for public comment about drafts of regulations). Once enacted, federal and state regulations have the force of law.

Case law is created in the context of litigation and judicial rulings. For example, a judge may need to interpret the meaning or application of existing law, resolve conflicts between laws, or fill gaps in existing laws. Such rulings by appellate courts become legal precedent or case law.

Constitutional law is dictated by the Constitution and includes numerous provisions that pertain to social work practice. Examples concern Fourth Amendment guidelines concerning citizens' right to privacy and protections against improper search and seizure (important in residential treatment programs) and Eighth Amendment protections against cruel and unusual punishment (important in juvenile and adult correctional facilities).

Executive orders may be issued by chief executives in federal, state, and local governments. This authority usually is based in federal and state statute. Executive orders resemble regulations.

Test-Taking Strategies Applied

This question requires social workers to be familiar with a landmark California court case related to duty to warn. Current guidelines concerning social workers' duty to disclose confidential information without client consent to protect third parties from harm were initially established by *Tarasoff v. Board of Regents of the University of California*. In 1976, the California Supreme Court ruled that mental health clinicians have a duty to protect potential victims if their clients make threats or otherwise behave as if they present a "serious danger of violence to another." In its ruling, the court determined that the need for mental health clinicians to protect the public was more important than protecting client confidentiality.

Knowledge Area

Unit IV—Professional Relationships, Values, and Ethics (Content Area); Confidentiality (Competency); Legal and/or Ethical Issues Regarding Confidentiality, Including Electronic Information Security (KSA)

76. D

Rationale

Social workers must be mindful of **value differences** which often arise with clients. Social workers' own values and beliefs can greatly influence social worker–client relationships. Culture, race, and ethnicity are strongly linked to values. *A social worker's self-awareness about his or her own attitudes, values, and beliefs and a willingness to acknowledge value differences are critical factors in working with clients.* A social worker is responsible for bringing up and addressing issues of cultural or other differences with clients.

Social workers should value and celebrate differences of others rather than ignoring or minimizing them. Social workers must have an awareness of personal values and biases and how they may influence relationships with clients. They must also understand their own personal and professional limitations, as well as acknowledge their own stereotypes and prejudices.

Test-Taking Strategies Applied

All of the response choices are plausible, but the correct one is most appropriate and relevant in this situation. Even though a qualifying word is not used, it is necessary to select the best action when value conflicts with clients arise. Referring clients to other practitioners implies that such conflicts cannot be successfully managed. It is common for social workers to have different beliefs and attitudes than their clients. Clients should not be penalized by having to reengage with other providers simply because their views differ. It is the responsibility of social workers to acknowledge and manage these conflicts.

Seeking supervision can be helpful in practice, but social workers should be able to address this situation independently. Supervision is not required in every instance in which social workers have value conflicts with clients, whereas the correct response choice is always needed.

Social workers should always respect clients' rights to self-determination. Self-determination relates to the differences in values between social workers and clients. These differences can impact all steps in the problem-solving process—engagement, assessment, planning, intervention, evaluation, and termination. Self-determination concerns clients' rights to make decisions and take actions in their lives. Role conflicts can also impact social workers' abilities to form therapeutic alliances and gather all relevant information during assessment—problems that will persist unless the impacts of these conflicts are examined.

Knowledge Area

Unit IV—Professional Relationships, Values, and Ethics (Content Area); Professional Development and Use of Self (Competency); The Influence of the Social Worker's Own Values and Beliefs on the Social Worker–Client/Client System Relationship (KSA)

77. B

Rationale

Social workers often are called upon to work with **mandated clients** and have to maximize their **self-determination** even when they enter services involuntarily. In instances when clients are receiving services involuntarily, social workers should provide information about the nature and extent of services and about the extent of clients' right to refuse service. This ethical standard recognizes that, even though involuntary clients are being pressured into services, they still have rights. First, social workers need to inform clients about the purpose and goals of the services, what model of intervention will be used, what research says about the benefits and risks of the services, and what the expectations of the client are as a participant in the services. Additionally, even when clients are mandated into services, social workers should inform clients about the extent of their right to refuse services. In particular, workers should clarify what the client is mandated to do and what the client may refuse to do. The worker should also help clarify the consequences if the client does not fulfill what has been.

Self-determination is not simply an either/or situation. Although social workers should recognize that self-determination may be imperfect for involuntary clients, workers are able to enhance self-determination through various strategies:

- Social workers may empower clients by helping them set goals and objectives that they genuinely want to pursue—even if they did not initially choose to participate in services.

- Social workers may offer clients a range of choices, including which methods and models of intervention will be used (e.g., individual vs. family counseling, cognitive vs. narrative therapy).
- In appropriate cases, social workers may advocate with authorities to honor client wishes and revise court orders or other mandates.

Test-Taking Strategies Applied

While it is critical for social workers to engage with mandated clients by empathizing with them and acknowledging perceived pressures, acknowledging their loss of control and lack of choice does not "maximize client self-determination." The other response choices are actions which give or try to give clients more choices. Acknowledging their current situations does not maximize the ability of clients to "have say" in the methods in which services are delivered.

This question has a qualifying word—EXCEPT—that is capitalized. Thus, the correct answer is the action which does not "maximize client self-determination." It is helpful to identify those actions which do provide more control to clients so they can be eliminated. The remaining response choice is correct—namely, it does not provide additional decision-making power to clients.

Knowledge Area

Unit IV—Professional Relationships, Values, and Ethics (Content Area); Professional Values and Ethical Issues (Competency); Techniques for Protecting and Enhancing Client/Client System Self-Determination (KSA)

78. C

Rationale

Intersectionality is the intersecting systems of privilege and oppression. **Privilege** is when people do not have to face an institutionalized form of oppression, and **oppression** is when they do have to face it. Just because one person has one form of privilege does not mean he or she only has privilege.

People can be oppressed and privileged in many different ways, such as due to their genders, sexual orientations, races, and so on. While a straight, White cisgender man has privilege, he may have a lower socioeconomic status and be oppressed for economic status. He also may have a physical or mental disability which results in oppression. This is an example of, intersectionality.

Race, gender, gender expression, sexual orientation, socioeconomic status, physical and mental ability, religion, language, age, physical attractiveness, occupation, and education are just some of the categories of intersectionality.

Test-Taking Strategies Applied

Social workers must be aware of privilege and oppression, which are shaped by racism, homophobia, ableism, and other institutionalized discrimination. This recall question requires knowledge that inequities are never the result of single, distinct factors. Rather, they are the outcome of intersections of different social locations, power relations, and experiences. While some of the incorrect response choices are true or contain important points, they are not the BEST (which is a qualifying word) definitions of intersectionality, which is the criteria used to select the correct answer.

Knowledge Area

Unit I—Human Development, Diversity, and Behavior in the Environment (Content Area); Diversity, Discrimination, and Stereotypes (Competency); Systemic (Institutionalized) Discrimination (e.g., Racism, Sexism, Ageism) (KSA)

79. D

Rationale

Dissociation is a mental process that severs connections among a person's thoughts, memories, feelings, actions, and/or sense of identity. Dissociation—losing the ability to recall or track a particular action (e.g., arriving at work but not remembering the last minutes of the drive)—is common and happens because the person is engaged in an automatic activity and is not paying attention to his or her immediate environment. However, dissociation can also be an **impact of trauma** as it serves as a protective element whereby the victim incurs distortion of time, space, or identity.

Dissociation helps distance the experience from the individual. People who have experienced severe or developmental trauma may have learned to separate themselves from distress to survive. At times, dissociation can be very pervasive and symptomatic of a mental disorder, such as Dissociative Identity Disorder (DID; formerly known as Multiple Personality Disorder). Diagnoses of Dissociative Disorders are closely associated with histories of severe childhood trauma.

There are many signs of dissociation including fixed or "glazed" eyes, sudden flattening of affect, long periods of silence, monotonous voice, stereotyped or repetitive movements, responses not congruent with situations, and/or excessive intellectualization.

Excessive guilt is another response to trauma. It attempts to make sense cognitively and gain control over a traumatic experience by assuming responsibility.

Intrusive thoughts and memories can also occur as a result of trauma. Experiencing, without warning or desire, thoughts and memories associated with the trauma can easily trigger strong emotional and behavioral reactions, as if the trauma was recurring in the present. The intrusive thoughts and memories can come rapidly, referred to as flooding, and can be disruptive at the time of their occurrence.

Depression can also result from guilty feelings associated with the trauma. Survivors often believe that others will not fully understand their experiences, leading to isolation and depression.

Test-Taking Strategies Applied

In the case scenario, there are many responses to trauma—substance use, aggression (perhaps tied to underlying anger), and memory gaps. However, no indicators of guilt or depression, such as crying, self-blaming, and lethargy, are mentioned. In addition, the case scenario does not describe the presence of intrusive thoughts, such as flashbacks. It is likely that the client would exhibit strong emotional or behavioral reactions to such memories. Instead, the client is unemotional, denying the impact of the abuse. This reaction is typical of dissociation.

Knowledge Area

Unit II—Intervention Processes and Techniques for Use Across Systems (Content Area); Biopsychosocial History and Collateral Data (Competency); The Impact of Stress, Trauma, and Violence (KSA)

80. B

Rationale

Clients who put themselves at risk pose a dilemma for social workers. At times, clients may refuse medical treatment or services or reject common-sense advice. Clients have the **right to self-determination** or to **refuse treatment/services**. However, there can be risks associated with doing so.

The dilemma lies in determining whether clients are competent, so social workers are responsible for assessing whether clients understand the consequences of their behaviors or actions.

Decisions about staying at home, going into hospitals, or moving to assisted living programs are often made for older adults. Whenever possible, clients must be supported to make these decisions themselves. This means, if competent, clients should be assisted to make these choices.

These are very important decisions, so a lot of care must be taken to check whether clients can make these decisions themselves. Usually social workers will assess clients' capacity, as social workers have been educated in cognitive functioning. Results of the assessment will help guide the actions of social workers as to the next appropriate steps with clients.

Test-Taking Strategies Applied

In the case scenario, the social worker has been informed by a collateral contact that the client is making a decision about which there are health and safety concerns. It is vital that the social worker determine whether the client understands the options available and is competent to make this decision. The social worker should neither encourage the client to move nor stand by the client's decision without further assessment of the situation, including determining client competency. Contacting the doctor is not appropriate as the client may be competent and has not given permission for such outreach to be made.

Knowledge Area

Unit IV—Professional Relationships, Values, and Ethics (Content Area); Professional Values and Ethical Issues (Competency); Client/Client System Competence and Self-Determination (e.g., Financial Decisions, Treatment Decisions, Emancipation, Age of Consent, Permanency Planning) (KSA)

81. A

Rationale

There are a number of contraindications to **family-centered social work practice**. These include, but are not limited to, when:

- There is an unstable member or members and the risk of stimulating intense affect in session might lead to decompensation or other adverse effects.
- There is violence in the family (elder abuse, domestic violence, child abuse).

- Family members are physically or emotionally destructive toward one another.
- Essential members of the family cannot or refuse to be included.
- Detoxification of a family member or the stabilization of a family member with psychosis is the goal.
- There is not a commitment to address issues by all family members or one member is being deceptive (e.g., one partner has not disclosed his or her plan to leave the relationship).

Test-Taking Strategies Applied

This question is focused on choosing appropriate treatment modalities for client problems. Family-centered social work practice recognizes that people do not exist in a vacuum and it is important, at times, to look at families as a whole, not just their members.

Three of the four response choices are contraindications of family therapy, making them incorrect. Only the first answer, the correct one, illustrates a reason to treat a family as a whole.

Boundaries occur at every level of a system. They influence the flow of information into and within a system. Using family systems theory, social workers can assist with establishing healthy structures in situations where they do not exist or are continually violated.

Knowledge Area

Unit II—Intervention Processes and Techniques for Use Across Systems (Content Area); Intervention Planning and Implementation (Competency); The Criteria Used in the Selection of Intervention/Treatment Modalities (e.g., Client/Client System Abilities, Culture, Life Stage) (KSA)

82. D

Rationale

A significant court decision for social workers concerning **privileged communication** was the landmark case of *Jaffe v. Redmond* (1996) in which the U.S. Supreme Court ruled that the clients of clinical social workers have the right to privileged communication in federal courts. In this case, a police officer sought counseling from a social worker after the officer killed a man involved in a fight. The social worker objected to a court order to disclose clinical notes she made during counseling sessions with the officer, arguing that the psychotherapist–client privilege protected the contents of the conversation. In its decision, the

Supreme Court concluded that clients in therapy must be able to predict with some degree of certainty whether particular discussions will be protected.

In various rulings, courts have identified numerous **exceptions to the client's right of privileged communication**. A number of these exceptions pertain to judicial proceedings, such as when a client introduces information in court that he or she received counseling for emotional problems resulting from a workplace accident that has led to a lawsuit for damages, or *when a social worker's testimony about a client is required so that the social worker can defend himself or herself against a lawsuit filed by the client*.

Disclosure of privileged information may also be permissible when a client threatens to commit suicide, shares information in the presence of a third party, is impaired and may pose a threat to the public (e.g., an impaired bus driver or airline pilot), threatens to injure a third party, and so on. Whether a social worker must disclose privileged information without a client's consent is often a matter of dispute and subject to relevant statutes, regulations, and judicial opinion.

Test-Taking Strategies Applied

Social workers must be aware of the instances in which they are allowed to breach privilege. Social workers who are being sued by clients have the right to defend themselves. They should only release information that is relevant to the allegations made against them. Even in these instances, social workers should encourage the courts to protect sensitive information by allowing only the judge to view it or keeping it under seal.

Knowledge Area

Unit IV—Professional Relationships, Values, and Ethics (Content Area); Confidentiality (Competency); Legal and/or Ethical Issues Regarding Confidentiality, Including Electronic Information Security (KSA)

83. B

Rationale

Prevention includes a wide range of activities—known as "interventions"—aimed at reducing risks or threats. **Primary, secondary, and tertiary prevention** are three terms that describe the range of possibilities.

Primary prevention aims to prevent disease or injury before it ever occurs. This is done by preventing exposures to hazards that cause disease or injury, altering unhealthy or unsafe behaviors that can lead to disease or injury, and increasing resistance to disease or injury should exposure occur.

Secondary prevention aims to reduce the impact of a disease or injury that has already occurred. This is done by detecting and treating disease or injury as soon as possible to halt or slow its progress, encouraging personal strategies to prevent reinjury or recurrence, and implementing programs to return clients to their original health and function to prevent long-term problems.

Tertiary prevention aims to soften the impact of an ongoing illness or injury that has lasting effects. This is done by helping clients manage long-term, often-complex health problems and injuries (e.g., chronic diseases, permanent impairments) in order to improve as much as possible their ability to function, their quality of life, and their life expectancy.

Test-Taking Strategies Applied

The question contains a qualifying word—BEST. In the case scenario, the client "is very worried about ensuring that the drug administration does not adversely affect her current routine." Her concern is the presenting problem and the social worker can assist the client to better understand what will be required by ensuring that she receives accurate and complete information about what is required. Psychoeducation is often used to help clients learn how to slow the progression of a disease or limit its long-term impacts through diet, medication, or exercise. She is in need of a tertiary prevention intervention.

The client may be worrying unnecessarily. Thus, providing information is the most effective strategy for determining whether there will be any impact to her current daily routine.

There is nothing in the case scenario that indicates that the client needs help navigating multiple service delivery systems, thereby making the provision of case management futile at this point. The client also does not need to make behavioral changes, so interventions aimed at such are not warranted. Lastly, psychotherapy aims to facilitate change and confront barriers that interfere with emotional and mental well-being. Support may be needed to assist the client while she understands changes in her medication regimen, but there is no indication that she needs psychotherapy due to her most pressing concern.

Knowledge Area

Unit III—Intervention Processes and Techniques for Use With Larger Systems (Content Area); Methods for Social Change (Competency); Primary, Secondary, and Tertiary Prevention Strategies (KSA)

84. C

Rationale

Social workers often serve as consultants for problems related to clients, services, organizations, and/or policies. **Consultation** is the utilization of an "expert" in a specific area to assist with developing a solution to the issue. Consultation is usually time limited and the advice of consultants can be used or not used by those who have formal decision-making power. *Although consultants do not have formal authority within agencies, they have informal authority as "experts" based upon their expertise and skill.* Formal authority comes from one's official position with agencies, with those at the top of organizational structures having more formal authority than those at the bottom.

Test-Taking Strategies Applied

As the social worker in the case scenario is a consultant, the source of his or her authority comes from professional expertise. This knowledge base evolves from both education and experience in the field. The incorrect answers are not sources of authority based on the social worker's role. The social worker is not an employee of the agency. There is no evidence that the consultation was mandated by the funder, just that funding data was used to illuminate the problem. Lastly, a consultant has no official position within an organizational structure. Thus, consultants usually do not appear on organizational charts or are depicted with dotted lines to show that they are advisory and not within the hierarchical structures.

Knowledge Area

Unit II—Intervention Processes and Techniques for Use Across Systems (Content Area); Intervention Planning and Implementation (Competency); Consultation Approaches (e.g., Referrals to Specialists) (KSA)

85. C

Rationale

Separation anxiety is normal in very young children (those between 8 and 14 months old). When this fear occurs in a child over age 6 years, is excessive, and lasts longer than 4 weeks, the child may have Separation Anxiety Disorder.

Separation Anxiety Disorder is a condition in which a child becomes fearful and nervous when away from home or separated from a parent or other caregiver. Some children also develop physical symptoms, such as headaches or stomachaches, at the thought of being separated. The fear of separation causes great distress to the child and may interfere with the child's normal activities, such as going to school or playing with other children.

Most mild cases of Separation Anxiety Disorder do not need medical treatment. In more severe cases, or when the child refuses to go to school, treatment may be needed. The **goals of treatment** include reducing anxiety in the child and developing a sense of security in the child and the caregivers. Treatment options include psychotherapy to help the child tolerate being separated from the caregiver without the separation causing distress or interfering with function. A type of therapy called **cognitive behavioral therapy** works to reshape the child's thinking (cognition) so that the child's behavior becomes more appropriate. Family therapy also may help teach the family about the disorder and help family members better support the child during periods of anxiety. Antidepressant or other antianxiety medications may be used to treat severe cases of Separation Anxiety Disorder.

There is no known way to prevent Separation Anxiety Disorder, but recognizing and acting on symptoms when they appear can minimize distress and prevent problems associated with not going to school. In addition, reinforcing a child's independence and self-esteem through support and approval may help prevent future episodes of anxiety.

Test-Taking Strategies Applied

The root cause of the problems experienced by the mother is her daughter's separation anxiety. Thus, appropriate intervention must focus on assisting the child to return to normal developmental functioning. A child with separation anxiety needs to be able to tolerate normal separation from caregivers without distress or impairment of functioning. A child with concomitant school refusal should return to school as quickly as possible. As the mother is the client, intervention should focus on helping her deal with the child's symptoms while seeking treatment for the daughter.

Suggesting that the woman tell her employer about her situation will not help to address the underlying problem. Job performance will continue to be impacted until the child's anxiety is managed. It is helpful for the woman not to feel isolated and understand that her emotional reaction is typical. However, this acknowledgement will also not address the problem. Placing the child on homebound instruction is contraindicated because it may prolong the child's symptoms and increase the severity of symptoms.

The question uses a qualifying word—MOST—to highlight that some of the response choices may be helpful to the client, but the correct answer is the one focused on addressing the presenting problem.

Knowledge Area

Unit II—Intervention Processes and Techniques for Use Across Systems (Content Area); Intervention Planning and Implementation (Competency); The Criteria Used in the Selection of Intervention/Treatment Modalities (e.g., Client/Client System Abilities, Culture, Life Stage) (KSA)

86. D

Rationale

Child development literature draws attention to the **importance of peer relationships in social development**, especially in adolescence, when peers may facilitate each other's antisocial behavior. It has often been assumed that peers are less important in early childhood, when relationships with family members are more influential. However, research shows clearly that even infants spend time with peers, and that some 3- and 4-year-olds are already having trouble being accepted by their peers.

Most infants and toddlers meet peers on a regular basis, and some experience long-lasting relationships with particular peers that start at birth. By 6 months of age, infants can communicate with other infants by smiling, touching, and babbling. In the second year of life, they show both prosocial and aggressive behavior with peers, with some toddlers clearly being more aggressive than others.

Although many investigators have described early peer relations, relatively little attention has been paid to the emotional, cognitive, and behavioral skills that underlie the ability to interact harmoniously with peers. Early peer relations depend on the following skills that develop during the first 2 years of life: (a) managing joint attention, (b) regulating emotions, (c) inhibiting impulses, (d) imitating another's actions, (e) understanding cause-and-effect relationships, and (f) linguistic competence.

Peer acceptance is affected by relationships at home with parents and siblings, the parents' own relationships, and families' levels of social support. However, peer acceptance is most directly affected by children's own behavior. Studies show that highly aggressive children are not accepted by their peers, but this may depend on gender.

There are clear links between very early peer relations and those that occur later in childhood. Peer acceptance in early childhood is a predictor of later peer relations. Children who were without friends in kindergarten were still having difficulties dealing with peers at the age of 10.

Thus, peers play important roles in children's lives. In fact, experiences in the first 2 or 3 years of life have implications for children's acceptance by their classmates in nursery school and the later school years. Children who are competent with peers at an early age, and those who show prosocial behavior, are particularly likely to be accepted by their peers.

Test-Taking Strategies Applied

Answering the question correctly requires knowledge of the policy mandate to mainstream as per the Individuals with Disabilities Education Act (IDEA). Mainstreaming means that schools put children with unique learning needs into classrooms with their peers without them. Students who are mainstreamed have higher self-esteem and develop better social skills. Their nondisability peers also become more tolerant and accepting.

Understanding that the goal of mainstreaming is to increase peer interactions with nondisabled peers will assist with selecting the correct answer. The age at which peer interactions start and the influences of peer relationships are not directly related to the aims of mainstreaming.

Family support, parental interactions, and sibling relationships are also not directly related to greater exposure with nondisabled peers in school settings. The idea that interactions lead to peer friendships which have positive effects is the most salient reason for inclusion of those with unique learning needs into classrooms with other students who are classified as disabled.

Knowledge Area

Unit I—Human Development, Diversity, and Behavior in the Environment (Content Area); Human Growth and Development (Competency); Theories of Human Development Throughout the Lifespan (e.g., Physical, Social, Emotional, Cognitive, Behavioral) (KSA)

87. B

Rationale

Advances in digital and other **electronic technology** used to deliver and communicate with and about clients, colleagues, and others have transformed the nature of social work practice. Social workers' use of digital and other technology has the potential to assist people in need. However, it poses new challenges for social workers. In 2015, ASWB published model regulatory standards related to the use of technology in an effort to help licensing and other regulatory boards understand best practices.

Some of the standards addressed **confidentiality** of clients, including those related to electronic information. Social workers should inform clients about risks associated with disclosure of confidential information on the Internet, social media sites, text-messaging sites, and videoconferencing sites, and the potential consequences. Social workers should also use proper safeguards, including encryption, when sharing confidential information using digital or other electronic technology.

Social workers should obtain client consent when using electronic search engines to gather information about the client, with the exception of emergency circumstances when such search may provide information to help protect the client or other parties who may be at risk.

Finally, social workers must develop confidentiality agreements for clients, including a summary of confidentiality exceptions. Social workers shall document client consent and acknowledgment of confidentiality agreements in client records.

Test-Taking Strategies Applied

Social workers must be aware of confidentiality practices in the current electronic age. This is a recall question, but the correct answer may be identified by remembering that strict ethical standards related to informed consent, release of information, and confidentiality often are waived when clients are a danger to self or others. Thus, client consent is required unless accessing electronic information will help to protect clients or others. Prohibiting use of electronic search engines, even with client consent, would not be prudent given that technology provides valuable information about clients in today's society.

Knowledge Area

Unit IV—Professional Relationships, Values, and Ethics (Content Area); Confidentiality (Competency); Legal and/or Ethical Issues Regarding Confidentiality, Including Electronic Information Security (KSA)

88. B

Rationale

Observation is probably the most common and the simplest method of data collection. It does not require much technical knowledge.

Although scientific controlled observation requires some technical skill, it is still often easier than other methods.

There are many advantages and disadvantages to observation. With other data collection methods like interviewing and surveying, information is provided by clients so there is no means to examine the accuracy of the data supplied. But in observation, social workers can directly check the accuracy by seeing it happening. Thus, data collected through observation is often more reliable than that collected through interviewing or surveying. Observation can also be useful in learning about phenomena which are not capable of giving verbal information about their behavior, feelings, and activities simply for the reason that they cannot speak, such as infants. Observation is indispensable in finding out information on infants who can neither understand questions by social workers nor express themselves verbally.

However, some occurrences may not be open to observation. Personal behaviors are usually done when others are not present. In addition, much can occur when observers are not present. One is also not sure that what is observed is the same as it appears to others. Two persons may judge the same phenomena differently. Lastly, observation is a time-intensive process, making it costly.

Test-Taking Strategies Applied

The question contains a qualifying word—MOST. While there is more than one concern, the correct answer is most significant about "using this approach." Observations are costly, but the expense does not appear to be prohibitive as the social worker is doing the data collection. No additional costs are incurred.

Behavior frequency is being collected. As the behavior was modified using operant conditioning, there is likely a well-defined behavior which can be directly observed. There can be ethical issues in the choice of any therapeutic technique. However, there is no indication that unethical practices were used. There are many punishments which are not adversive, such as time out. Also, the question is asking about "this approach"—observation—not the behavioral strategy.

The case scenario states that the behavior has a "high rate" or occurs frequently. It is likely that many behaviors will be occurring when the social worker is not present. The social worker will need to get information on what is happening when the client is alone or not with the social worker as the client may be acting differently in these situations. Self-monitoring or self-reports—not direct observation—can be helpful in these instances.

Knowledge Area

Unit II—Intervention Processes and Techniques for Use Across Systems (Content Area); Intervention Planning and Implementation (Competency); The Principles of Active Listening and Observation (KSA)

89. D

Rationale

Erik Erikson maintained that personality develops in a predetermined order. He was interested in how children socialize and how this affects their sense of self. He saw personality as developing throughout the life course and looked at identity crises as the focal point for each stage of human development.

According to Erikson, there are eight stages of **psychosocial development**, with two possible outcomes. Successful completion of each stage results in a healthy personality and successful interactions with others. Failure to successfully complete a stage can result in a reduced ability to complete further stages and, therefore, a more unhealthy personality and sense of self. These stages, however, can be resolved successfully at a later time.

Industry versus inferiority occurs during childhood between the ages of 6 and 11 and is the fourth stage of psychosocial development. School and social interaction play an important role during this time of a child's life. Through social interactions, children begin to develop a sense of pride in their accomplishments and abilities. During the earlier stages, a child's interactions centered primarily on caregivers, family members, and others in their immediate household. As the school years begin, the realm of social influence increases dramatically. Friends and classmates play a role in how children progress through the industry versus inferiority stage.

At earlier stages of development, children were largely able to engage in activities for fun and to receive praise and attention. Once school begins, actual performance and skill are evaluated. Grades and feedback from educators encourage kids to pay more attention to the actual quality of their work.

During the **industry versus inferiority** stage, children become capable of performing increasingly complex tasks. As a result, they strive to master new skills. Children who are encouraged and commended by parents and teachers develop a feeling of competence and belief in their skills. Those who receive little or no encouragement from parents, teachers, or peers will doubt their ability to be successful.

According to Erikson, this stage is vital in developing self-confidence. During school and other social activities, children receive praise and attention for performing various tasks such as reading, writing, drawing, and solving problems. *Kids who do well in school are more likely to develop a sense of competence and confidence. They feel good about themselves and their ability to succeed.*

Children who struggle with schoolwork may have a harder time developing these feelings of sureness. Instead, they may be left with feelings of inadequacy and inferiority.

At this stage, it is important for both parents and teachers to offer support and encouragement. However, adults should be careful not to equate achievement with acceptance and love. Unconditional love and support from adults can help all children through this stage, but particularly those who may struggle with feelings of inferiority.

Children who are overpraised, on the other hand, might develop a sense of arrogance. Clearly, balance plays a major role at this point in development. Parents can help kids develop a sense of realistic competence by avoiding excessive praise and rewards, encouraging efforts, and helping kids develop a growth mind-set. Even if children struggle in some areas of school, encouraging kids in areas in which they excel can help foster feelings of competence and achievement.

Test-Taking Strategies Applied

The question contains a qualifying word—MOST. In order to select the correct answer, it is necessary to recall Erikson's stages of psychosocial development. The incorrect answers reflect problems associated with other psychosocial crises throughout the life course. **Trust versus mistrust** occurs in the first year of life and is the first stage. **Intimacy versus isolation** happens in young adulthood when there is a longing for long-term relationships with others. Lastly, *initiative versus guilt* begins at age 3 until age 6. In the case scenario, the boy is in third grade, making him too old for this stage and appropriate for struggles associated with industry versus inferiority.

When age is included in a question, it is usually critical to selecting the correct answer. In addition, even though Erikson is not explicitly mentioned, the question asks about a "psychosocial problem." Erikson is a well-known theorist in this area and all the answers are associated with negative outcomes of his stages. Thus, his work should be used to distinguish the correct answer from the incorrect ones. Often the names of theorists are not mentioned in questions. However, reasoning using their work is essential to successfully selecting the correct answers.

Knowledge Area

Unit I—Human Development, Diversity, and Behavior in the Environment (Content Area); Human Growth and Development (Competency); Theories of Human Development Throughout the Lifespan (e.g., Physical, Social, Emotional, Cognitive, Behavioral) (KSA)

90. A

Rationale

Informed consent is most often thought of in the context of the contracting stage with a client, which comes at the beginning of the professional relationship. *To be effective, informed consent should be seen as an ongoing process. Informed consent can be integrated into each session with a client, or at regular/periodic intervals throughout a professional relationship. As the goals of the relationship change, informed consent should be revisited.*

Informed consent is the process through which social workers discuss with clients the nature of the social worker/client relationship. Through informed consent, the social worker and client outline what the client can expect from the professional relationship, as well as what the social worker expects from the client's participation. Informed consent often includes a discussion of basic protocols, such as how to make or cancel appointments, or the best way to contact the social worker. The process should also involve outlining what work will be done with and for the client, and what expectations there are for client involvement. Integral to the informed consent process is a discussion of client confidentiality.

Using simple language, appropriate to the developmental and language needs of the client, the social worker needs to explain to the client that he or she will generally keep information private, but that there are specific instances when the social worker is required to break client confidentiality. It is at this point that the social worker should highlight that if he or she suspects child maltreatment based on information received from the client, the social worker must break client confidentiality to make a report of the suspicion to child protective services.

In some agencies or practice settings, informed consent involves the client signing a form that acknowledges receipt of certain information. Although a written tool is a good idea, it is important that there be additional methods for ensuring informed consent. In all cases, with or without written informed consent tools, the social worker and client should discuss, face-to-face, expectations for confidentiality and when confidentiality will be breached. The social worker should use language the client can understand. As with other forms of communication with clients, it is important to ensure that the client understands what is said with regard to informed consent.

Test-Taking Strategies Applied

The qualifying word—BEST—indicates that more than one listed answer may be informative or useful, but the correct one is that which most effectively "informs clients of the nature and expectations of the social worker/client relationship."

None of the incorrect answers speak to exchanges between social workers and clients about consent policies. They simply provide clients with, or have clients sign, written materials, which is not sufficient for informed consent. Clients should have the opportunity to ask questions and have policies explained in clear, concise ways which are easy to understand. The correct answer also acknowledges that informed consent is an ongoing process and does not just occur at intake.

Knowledge Area

Unit IV—Professional Relationships, Values, and Ethics (Content Area); Confidentiality (Competency); The Principles and Processes of Obtaining Informed Consent (KSA)

91. C

Rationale

Object relations is a variation of psychoanalytic theory that diverges from Sigmund Freud's belief that humans are motivated by sexual and aggressive drives, suggesting instead that humans are primarily motivated by the need for contact with others—the need to form relationships. The aim of a clinical social worker using object relations theory is to help a client in therapy uncover early mental images that may contribute to any present difficulties in relationships with others and adjust them in ways that may improve interpersonal functioning. In the context of object relations theory, the term "objects" refers not to inanimate entities, but to significant others with whom a client relates, usually a mother, father, or primary caregiver. In some cases, an object may also be used to refer to a part of a person, such as a mother's breast, or to the mental representations of significant others.

Object relations theorists stress the importance of early family interactions, primarily the mother–infant relationship, in personality development. It is believed that infants form mental representations of themselves in relation to others and that these internal images significantly influence interpersonal relationships later in life. Since relationships are at the center of object relations theory, the client–social worker alliance is important to the success of therapy.

Internal objects are formed during infancy through repeated experiences with one's caregiver. The images do not necessarily reflect reality but are subjectively constructed by an infant's limited cognitive abilities. In healthy development, these mental representations evolve over time; in unhealthy development, they remain at an immature level. The internal images have enduring qualities and serve as templates for future relationships.

Central to object relations theory is the notion of **splitting**, which can be described as *the mental separation of objects into "good" and "bad" parts. This is a process of "psychic economy" whereby a complex situation is simplified by separation rather than resolution.*

Infants first experience splitting in their relationship with the primary caregiver: The caregiver is "good" when all the infant's needs are satisfied and "bad" when they are not. Initially, these two aspects of the object (the caregiver) are separated in the mind of the infant, and a similar process occurs as the infant comes to perceive good and bad parts of the self. If the mother is able to satisfactorily meet the needs of the infant or—in the language of object relations—if the mother is "good enough," then the child begins to merge both aspects of the mother, and by extension the self, into an integrated whole.

Isolation is a state of separation from others. Intimacy versus isolation is one of Erikson's psychosocial stages of development which occurs in early adulthood.

Resistance is an attempt to prevent action or refuse to accept something new. Clients often display resistance during the problem-solving process as they are not ready to change or are fearful about addressing long-standing issues in their lives.

Rapprochement is broadly defined as the reestablishment of happy relationships. It is also the name of a subphase in object relations theory which occurs when a child is about 15 months old and once again becomes close to the primary caregiver (usually the mother), though he or she is beginning to differentiate oneself. Physical mobility demonstrates psychic separateness, but the toddler may become tentative, wanting the caregiver to be in sight so that exploration can occur.

Test-Taking Strategies Applied

This is a recall question which relies on social workers understanding object relations theory. Questions on the examination may focus on general underlying principles of theories, as well as key terms. It is not necessary to memorize terms, but being able to identify them when they are listed is essential. Often ones that look correct, just based on their wording, are not. For example, in this question, "isolation" may seem to fit as it implies separation. However, it is not the correct answer as "splitting" is the formal name of this process. Thus, social workers must know specific terms associated with all the major theories studied.

Knowledge Area

Unit I—Human Development, Diversity, and Behavior in the Environment (Content Area); Human Growth and Development (Competency); Psychoanalytic and Psychodynamic Approaches (KSA)

92. C

Rationale

When there is **addiction in a family system**, members typically adapt to the person with the substance use problem by taking on roles that help reduce stress, deal with uncertainty, and allow the family to function. There is a problem with taking on these roles. While they tend to reduce stress, they allow the member with the addiction to continue his or her behavior. The following are roles that family members often take on in these relationships.

The Enabler: The enabler is a family member who steps in and protects the addict from the consequences of his or her behavior. The motivation for this may not be just to protect the addict, but to prevent embarrassment, reduce anxiety, avoid conflict, or maintain some control over a difficult situation. The enabler may try to clean up the messes caused by the addict and make excuses for him or her, thus minimizing the consequences of addiction.

The Mascot: The mascot attempts to use humor as a means to escape from the pain of the problems caused by addiction. He or she will often act out by "clowning around," cracking jokes, or making light of serious situations. While the mascot can certainly help lighten up a desperate situation, the real intent is to ease tension, in order to keep the peace. Many comedians come from dysfunctional homes.

The Scapegoat: *The scapegoat is a family member who creates other problems and concerns in order to deflect attention away from the real issue.* This can be through misbehavior, bad grades, or his/her own substance abuse. Oftentimes, the scapegoat is very successful at distracting the family and others from the addiction.

The Lost Child: The lost child is a family member who appears to be ignoring the problem completely. There could be a fight, with yelling and screaming, and the lost child will be absent or secluded from the situation. He or she is often perceived as the "good" child because much time is spent alone with books or involved in isolated activities. While the lost child will not be successful at drawing attention away from the family problem, he or she is able to avoid stress personally.

The Hero: The hero is a family member who attempts to draw attention away from the addict by excelling, performing well, and generally being "too good to be true." The hero has a hope that somehow his or her behavior will help the addict to stop using. Additionally, the hero's performance-based behavior helps to block emotional pain and disappointment.

Test-Taking Strategies Applied

This is a recall question about "survival" roles in families with members who have addictions. Families are organized around roles, rules, rituals, boundaries, and hierarchies. Structure serves to promote their well-being and the happiness of their members. But addiction in families distorts their structure, and family members assume roles that naturally do not belong to them. Members abandon their identities and needs and become enmeshed in the lives of those who are addicted. Each of the roles listed as response choices aims to release stress related to addiction.

The hero, like the scapegoat, attempts to draw attention away from the problem, with the former role doing so by excelling and the latter one distracting through misbehavior. The hero is not a provided response choice, so the scapegoat is the correct answer.

Knowledge Area

Unit I—Human Development, Diversity, and Behavior in the Environment (Content Area); Human Growth and Development (Competency); Addiction Theories and Concepts (KSA)

93. A

Rationale

Social workers vary in their approach to relational practice. However, it is important that social workers recognize clients as unique individuals with diverse perspectives and values. The principle of **individualization** plays a key role in the social worker–client relationship as *various problems, needs, goals, and values of clients require different patterns of relationships with social workers and different methods of helping.*

Self-determination is an ethical principle that recognizes the rights and needs of clients to be free to make their own choices and decisions.

Mutuality is the recognition that social workers and clients have commonality as human beings and there is a shared potential and willingness for vulnerability and interdependency.

Reciprocity describes instances when clients make gestures of care to social workers as positive responses to the care they receive from social workers. These gestures may be tangible acts such as handshakes, thank you cards, or expressions of concern, but they also may be more subtle expressions of caring. Reciprocity is taking the other's perspective (rather than one-sidedness), and the underlying acknowledgement of equality of interest of all parties.

Test-Taking Strategies Applied

This is a recall question which relies on social workers understanding various terms related to the helping relationship and its dynamics. Mutuality and reciprocity involve the interplay between clients and social workers, with two parties needing to be part of the dynamic. The question is asking about an acknowledgement or recognition, so individualization and self-determination are better candidates since an interaction is not mentioned. Self-determination relies on actions by the client and the question asks about views of the social worker, so individualization can be identified as the correct answer as it is most closely linked to the provided description.

Knowledge Area

Unit IV—Professional Relationships, Values, and Ethics (Content Area); Professional Development and Use of Self (Competency); The Components of the Social Worker–Client/Client System Relationship (KSA)

94. D

Rationale

The Individuals with Disabilities Education Act (IDEA) requires that all children with disabilities be educated in the **least restrictive environment** (LRE) that is appropriate. The spirit of this requirement is to ensure that children are not unnecessarily removed from the regular classroom or isolated from other nondisabled children of their age.

To the maximum extent appropriate, children with disabilities, including children in public or private institutions or other care facilities, must be educated with children who are not disabled. Thus, special classes, separate schooling, or other removal of children with disabilities from the regular educational environment can only occur when the nature or severity of the disability of a child is such that education in regular classes with the use of supplementary aids and services cannot be achieved satisfactorily.

The IDEA mandates that every student with a disability should be given the opportunity to start out in a general education classroom; if that environment does not allow for success and a more restrictive environment is deemed appropriate, then good reason must be given as to why the LRE is not working. This decision should be a main topic of discussion in Individual Education Planning (IEP) meetings.

LRE decisions are made based on children's learning needs and vary from child to child. IDEA also requires that schools provide a full continuum of services ranging from regular classrooms with support to special classes, and special school placements, as needed.

Test-Taking Strategies Applied

The case scenario describes a situation where a school official has an opinion contrary to the student's legal right under IDEA. The student's needs "can be adequately met in either the regular classroom with additional supports or a separate resource room for students who require special assistance." The right to be served in the LRE should be the guiding principle in making decisions about needed level of care.

The child's preferences do not take precedent over the legal right to obtain supports in the regular classroom, so meeting with the child is not needed to resolve the presenting conflict. The guidance counselor's feelings also do not negate the rights of the child, as his or her academic needs can be met in the regular classroom with additional supports. Thus, understanding the guidance counselor's recommendations is not necessary. Lastly, suggesting ways to maintain friendships assumes that the child will be receiving instruction in a resource room, which is in violation of the IDEA.

Social workers must advocate for client rights when they are threatened or violated by others. Being knowledgeable about laws which must be followed when assessing and deciding needed level of care is critical.

Knowledge Area

Unit II—Intervention Processes and Techniques for Use Across Systems (Content Area); Assessment Methods and Techniques (Competency); Placement Options Based on Assessed Level of Care (KSA)

95. D

Rationale

Central to successful **interdisciplinary collaboration** is dialogue among members. Dialogue is a communications process that facilitates thinking and questioning together. In dialogue, conversations focus on surfacing assumptions, goals, and values, and summarizing disparate ideas in search of connections. This type of strategic conversation allows for further exploration and clarification of different vantage points, thus allowing for the development of new knowledge. Information sharing is increased and expertise within the group begins to surface, leading to a new valuation of difference as a context for innovation.

Listening to and observing team members to recognize their values, goals, and ways of communicating are critical actions to engage in if mutually beneficial partnerships are to develop. This takes time and effort. Formal and informal interactions can be opportunities for learning about the diversity of styles and perceptions within a team.

The current context of different mental models of collaboration and status differences between team members, combined with the need to communicate regularly to reach agreements, reflects the complexity of skill and effort needed for effective collaboration. There are no easy answers or shortcuts.

Test-Taking Strategies Applied

The incorrect answers require the social worker to stay silent about a core professional value—self-determination. In interdisciplinary collaboration, social workers should never adopt "groupthink," ignoring their own values and beliefs. Supporting a proposal or not speaking out against an action that may be detrimental or does not respect the rights of clients is wrong. In practice, social workers can speak to their supervisors about problems, but this answer does not let others in the group know about the concerns, which is critical.

Knowledge Area

Unit IV—Professional Relationships, Values, and Ethics (Content Area); Professional Development and Use of Self (Competency); The Influence of the Social Worker's Own Values and Beliefs on Interdisciplinary Collaboration (KSA)

96. A

Rationale

Major Neurocognitive Disorder (formerly called Dementia) and **Delirium** are prevalent mental disorders in those who are elderly.

While Major Neurocognitive Disorder is prevalent in the community, hospitals, and nursing homes, Delirium is seen most often in acute care hospitals. It is imperative that social workers be adept at recognizing, evaluating, and managing clients with these syndromes.

The differential diagnosis hinges on a careful clinical evaluation. The first step is to recognize which of the syndromes is present. Major Neurocognitive Disorder is defined by a chronic loss of intellectual or cognitive function of sufficient severity to interfere with social or occupational function. Delirium is an acute disturbance of consciousness marked by an attention deficit and a change in cognitive function. It is important to recognize that these syndromes are not mutually exclusive, as Major Neurocognitive Disorder can coexist with Delirium and other disorders, such as Major Depressive Disorder.

When a client presents with new cognitive complaints, the first consideration is whether this condition represents Major Neurocognitive Disorder or Delirium. Generally, a major difference between Delirium and Major Neurocognitive Disorder is the rapidity of onset: Progression of symptoms is usually acute in Delirium, rather than insidious and slowly progressive as in Major Neurocognitive Disorder. Additionally, Delirium may cause disturbance in the level of consciousness, attention, and vital signs, whereas Major Neurocognitive Disorder should not. The *DSM-5* defines Delirium as a disturbance from baseline in attention, awareness, and cognition over a short period of time, with fluctuation in severity throughout the day. These changes must not be explained by another Neurocognitive Disorder, and there must be evidence that the condition is not explained by another condition such as infection, or Substance Intoxication and Withdrawal.

Test-Taking Strategies Applied

This is a recall question about the differences between Delirium and Major Neurocognitive Disorder. Social workers must be able to make differential diagnoses as many of the response choices related to the competency of assessment and diagnosis have similar symptoms. Picking among them will require knowing how disorders differ from one another.

A significant difference which is used to diagnose Delirium is the rapid onset of symptoms. Major Neurocognitive Disorder causes a more gradual progression of impairment. Alertness and orientation also fluctuate and are variable throughout the day when a client has Delirium. In Major Neurocognitive Disorder, a client may have issues with alertness or orientation, but his or her symptomology should be stable throughout the day.

The severity of the memory loss, family history, and the impact of the symptoms are not the best methods "to differentiate" between these diagnoses.

Knowledge Area

Unit II—Intervention Processes and Techniques for Use Across Systems (Content Area); Biopsychosocial History and Collateral Data (Competency); Symptoms of Neurologic and Organic Disorders (KSA)

97. C

Rationale

A **functional behavior assessment** is a comprehensive and individualized strategy to identify the purpose or function of a client's problem behavior(s), develop and implement a plan to modify variables that maintain the problem behavior, and teach appropriate replacement behaviors using positive interventions. While there are a variety of techniques available to conduct a functional behavioral assessment, the first step in the process, regardless of technique, is to define the behavior in concrete terms.

Before a functional behavioral plan can be implemented, it is necessary to pinpoint the behavior causing problems and to define that behavior in concrete terms that are easy to communicate and simple to measure and record. Behavior must be in specific, observable, and measurable terms. Simply stating that a client is aggressive is too vague. Instead, for example, a social worker should specify that a client pokes, hits, and kicks other students with her feet or hands during lunch period.

It may be necessary to carefully and objectively observe client behavior in different settings and during different types of activities, and to conduct interviews with others in order to pinpoint the specific characteristics of a behavior. Once a problem behavior has been defined concretely, it is possible to devise a strategy for determining the functions of this behavior.

Test-Taking Strategies Applied

The question contains a qualifying word—FIRST. While there may be more than one appropriate action by a social worker listed, the correct answer is the initial step in conducting a functional behavioral assessment. Determining why intervention is needed now and explaining the limits of confidentiality occur during engagement with a client. Engagement occurs prior to assessment in the problem-solving process. However, the question is asking about the first action taken "when completing a functional behavioral assessment"—not ever with a client. When doing a functional behavioral assessment, a problem behavior is defined in measurable terms; data is collected and analyzed; a hypothesis is formulated; and an intervention plan is developed, implemented, and monitored, respectively. Thus, the first action taken by a social worker is to define a problem behavior in measurable terms. Identifying antecedents may be important if an operant approach is being used, but this action would occur after the behavior has been defined and data has been collected.

Knowledge Area

Unit II—Intervention Processes and Techniques for Use Across Systems (Content Area); Assessment Methods and Techniques (Competency); Techniques and Instruments Used to Assess Clients/Client Systems (KSA)

98. A

Rationale

Shared power views clients as experts on their lives, cultures, dreams, experiences, and goals. This perspective mandates that social workers assume power only over the limited activities in which they are trained while clients retain power to direct the work.

Often shifting views on expertise and interest in sharing power do not come easily. In the United States, there is a strong socialization to value expertise. Thus, social workers' values and contributions are seen through the lens of expertise. Social workers are educated and socialized in professional programs to become respected members of a profession. They are often pushed to adopt "expert" roles.

Additionally, some clients may want social workers to be experts on their lives and relationships—just as they want doctors to dictate their medical care. Adopting the "expert" role can obscure client ownership or participation in the work.

Most social work services are delivered in agency settings. These settings, which are traditionally operated with "top down" approaches, place service recipients at the bottom of hierarchies with little say in many decisions.

Social workers must recognize that the only experts on experiences are those who have lived them. Social workers honor this wisdom by sharing power within therapeutic relationships. Systems that rely on expertise can be humiliating, insulting, or patronizing, and inspire disillusionment in those served.

Test-Taking Strategies Applied

The question contains a qualifying word—NOT—that requires social workers to select the response choice which is not a threat to shared power.

When NOT is used as a qualifying word, it is often helpful to remove it from the question and eliminate the three response choices which are threats. This approach will leave the one response choice which is NOT a threat to having shared power with clients.

While objectivity is important in social work practice, it is not directly related to shared power, which views clients as experts in their lives. Objectivity should not be used to justify beliefs that clients cannot solve their own problems.

Knowledge Area

Unit IV—Professional Relationships, Values, and Ethics (Content Area); Professional Development and Use of Self (Competency); The Dynamics of Power and Transparency in the Social Worker–Client/Client System Relationship (KSA)

99. C

Rationale

Behavior modification is the generic term given to any process derived from **learning theory** where the goal is to change client behavior. To understand behavior modification, it is necessary to understand the two main concepts that it is based on: classical and operant conditioning. **Classical conditioning** refers to the pairing of naturally occurring stimulus-response chains with other stimuli in order to produce a similar response. **Operant conditioning** is recognition that behaviors have antecedents and consequences—and are increased or decreased by reinforcement or punishment, respectively.

Biofeedback is the process of learning to voluntarily influence physiological processes by making changes in cognition. It provides a visible and experiential demonstration of the mind–body connection. Biofeedback is also a therapeutic tool to facilitate learning self-regulation of autonomic functions for improving health.

Modeling is learning by observing or imitating. There are different types of modeling techniques to assist learners.

Shaping refers to the reinforcement of behaviors that approximate or come close to desired new behaviors. The steps involved are often called successive approximations because they successively approximate or get closer and closer to desired behaviors. This technique works well for phobias and anxiety-related disorders as the process of shaping can involve the creation of a hierarchy ranging from the least feared situation to the most feared situation. Rewards to greater incremental exposure are provided as a means to confront fears.

Flooding is a form of behavior therapy based on the principles of respondent conditioning. It is sometimes referred to as exposure therapy or prolonged exposure therapy. As a psychotherapeutic technique, it is used to treat phobia and Anxiety Disorders including Posttraumatic Stress Disorder. It works by exposing clients to their painful memories, with the goal of reintegrating their repressed emotions with their current awareness.

Test-Taking Strategies Applied

The question requires recall knowledge about behavioral techniques. Shaping is used when it may be, or has been, difficult to achieve a goal or demonstrate a behavior. Shaping allows the goal or behavior to be achieved in steps, each reinforced positively. After a client achieves each successive step of the behavior or goal, a reward is received and the next one is presented until the desired end result is reached. If there is difficulty in a client reaching the steps, they should be broken down into smaller increments.

While behaviors may be broken down when they are modeled, there is no mention of the social worker demonstrating them or the client observing or imitating the social worker in the case scenario presented.

Knowledge Area

Unit I—Human Development, Diversity, and Behavior in the Environment (Content Area); Human Growth and Development (Competency); Theories of Human Development Throughout the Lifespan (e.g., Physical, Social, Emotional, Cognitive, Behavioral) (KSA)

100. C

Rationale

The **dynamics of loss, separation, and grief** are different for all who experience them. However, the stages of grief and mourning are universal and are experienced by people from all walks of life, across many cultures. Mourning occurs in response to terminal illness, the loss of a close relationship, or the death of a valued being, human, or animal. There are five stages of grief that were first proposed by Elisabeth Kübler-Ross. *The five stages of grief and loss are denial and isolation, anger, bargaining, depression, and acceptance.*

Denial and isolation

The first reaction to learning about the terminal illness, loss, or death of a cherished loved one is to deny the reality of the situation. "This isn't happening, this can't be happening." It is a typical reaction to rationalize overwhelming emotions. It is a defense mechanism that buffers the immediate shock of the loss.

Anger

As the masking effects of denial and isolation begin to wear, reality and its pain reemerge. The intense emotion is redirected and expressed instead as anger. The anger may be aimed at inanimate objects, complete strangers, friends, or family. Anger may be directed at a dying or deceased loved one.

Bargaining

The normal reaction to feelings of helplessness and vulnerability is often a need to regain control:

- If only we had sought medical attention sooner ...
- If only we got a second opinion from another doctor ...
- If only we had tried to be a better person toward them ...

This is a weaker line of defense to protect from the painful reality.

Depression

Depression can be a reaction to practical implications relating to loss or a quiet preparation to separate and bid farewell to loved ones.

Acceptance

Not everyone reaches acceptance as death may be sudden and unexpected or it is not possible to see beyond anger or denial. Acceptance is often marked by withdrawal and calm.

Not everyone goes through the stages in the same order or experiences all of them. Different lengths of time are needed to work through each stage. It is important for social workers to not judge how a person experiences his or her grief, as each person will experience it differently.

Throughout each stage, a common thread of hope emerges: As long as there is life, there is hope. As long as there is hope, there is life.

Test-Taking Strategies Applied

This is a recall question which relies on social workers knowing about the stages of grief and mourning. While Elisabeth Kübler-Ross is not explicitly stated, it is useful to think of her model. Often the names of theorists are not included in questions, but it is necessary to refer to their work to assist in selecting the correct answers. Social work is built on hope, the belief that certain things can happen and are always possible. Thus, viewing hope as present throughout the stages of grief and mourning is consistent with social work ideology.

Knowledge Area

Unit II—Intervention Processes and Techniques for Use Across Systems (Content Area); Biopsychosocial History and Collateral Data (Competency); The Dynamics and Effects of Loss, Separation, and Grief (KSA)

101. D

Rationale

Social workers must ensure that they do not engage in **dual or multiple relationships** that may impact on the treatment of clients. *Dual or multiple relationships occur when social workers relate to clients in more than one relationship, whether professional, social, or business. Dual or multiple relationships can occur simultaneously or consecutively.*

Social workers should be alert to, and avoid, conflicts of interest that interfere with the exercise of professional discretion and impartial judgment. Social workers should inform clients when a real or potential conflict of interest arises and take reasonable steps to resolve the issue in a manner that makes clients' interests primary and protects clients' interests to the greatest extent possible. In some cases, protecting clients' interests may require termination of the professional relationship with proper referral of clients. Social workers should not take unfair advantage of any professional relationship or exploit others to further their personal, religious, political, or business interests.

Social workers should not engage in dual or multiple relationships with clients or former clients in which there is a risk of exploitation or potential harm to a client. In instances when dual or multiple relationships are unavoidable, social workers should take steps to protect clients and are responsible for setting clear, appropriate, and culturally sensitive boundaries.

Test-Taking Strategies Applied

The case scenario suggests that a former client would like to enter into a new relationship with a social worker. While this new relationship is professional in nature, it still reflects the existence of a dual relationship. While perhaps not readily apparent, the former client may be harmed by this relationship with the social worker. For example, the client may need treatment again in the future. Being a co-facilitator with the social worker would preclude him or her from providing services, thereby eliminating the availability of a clinical support for the former client if needed. In addition, the client may personalize or feel that examples provided by the social worker during group sessions relate to her own service provision. While the former client is not currently receiving services from the social worker, dual or multiple relationships can occur consecutively such as described in the case scenario.

Co-facilitating, even for a short time, would be inappropriate. In addition, assisting the former client in preparing for the group is also problematic. The former client may experience anxiety during this process and confuse the social worker's support with a therapeutic alliance. It is best for the social worker to keep involvement, even encouragement, to a minimum.

Knowledge Area

Unit IV—Professional Relationships, Values, and Ethics (Content Area); Professional Values and Ethical Issues (Competency); Ethical Issues Related to Dual Relationships (KSA)

102. C

Rationale

The function of **silence**, like its meaning, is culturally defined. There are vast **differences in culture, race, and/or ethnicity** with regard to its use. It has a "linkage" function in that it can bind people together as well as isolate. Being silent with others can indicate rapport, respect, and comfort as it acknowledges solidarity or that no conversation is needed. Silence can also have an "affecting" function, meaning that it has the power to affect others for both good and ill. Silence can be interpreted as indifference, causing negative feelings by others who observe it. Conversely, it can also be seen as a sign of respect, viewed positively.

Assumptions should not be made that those who are silent are not benefitting from others' participation or not actively engaged. For some, silence is seen as an opportunity given to others to speak or express their ideas. This dialogue by others mutually benefits those who do not verbalize. Silence also can indicate assent—there may be no need to verbally affirm what is said as remaining quiet is seen as having the same effect. Silence may be viewed as a way to retain harmony among the group.

Silence can be seen as a way to agree with others without vocalizing. This indirect form of communication is more common among some cultures, including those who are Asian. In addition, some cultures are more collectivist, placing the views of larger groups as more important than those of individual members. Thus, remaining silent is seen as a sign of respect even when having an opposing view. Dissenting opinions are viewed as having possible negative repercussions for the work of the overall group, which is prioritized.

Test-Taking Strategies Applied

In the case scenario, there is no indication of the race, culture, and/or ethnicity of other group members. However, the recent immigration of the youth may have been mentioned as an indication that her participation may be influenced by different cultural, racial, and/or ethnic norms. Some races, cultures, and/or ethnicities are more dominant and pervasive than others. This influences how people in both dominant and minority cultures interact; this, in turn, can impact on a group's interactions. It is the social worker's job as facilitator to encourage participation and challenge behavior which inhibits it. The facilitator is not responsible for what a member chooses to say or withhold in a group—clients should not be forced to participate. *What a social worker can and must do is create an environment in the group where clients can choose to contribute and where it is safe for them to do so.* Thus, a social worker must challenge and dilute any negative impacts of prejudice which may arise in the group due to differences in communication styles. Ensuring that any negative effects of social prejudice are not tolerated will create a "safe space" where group members can choose to express their opinions if they wish.

Knowledge Area

Unit I—Human Development, Diversity, and Behavior in the Environment (Content Area); Diversity, Discrimination, and Stereotypes (Competency); The Effect of Culture, Race, and Ethnicity on Behaviors, Attitudes, and Identity (KSA)

103. B

Rationale

Engagement within the context of **building and maintaining helping relationships** is defined as a point at which clients view treatment as a meaningful and important process. It involves developing agreement with social workers on the goals and tasks of treatment. Engagement can also be described as the time when the therapeutic relationship or therapeutic alliance forms between social workers and clients. The engagement process is sometimes described using words like *cooperation, collaboration, participation*, or *buy in*. During the engagement process, clients' worldviews including their values, core beliefs, and ways of life are challenged in order to facilitate substantive change.

As clients realize the need to change, resistance can occur. **Resistance** to change can occur throughout the problem-solving process as it helps clients to protect the status quo. Closely related to resistance is **ambivalence**, which is a condition of both wanting and not wanting a particular change. Social workers must be alert to the forces of ambivalence and, when necessary, assist clients in working through these blocks to decision making and action. Such work involves various interviewing and therapeutic techniques, but initially it is critical that clients feel that social workers are there to help and will not be judging or giving advice.

Test-Taking Strategies Applied

Material in quotation marks deserves particular attention and usually relates to the answer. The client's comment may result from apprehension about the ability to make change or fear of the therapeutic process. Being reluctant to tell others about problems is typical and should not be viewed as a therapeutic issue. The client is in the beginning phase of treatment (engagement) where the goal is to build a strong helping relationship with the social worker. Ignoring the comment may send a message to the client that the articulated feelings are not important and asking about other situations distracts from the situation at hand. The best way to deal with any resistance or apprehension is by educating the client about what will happen in the future.

Knowledge Area

Unit IV—Professional Relationships, Values, and Ethics (Content Area); Professional Development and Use of Self (Competency); The Principles and Techniques for Building and Maintaining a Helping Relationship (KSA)

104. C

Rationale

Defense mechanisms are psychological mechanisms aimed at reducing anxiety. They were first discussed by Sigmund Freud as part of his psychoanalytic theory and further developed by his daughter, Anna Freud. Often unconscious, defense mechanisms are used to protect clients from psychological pain or anxiety. While such mechanisms may be helpful in the short term, alleviating suffering that might otherwise incapacitate, they can easily become a substitute for addressing the underlying cause and so lead to additional problems. The solution, therefore, is to address the underlying causes of the pain these mechanisms are used to defray.

Sublimation is a mature type of defense mechanism where socially unacceptable impulses or idealizations are unconsciously transformed into socially acceptable actions or behavior. It causes "id" impulses to be channeled into refined and civilized behavior. Alfred Adler called sublimation "the healthy defense mechanism" because it produced socially beneficial outcomes for humanity.

Test-Taking Strategies Applied

This is a recall question on the defense mechanisms. It is not necessary to memorize the definitions of the defense mechanisms, but their meanings should be familiar.

Often questions on defense mechanisms include case scenarios which describe clients' behavior. Thus, social workers must be able to distinguish between the defense mechanisms based on client verbalizations and actions using the situational contexts as clues.

Knowledge Area

Unit I—Human Development, Diversity, and Behavior in the Environment (Content Area); Effects of the Environment on Systems' Behavior (Competency); Psychological Defense Mechanisms and Their Effects on Behavior and Relationships (KSA)

105. C

Rationale

Defense mechanisms are psychological mechanisms aimed at reducing anxiety. They were first discussed by Sigmund Freud as part of his psychoanalytic theory and further developed by his daughter, Anna Freud. Often unconscious, defense mechanisms are used to protect clients from psychological pain or anxiety. While such mechanisms may be helpful in the short term, alleviating suffering that might otherwise incapacitate, they can easily become a substitute for addressing the underlying cause and so lead to additional problems. The solution, therefore, is to address the underlying causes of the pain these mechanisms are used to defray.

Conversion is a defense mechanism which occurs when cognitive tensions manifest themselves in physical symptoms. The symptom may be symbolic and dramatic and often acts as a communication about the situation. Extreme symptoms may include paralysis, blindness, deafness, becoming mute, or having a seizure. Lesser symptoms include tiredness, headaches, and twitches. For example, a client's arm becomes suddenly paralyzed after he or she has been threatening to hit someone else.

Conversion is different from psychosomatic disorders where real health changes are seen (such as the appearance of ulcers). It also is more than malingering, where conscious exaggeration of reported symptoms is used to gain attention. With time, symptoms will go away, especially if clients' stress is reduced, such as by taking them away from the initial, anxiety-provoking situations.

Test-Taking Strategies Applied

This is a recall question on the defense mechanisms. It is not necessary to memorize the definitions of the defense mechanisms, but their names should be familiar. The correct answer could have been obtained simply by recognizing that conversion was a defense mechanism.

Often questions on defense mechanisms include case scenarios which describe clients' behavior. Thus, social workers must be able to distinguish between the defense mechanisms based on client verbalizations and actions using the situational contexts as clues.

Knowledge Area

Unit I—Human Development, Diversity, and Behavior in the Environment (Content Area); Effects of the Environment on Systems' Behavior (Competency); Psychological Defense Mechanisms and Their Effects on Behavior and Relationships (KSA)

106. C

Rationale

Crises are defined as an acute disruption of psychological homeostasis in which a client's usual coping mechanisms fail and there exists evidence of distress and functional impairment. The *subjective reaction* to life experiences dictates clients' abilities to cope or function. The main cause of a crisis is a stressful, traumatic, or hazardous event, but two other conditions must be present—(a) a client's perception of the event causes considerable upset or disruption and (b) a client is unable to resolve the disruption by previously used coping skills. Thus, it is a client's subjective experience that signals whether a crisis exists as it is the way that these experiences are perceived by a client that cause a crisis. Clients can encounter life stressors (deaths, health issues, etc.), but it is only if these events are perceived as threats or beyond coping abilities that crises occur.

Test-Taking Strategies Applied

The question requires knowledge about the **difference between subjective and objective data** in assessment and treatment planning.

While all of the response choices may be helpful in gathering information relevant to a client's state, a crisis is a subjective experience. Many clients experience adversity and cope. Only the correct response choice involves speaking with the client directly to understand her feelings about recent events. Two incorrect answers involve reviewing or obtaining objective, not subjective, information related to her physical/neurological condition. The remaining incorrect response choice relies on speaking to collaterals whose views about the current happenings may be different, and are less relevant, than the client's.

Knowledge Area

Unit II—Intervention Processes and Techniques for Use Across Systems (Content Area); Biopsychosocial History and Collateral Data (Competency); Biopsychosocial Responses to Illness and Disability (KSA)

107. A

Rationale

Clients may be unaware about the dangers of sharing **confidential information**, especially via electronic means. Advances in digital and other **electronic technology** provide new challenges for social workers and their clients. In 2015, ASWB published model regulatory standards related to the use of technology in an effort to assist licensing and other regulatory boards to understand best practices.

These standards state that *social workers should inform clients about risks associated with disclosure of confidential information on the Internet, social media sites, text-messaging sites, and videoconferencing sites, and the potential consequences*. It is important that clients understand all risks associated with their actions.

Test-Taking Strategies Applied

Social workers must be aware of the practice implications associated with technology use by themselves and their clients. Social workers have to keep client information confidential, but they also need to ensure that clients understand confidentiality limits of their own actions. This is a recall question, but the correct answer may be identified by seeing that it is most helpful to clients by educating them about technological dangers. Social workers are often called upon to educate clients so that they can make more informed decisions.

The social worker should share the concerns and not discourage the client from using Internet dating sites completely. These sites are ways that people connect in this technological age. However, the client must understand the dangers of sharing personal information so freely. There is no indication that the client has poor boundaries as perhaps the client is just not aware of or educated about the perils which can arise from such disclosures.

Knowledge Area

Unit IV—Professional Relationships, Values, and Ethics (Content Area); Confidentiality (Competency); Legal and/or Ethical Issues Regarding Confidentiality, Including Electronic Information Security (KSA)

108. B

Rationale

Emotional and psychological trauma result from extraordinarily stressful events that destroy a sense of security, making a client feel helpless and vulnerable in a dangerous world.

Traumatic experiences often involve a threat to life or safety, but any situation that leaves a client feeling overwhelmed and alone can be traumatic, even if it does not involve physical harm. It is not the objective facts that determine whether an event is traumatic, but a subjective emotional experience of the event.

A number of risk factors make clients susceptible to emotional and psychological trauma. Clients are more likely to be traumatized by a stressful experience if they are already under a heavy stress load or have recently suffered a series of losses.

Emotional and psychological trauma can be caused by one-time events or ongoing, relentless stress.

Not all potentially traumatic events lead to lasting emotional and psychological damage. Some clients rebound quickly from even the most tragic and shocking experiences. Others are devastated by experiences that, on the surface, appear to be less upsetting.

Clients are also more likely to be traumatized by a new situation if they have been traumatized before—especially if the earlier trauma occurred in childhood. Experiencing trauma in childhood can have a severe and long-lasting effect. Children who have been traumatized see the world as a frightening and dangerous place. When childhood trauma is not resolved, this fundamental sense of fear and helplessness carries over into adulthood, setting the stage for further trauma.

An event will most likely lead to emotional or psychological trauma if it happened unexpectedly; there was no preparation for it; there is a feeling of having been powerless to prevent it; it happened repeatedly; someone was intentionally cruel; and/or it happened in childhood.

Test-Taking Strategies Applied

The question contains a qualifying word—MOST. Emotional or psychological trauma may occur as a result of events in adulthood or those which were anticipated/preventable. However, events which happen unexpectedly with no preparation or warning are those which are associated with the greatest negative impacts. Clients who feel that there is no way to prevent these traumatic circumstances are likely to feel ongoing danger or that they are vulnerable for repeated incidents in the future.

Knowledge Area

Unit II—Intervention Processes and Techniques for Use Across Systems (Content Area); Biopsychosocial History and Collateral Data (Competency); The Impact of Stress, Trauma, and Violence (KSA)

109. C

Rationale

Structural family therapy (SFT) is similar to other types of family therapies that view the family unit as a system that lives and operates within larger systems, such as a culture, the community, and organizations. This system—ideally—grows and changes over time. But sometimes a family gets "stuck," often resulting from behavioral or mental health issues of one of its family members.

Rather than focus on the individual's pathology, however, SFT considers problems in the family's structure—a dysfunction in the way the family interacts or operates. SFT does not maintain that the family's interactions, or "transactions," cause the pathology, but rather that the family's transactions support or encourage the symptoms. Transactions are simply patterns of how family members routinely interact with each other. Through its transactions, a family establishes a set of rules for its daily functioning, and these rules form its "structure." A social worker employing SFT must first assess a family's interactions, figuring out a family's hierarchy and alliances within a family. The social worker composes a map or flow chart describing the process that a family unconsciously follows.

Ultimately, the social worker's goal is to change or modify the family map or structure—to get it "unstuck" from its harmful transactions that are supporting and amplifying certain issues or problems.

Social workers using SFT delineate proper "boundaries" between family members and their transactions or interactions.

When boundaries are crossed, ignored, and distorted, the family's structure becomes dysfunctional.

Social workers using SFT identify a wide range of family dysfunctional communication and interaction patterns. Unlike more traditional approaches that prescribe a supportive, empathetic-listening approach to therapy, social workers using SFT get involved with a family's transactions. In this unique role, and in the context of the therapeutic setting, a social worker will provoke the family members to interact and speak about the problem or issue. The therapist asks questions, points out harmful transactions, and uncovers not only dysfunctional patterns, but positive behaviors or personal qualities that are ignored or overlooked by a family.

During interactions that take place in therapy, hidden conflicts become apparent, inappropriate or counterproductive transactional patterns are observed, and, finally, ways to help a family change or restructure interactions are made.

To assist with understanding the family system, social workers will ask for "live" displays of concerns called *enactments*. The family will be encouraged to engage in a difficult communication so that social workers can best identify the current problematic patterns and dynamics. SFT focuses on family interaction in the "here and now." It is less concerned with how their interactional styles evolved.

Test-Taking Strategies Applied

While several response choices may appear appropriate, the correct one is most closely associated with SFT. This approach focuses on the boundaries, communication patterns, and interactions between family members. Obtaining information about childhood events or past feelings is not viewed as being as helpful as "enactments" or observing current relational communication between members. Using this technique, a social worker takes a very active role to provoke conflict and point out maladaptive behavior.

While the mother's current mental status may be a concern and requires assessment, it is not the correct answer as it does not most directly relate to an SFT approach.

Knowledge Area

Unit II—Intervention Processes and Techniques for Use Across Systems (Content Area); Intervention Planning and Implementation (Competency); Family Therapy Models, Interventions, and Approaches (KSA)

110. D

Rationale

Peer supervision enables social workers to go beyond individual limitations and to expand on their knowledge, skills, and experiences. It involves groups of social workers with the same knowledge, skill levels, and statuses meeting regularly to discuss challenges in the profession, self-exploration, diversity and culture, new interventions and solutions, and ethical dilemmas or situations in the workplace. Peer supervision groups do not have defined leaders. As a result of peer supervision, social workers may feel validated, discuss difficult situations, self-explore, and learn different interventions and perspectives. Peer supervision counteracts burnout and social isolation as members are supported and feel group cohesion.

Members also learn to practice supervisory skills for when they become supervisors in the field. They are able to do this because they practice *giving and receiving feedback* as well as boundary management. Peer groups serve as trusting environments where social workers talk about their mistakes and feelings in the field.

Test-Taking Strategies Applied

The question contains a qualifying word—PRIMARY—that requires identification of the main way in which social workers "learn" in peer supervision. **Modeling** is demonstration of a skill or task which may occur in peer supervision, but is not the primary method for learning. **Summative evaluation** focuses on assessing outcomes, which is not the aim of peer supervision. Peer supervision is not evaluative in nature. **Positive reinforcement** is a technique to increase behavior frequency by adding a desirable stimulus. For example, praising actions can be very rewarding, making it likely that social workers will do them again. While peer supervision can be supportive, it is not the "PRIMARY method for learning" within these venues.

Feedback, specifically **formative feedback**, which is characterized as nonevaluative and supportive, is regarded as crucial to improving knowledge and skill acquisition in peer supervision. Formative feedback represents information communicated to social workers by peers that is intended to modify thinking or behavior. Formative indicates that it is occurring while social workers are experiencing difficulties with client situations, not after treatment has ended. It is instructional rather than evaluative. Feedback from others who have had similar experiences is the main method through which social workers gain new knowledge and develop their skills in peer supervision.

Knowledge Area

Unit III—Intervention Processes and Techniques for Use With Larger Systems (Content Area); Supervision and Administration (Competency); Models of Supervision and Consultation (e.g., Individual, Peer, Group) (KSA)

111. A

Rationale

Self-determination is a cornerstone of the social work profession. Self-determination is built on the values of autonomy and respect for the dignity and worth of all people. So, given the primacy of self-determination, it is necessary to examine how its mandate can be met when working with clients who are mandated to receive services.

Social workers respect and promote the right of clients to self-determination and assist clients in their efforts to identify and clarify their goals. Social workers may limit clients' right to self-determination when, in the social workers' professional judgment, clients' actions or potential actions pose a serious, foreseeable, and imminent risk to themselves or others (*NASW Code of Ethics, 2008—1.02 Self-Determination*).

Posing "a serious, foreseeable, and imminent risk to themselves or others" typically applies to situations of suicidal or homicidal ideation. Thus, the *NASW Code of Ethics* is giving priority to the principle of protecting life over the principle of respecting self-determination. This could include initiating processes that may result in involuntary admission for psychiatric treatment as a last resort.

This ethical standard does not say social workers may ignore self-determination. It says they may limit self-determination. Implicit in this language is the notion of the "least intrusive" course of action. In instances when clients are receiving services involuntarily, social workers should provide information about the nature and extent of services and about the extent of clients' right to refuse service (*NASW Code of Ethics, 2008—1.03 Informed Consent*).

This standard recognizes that, even though involuntary clients are being pressured into services, they still have certain rights. First, social workers need to inform clients about the services being offered. For instance, social workers should inform them about the purpose and goals of the services, models of intervention used, research about benefits and risks, and expectations as participants in services. Social workers should inform clients about the extent of their right to refuse services. Social workers should also help clarify the consequences if clients do not fulfill what has been mandated.

Self-determination is not simply an either/or situation. Honoring self-determination as much as possible may be more difficult with some clients than with others. Although social workers should recognize that self-determination may be imperfect for involuntary clients, workers are able to enhance self-determination through various intervention strategies:

- Social workers can empower clients by helping them set goals and objectives that they genuinely want to pursue—even if they did not initially choose to participate in services.
- Social workers may be able to offer clients a range of choices about which methods of intervention will be used (e.g., individual vs. family counseling).
- Social workers may be able to have clients pick their choice of practice modality (cognitive vs. narrative therapy).

In addition, social workers must engage clients by empathizing and acknowledging pressures placed on them, building trust, and validating concerns, so clients are more willing to participate in services. In appropriate instances, social workers can advocate with authorities to honor client wishes and revise court orders or other mandates in attempts to promote self-determination.

Test-Taking Strategies Applied

The question contains a qualifying word—EXCEPT—that requires social workers to select the response choice which would not promote client self-determination during planning in the problem-solving process. When EXCEPT is used as a qualifying word, it is often helpful to remove it from the question and eliminate the three response choices which must be done as per ethical standards. This approach will leave the one response choice which is not required.

In the case scenario, the social worker is "developing a contract." A contract is another name for an intervention or service plan and outlines goals, objectives, time frames for completion, and so on. It is done during the planning step of the problem-solving process, following engagement. While it is important for a mandated client to understand the contents of a court order related to treatment, such a review usually occurs prior to planning; for example, it may be part of the informed consent process at the onset of the therapeutic relationship. In addition, explaining directives contained in the order to the client does not "promote self-determination," which is the lens through which each response choice must be evaluated.

Knowledge Area

Unit IV—Professional Relationships, Values, and Ethics (Content Area); Professional Values and Ethical Issues (Competency); Client/Client System Competence and Self-Determination (e.g., Financial Decisions, Treatment Decisions, Emancipation, Age of Consent, Permanency Planning) (KSA)

112. B

Rationale

Policies, procedures, regulations, and laws can have a profound impact on social work practice. Social workers who treat clients involved with the legal system must be aware of problems that can arise prior to, during, and after the delivery of services. Many of these issues can be avoided by clarifying and defining the nature of a social worker's role. For example, some clients may be uncertain about what to expect from psychotherapy or have unrealistic hopes. Ethically, a social worker is expected to work jointly with clients in the development of treatment plans. By discussing what can and cannot be provided, clients are offered realistic portrayals of what may be expected from therapy, which may assist in deciding whether to work with a particular social worker.

Test-Taking Strategies Applied

In this case scenario, the client appears to be directing the social worker, and her behavior suggests that she believes the social worker is obligated to contact the attorney. In fact, the social worker would have no such obligation and would be wise to decline the client's request, in order to clarify the social worker's role and to better understand the client's expectations. If the social worker elects to contact the attorney prior to discussing the specifics and implications with the client, there is a risk that the client may interpret the social worker's action as an implied agreement to become involved in the legal matter. If the social worker and client ultimately determined that the client's expectations were inconsistent with the social worker's understanding of his or her role, there may be a need for a referral to another professional who is better suited to the client's needs.

The incorrect answers all focus on contacting the attorney or viewing the client's lack of information as resistance to discussing the legal matter.

There is no indication that the client is being resistant and to assume so is adding material to the question.

Knowledge Area

Unit IV—Professional Relationships, Values, and Ethics (Content Area); Professional Values and Ethical Issues (Competency); Legal and/or Ethical Issues Related to the Practice of Social Work, Including Responsibility to Clients/Client Systems, Colleagues, the Profession, and Society (KSA)

113. C

Rationale

In order to facilitate change through the problem-solving process, a social worker must use various **verbal and nonverbal communication techniques** to assist clients to understand their behavior and feelings. In addition, to ensure that clients are honest and forthcoming during this process, social workers must build trusting relationships with clients. These relationships develop through effective verbal and nonverbal communication. Social workers must be adept at using both forms of communication successfully, as well as understanding them, because verbal and nonverbal cues will be used by clients throughout the problem-solving process. Insight into their meaning will produce a higher degree of sensitivity to clients' experiences and a deeper understanding of their problems.

A social worker should also display *genuineness* in order to build trust. Genuineness is needed in order to establish a therapeutic relationship. It involves listening to and communicating with clients without distorting their messages, and being clear and concrete in communications.

Another method is the use of *positive regard*, which is the ability to view a client as being worthy of caring about and as someone who has strengths and achievement potential. It is built on respect and is usually communicated nonverbally.

Communication is also facilitated by *listening, attending, suspending value judgments*, and helping clients develop their own resources. A social worker should always be aware of *culturally appropriate communication* behaviors. It is also essential to be clear to establish *boundaries* with clients to facilitate a safe environment for change.

Test-Taking Strategies Applied

Material in quotation marks deserves particular attention and usually relates to the answer. The client–social worker interaction in the case scenario is occurring in the first session. The first session focuses on engagement or building a therapeutic alliance. The correct response choice is the one which addresses the client's belief that he is a failure and his comment about not understanding "how things got so bad." The incorrect response choices may be actions that will be taken at some time during the problem-solving process, but do not make him feel that the social worker understands his situation. The question asks for the social worker's response to his statements. Central to the formation of a therapeutic alliance is displaying *empathy*, which the social worker is doing in the correct answer.

Knowledge Area

Unit II—Intervention Processes and Techniques for Use Across Systems (Content Area); Intervention Planning and Implementation (Competency); The Principles and Techniques of Interviewing (e.g., Supporting, Clarifying, Focusing, Confronting, Validating, Feedback, Reflecting, Language Differences, Use of Interpreters, Redirecting) (KSA)

114. D

Rationale

Relying on the **expertise of other professions** when needed can reduce major liability risks for social workers. For example, in situations which require medical or other expertise, social workers should look to obtain appropriate guidance from others or else clients may be harmed. If such consultation does not occur, social workers breach **standards of care** through acts of omission (not acting when they should have done so).

Under the common law doctrine of standard of care, courts usually seek to determine what a typical, reasonable, and prudent (careful) social worker with the same or similar education and training would have done under the same or similar conditions. In many instances, establishing the standard of care is easy. But in other instances, it is not easy to establish what constitutes ordinary, reasonable, and prudent practice. Well-educated, skilled, thoughtful, and careful social workers may disagree with colleagues about the best course of action in complex circumstances, perhaps because of their different schools of thought, training, and experience.

Test-Taking Strategies Applied

In the case scenario, the social worker has "a lack of knowledge about this medical condition and the medication prescribed," which is causing dramatic mood changes in the client. Thus, the social worker has an ethical responsibility to learn more through consultation with an appropriate medical professional. Failure to seek consultation may adversely affect the client.

The reason for the contact is for the social worker to learn more about the medical condition and medication. The social worker is not collaborating, which is defined as working with another to produce or create something. Joint work by both the social worker and physician is not occurring. There is also no indication that the physician is the treating medical professional of the husband, so the social worker's action is not an effort to enhance coordination of services. Similarly, the social worker and physician are not part of a team, so the action is not aimed at team building.

Knowledge Area

Unit II—Intervention Processes and Techniques for Use Across Systems (Content Area); Intervention Planning and Implementation (Competency); Consultation Approaches (e.g., Referrals to Specialists) (KSA)

115. A

Rationale

Enhanced **coordination of client services** can be achieved through the use of alternative funding approaches. Blending or braiding funding across related programs and across multiple agencies is a basic way that state and local agencies can more effectively serve the holistic needs of clients, more efficiently target high-priority performance goals, and streamline administrative requirements. *Blending and braiding of fiscal resources aim to enhance service coordination to meet the holistic needs of clients.*

Some jurisdictions, particularly at the local level, have successfully used blended and braided funding, but *federal categorical limitations make taking this concept to a larger scale difficult*. The terms "blending" and "braiding" are used frequently, often together, and generally with little definition. However, they refer to two very different approaches to fiscal coordination.

Blending funding involves comingling the funds into one "pot" where social workers can draw down service dollars, personnel expenses can be paid, or other program needs can be met. When funding is blended, it goes into the "pot," and when it is pulled back out to pay for an expense, there is no means for the fiscal manager to report which funding stream paid for exactly which expense. Blending funding is politically challenging. Some funding streams cannot be blended. Other funding streams will require the funder to allow an exception to how the reporting normally functions. Instead of the usual reporting, funders can opt to accept reports on services and outcomes across the population being served, rather than exactly which children, youth, and families received services with their dollars. To blend funding, social workers need to work closely with funders and ensure that reporting requirements are met. Though it is challenging politically, once funders are on board, blended funding is less challenging to implement than braided funding. There is significantly less workload, as the tracking and accountability happens across all of the funding streams. *Rather than reporting to funders on their funding stream alone, reporting is done on how the collective funds are used. Blended funding can allow you to pay for services that may not be allowable with more categorical funding approaches. However, for many funders, the flexibility associated with blending makes it seem too "risky" as it often looks like supplanting, and they end up with less detailed information about how each of their dollars have been spent.*

Braided funding involves multiple funding streams utilized to pay for all of the services needed by a given population, with careful accounting of how every dollar from each funding stream is spent. The term "braiding" is used because multiple funding streams are initially separate, brought together to pay for more than any one funding stream can support, and then carefully pulled back apart to report to funders on how the money was spent. Braided funding is often the only option. Federal funding streams require careful tracking of staff time and expenses, to ensure that a federal funding stream only pays for those things directly associated with the intent of the funding. *Consequently, when multiple funding streams are paying for a single program or system, the system will need to be carefully designed to allow for sufficient reporting to ensure each funding stream is only paying for activities eligible under that funding stream. Braided funding requires significant effort to create the systems for tracking how funding is utilized.*

The design of a braided funding system that can respond to the individualized needs of many types of clients will require social workers to decide which services will be paid for by which funding streams. Ideally, this decision happens after the needs of the individual or family being served are identified, so that the funding does not drive the services being provided. This type of braided model requires a clear understanding of the eligible populations and the eligible services, so that decisions on how to fund the services can be made post hoc, rather than prior to discussing service needs with the families. The design of a braided funding program is simpler than the design of a braided funding system. Programs typically have clearly defined services that are provided and sometimes have very defined populations who are eligible for services.

Test-Taking Strategies Applied

The question contains a qualifying word—TRUE. It is even capitalized to assist with identifying the distinguishing factor of the correct response from the rest. Each statement must be read carefully and evaluated as to its accuracy. The correct answer is identified through the process of elimination, with each false assertion being excluded.

Blending is often not preferred by funders as they receive less detail about how monies are spent, while braiding is frequently not seen as possible due to the burden of the tracking associated with its implementation. It requires detailed reporting to ensure each funding stream is only paying for eligible activities. Thus, only the first statement is true as both blending and braiding are difficult to administer due to federal categorical limitations.

Knowledge Area

Unit III—Intervention Processes and Techniques for Use With Larger Systems (Content Area); Program Development and Research (Competency); Methods of Service Delivery (KSA)

116. D

Rationale

Operant conditioning attempts to understand complex human behavior without studying the internal mental thoughts and motivations.
B. F. Skinner based his theory of conditioning on the preexistent theory called "Law of Effect" or the belief that responses that produce satisfying effects become more likely to occur again and responses that produce discomforting effects become less likely to occur again.

Punishment has as its objective to decrease the rate of certain undesired behavior from occurring again. Punishment can be further classified into two major parts—positive and negative.

Positive punishment focuses on decreasing the undesired behavior by presenting negative consequences once undesired behavior has been exhibited. When subjected to negative consequences, individuals are less likely to repeat the same behavior in the future.

Negative punishment focuses on undesired behavior by removing favorite or desired items. When desired stimuli are removed, there is less chance of the behavior occurring again in the future.

Reinforcement aims to strengthen or increase behavior frequency.

Positive reinforcement increases the likelihood that behavior will occur again in the future by pairing it with desirable stimuli (reinforcers).

Negative reinforcement increases the probability that behavior will occur again in the future by removing negative stimuli.

Test-Taking Strategies Applied

This is a recall question which relies on social workers understanding various operant conditioning techniques. Negative punishment is when a desirable stimulus is removed following an undesirable behavior for the purpose of decreasing or eliminating the behavior. In the case scenario, the client takes away her daughter's cell phone (a desirable stimulus) with the desire to decrease her homework incompletion and tardiness (targeted behaviors).

Knowledge Area

Unit I—Human Development, Diversity, and Behavior in the Environment (Content Area); Human Growth and Development (Competency); Theories of Human Development Throughout the Lifespan (e.g., Physical, Social, Emotional, Cognitive, Behavioral) (KSA)

117. C

Rationale

Reimbursement methodologies can have a dramatic impact on the delivery of services. Social workers must be aware of different payment policies and the implications of each.

Capitation is based on a payment per person, rather than a payment per service provided. There are several different types of capitation, ranging from relatively modest per person per month case management payments to assist with care coordination to per person per month payments covering all professional services (professional, facility, pharmaceutical, clinical laboratory, durable medical equipment, etc.). There may also be particular services that are "carved out" of such payments. These may be handled on either a fee-for-service basis or by delegation to a separate benefit management company. Capitation is often used as a means of controlling growth in the cost of care.

Fee-for-service is a payment model where services are unbundled and paid for separately. It gives an incentive to provide more treatments because payment is dependent on the quantity of care, rather than quality of care. Similarly, when clients are shielded from paying (cost-sharing) by health insurance coverage, they are incentivized to welcome any medical service that might do some good. Fee-for-service is the dominant physician payment method in the United States.

In a **bundled payment** methodology, a single, "bundled" payment covers services delivered by two or more providers during a single episode of care or over a specific period of time. For example, if a client has cardiac bypass surgery, rather than making one payment to the hospital, a second payment to the surgeon, and a third payment to the anesthesiologist, the payer would combine these payments for the specific episode of care (i.e., cardiac bypass surgery). In some cases, one entity (for instance, an accountable care organization) may receive the bundled payment and subsequently apportion the payment among participating providers. In other cases, the payer may pay participating providers independently, but adjust each payment according to negotiated, predefined rules in order to ensure that the total payments to all of the providers for all of the defined services do not exceed the total bundled payment amount. This latter type of payment methodology is frequently referred to as "virtual" bundling. Bundled payment arrangements are a type of risk-contracting. If the cost of services is less than the bundled payment, participating providers retain the difference. But if the costs exceed the bundled payment, providers are not compensated for the difference.

Shared savings models can be roughly divided into two categories. In the first category, if the actual total costs of all care received by clients is lower than budgeted costs, the entities responsible for their care receive a percentage of the difference between the actual and budgeted costs (i.e., a "share of the savings"). However, if actual total cost exceeds the budgeted costs, the entities are not on the hook for any portion of the difference. Because the entities are only at risk for additional revenue, shared savings arrangements are sometimes said to involve only "upside" risk.

Test-Taking Strategies Applied

This is a recall question which relies on social workers understanding the effects that policies, procedures, regulations, and laws have on practice. Reimbursement methodologies can dramatically impact the ways in which services are coordinated and delivered. The question focuses on a single payment for multiple services. Fee-for-service would be excluded as it represents a separate reimbursement for each service provided. There is no mention of savings in the question, eliminating the last response choice.

Capitation should not be confused with bundled payments. Capitation is an actuarially determined payment per client who may or may not use services. The distinction between capitation and bundled payment is that capitation pays the same amount regardless of what clients need clinically or receive. The calculation of the capitation amount derives from actuarial principles of insurance. The big risk in capitation is incidence risk. The question asks about "services provided," making bundled payment the correct answer over capitation.

Knowledge Area

Unit III—Intervention Processes and Techniques for Use With Larger Systems (Content Area); Program Development and Research (Competency); Methods of Service Delivery (KSA)

118. A

Rationale

Cultural identity is often defined as the identity of a group, culture, or an individual, influenced by one's belonging to a group or culture. Certain ethnic and racial identities may also have privilege.

Cultural, racial, and ethnic identities are important, particularly for those who are members of minority groups. They may instill feelings of belonging to a particular group or groups and identification with that group (i.e., shared commitment and values). Cultural, racial, and ethnic identities are passed from one generation to the next through customs, traditions, language, religious practice, and cultural values. Cultural, racial, and ethnic identities are also influenced by the popular media, literature, and current events.

Self-esteem or image can be negatively impacted by cultural issues, especially when practices interfere with childhood development, such as being subject to criticism or abuse; missing out on experiences that would foster a sense of confidence and purpose; and/or receiving little or no positive reinforcement for accomplishments. In adulthood, cultural beliefs may compound life changes by further stigmatizing losing a job or changing jobs, ending an intimate relationship, having legal or financial troubles, struggling with addiction or substance abuse, having children with emotional troubles, developing physical health concerns, and so on.

People with poor self-image may work with social workers on becoming more assertive, confident, and self-aware. Finding a sense of accomplishment is a huge boost to self-esteem, and therapy can help clients identify specific activities that boost confidence and competence. In addition, many social workers focus on helping people develop self-compassion so that they can develop more realistic, achievable goals for themselves and treat themselves with kindness and encouragement.

Universalization is a supportive intervention used by social workers to reassure and encourage clients. Universalization places client experiences in the context of other individuals who are experiencing the same or similar challenges, and seeks to help clients grasp that their feelings and experiences are not uncommon given the circumstances. A social worker using this supportive intervention intends to "normalize" client experiences, emotions, and reactions to presenting challenges. By normalizing client experiences, social workers attempt to help avert client natural feelings of shame due to feeling alone or judged.

Test-Taking Strategies Applied

The case scenario requires the correct answer to be chosen as it is "most effective." As the poor self-image of the client is presented as a problem, it is necessary to select a response which will help the client see that she is not alone or to blame for her situation. The incorrect answers may be actions that the social worker will take, but they are not the most critical. The woman has not felt that she had any other choice than to stay married. She may have been skeptical and cautious about seeking help for fear of being mistreated or misunderstood. Thus, trust is an important element in establishing a therapeutic alliance. The client needs to know that the social worker can be trusted and is competent to help her. Only the correct answer helps build trust and rapport by helping her to see that the social worker accepts and understands her situation.

Knowledge Area

Unit I—Human Development, Diversity, and Behavior in the Environment (Content Area); Diversity, Discrimination, and Stereotypes (Competency); The Effect of Culture, Race, and Ethnicity on Behaviors, Attitudes, and Identity (KSA)

119. A

Rationale

Long-term **alcohol dependence** leads to a variety of moderate to severe health problems. The longer and heavier the consumption, the worse the physical results become. "**Wet brain**" is another way of describing a condition called **Wernicke-Korsakoff syndrom**e. It is caused by a deficiency in vitamin B_1 (thiamine). If "wet brain" is allowed to progress too far, it will not be possible to recover from it.

Wernicke-Korsakoff syndrome is actually a combination of two separate conditions: **Wernicke's encephalopathy** and **Korsakoff psychosis**. These two disorders combine to produce a variety of symptoms including confusion, changes to vision, loss of muscle coordination, difficulty swallowing, and speech problems. Hallucinations, loss of memory, confabulation (occurs as clients make up stories to compensate for their memory loss), inability to form new memories, inability to make sense when talking, and apathy are due to Korsakoff psychosis. It is possible for clients who are alcoholic to develop either Korsakoff psychosis or Wernicke's encephalopathy independently.

It is usual for the effects of Wernicke's encephalopathy to become noticeable first of all. These symptoms tend to come on suddenly. The first sign that something is wrong will be that a client appears confused. This can be hard to diagnose in a client who is habitually intoxicated. This confusion differs from drunken confusion because it lasts even when a client has not been drinking. Later the symptoms of Korsakoff psychosis will also become noticeable. In the beginning, only the ability to form new memories will be damaged, so a client can still appear quite lucid.

Clients who are alcoholic have poor dietary habits; over a long time, this will lead to nutritional deficiencies. Lack of thiamine in the diet interferes with glucose metabolism, which can then lead to atrophy in the brain. Wernicke's encephalopathy occurs due to damage to the thalamus and hypothalamus. Korsakoff psychosis occurs because of damage to those parts of the brain where memories are managed.

If wet brain syndrome has been allowed to progress too far, there may be little that can be done to reverse the effects. *Thiamine injections can improve things greatly and may restore a client back to full recovery*. Those who have developed the chronic form of wet brain will be far less likely to recover. In some cases, the best that can be done is prevention of any further deterioration.

The only possible cure for wet brain syndrome is complete abstinence from alcohol. Most of those who do find their way into recovery will be able to regain all functioning that was lost due to Wernicke-Korsakoff syndrome. Other clients will have to deal with lingering effects of the damage, but should be able to adapt and find a good life away from alcohol.

Test-Taking Strategies Applied

The question contains a qualifying word—BEST—that requires social workers to select the response choice which will optimally treat the root cause of the symptoms listed. While some of the incorrect response choices may be helpful to the client, only the correct answer addresses the reason for the wet brain symptoms. Cognitive rehabilitation and physical therapy address the manifestations of the vitamin B_1 (thiamine) deficiency, but not the underlying problem. There is also no justification for antipsychotic medications as delusion or hallucinations by the client were not mentioned in the question.

Knowledge Area

Unit I—Human Development, Diversity, and Behavior in the Environment (Content Area); Human Growth and Development (Competency); Addiction Theories and Concepts (KSA)

120. B

Rationale

There are many ethical standards, including those on touching clients, that speak to **professional boundary issues** that social workers face in practice. Often the maintenance of appropriate boundaries can be challenging for social workers. Social workers should not engage in physical contact with clients when there is a possibility of psychological harm to the client as a result of the contact (such as cradling or caressing clients). Social workers who engage in appropriate physical contact with clients are responsible for setting clear, appropriate, and culturally sensitive boundaries that govern such physical contact. The 2008 *NASW Code of Ethics* leaves the door open, but cautions social workers that they bear responsibility for ensuring that no negative consequences ensue.

The language leaves open the possibility that, when used responsibly, touch might occasionally make clinical sense, perhaps by helping a client stay grounded or feel less isolated or overwhelmed.

However, social workers using touch within the context of a therapeutic alliance must always carefully consider clients' factors, such as presenting problems and symptoms, personal touch and sexual history, ability to differentiate types of touch, and clients' ability to assertively identify and protect their boundaries, as well as the gender and cultural influences of both clients and social workers.

Social workers should have clear policies about touching, self-disclosure, and other boundary areas which are applied consistently to client situations. One of the most effective ways to establish clear professional boundaries is for a social worker's behavior to set the standard for meetings with clients. Appropriate dress and behavior should be displayed and talk should not include a social worker discussing his or her personal life.

Test-Taking Strategies Applied

The case scenario describes a client's reaction to a hesitation by a social worker to a hug *at the end of a session*. There is no indication that physical touch has been discussed between the client and social worker in this or any prior interaction. The client may be accusing the social worker of being homophobic due to an exchange with someone else in the past.

In the case scenario, it is necessary for the social worker to explain her policy on physical touch, as well as other boundary issues. Educating clients about the 2008 *NASW Code of Ethics* is essential so they can better understand therapeutic or helping alliances and not confuse them with friendships or romantic relationships. None of the incorrect responses include this critical education.

It would not be appropriate to explore the client's belief about being rejected based on her sexual orientation when the session is ending. In addition, there is no indication that the client's statement is anything other than a misunderstanding about professional boundaries between the social worker and client. The client may not realize that the social worker has a policy which is applied to all clients.

Continuing to hug the client would be contraindicated, especially given the accusation. It violates the social worker's policy on physical contact and treats this client differently than others.

Simply telling the client that the social worker is not homophobic does not provide an explanation for the hesitation. It also misses the opportunity to educate the client about the importance of maintaining professional boundaries and differentiating the therapeutic alliance from other personal relationships.

Knowledge Area

Unit IV—Professional Relationships, Values, and Ethics (Content Area); Professional Values and Ethical Issues (Competency); Professional Boundaries in the Social Worker–Client/Client System Relationship (e.g., Power Differences, Conflicts of Interest, etc.) (KSA)

121. D

Rationale

Xenophobia is a severe aversion to foreigners, strangers, their politics, and their cultures. Often, the term "xenophobia" is used interchangeably with racism, yet the two are actually different. While racism defines prejudice based solely on ethnicity, ancestry, or race, xenophobia covers any kind of fear related to **differences in culture, race, and/or ethnicity**, as well as other ways of being different. Those with xenophobia do not understand or accept that their condition is based in fear, yet it is the perceived threat of losing one's own identity, culture, and imagined superiority or purity that is the cause.

If left untreated, xenophobia can have seriously detrimental effects. An individual who is xenophobic is liable to pass along his or her highly generalized and ungrounded perceptions to children and family members. Some symptoms of a xenophobic person include:

- Feelings of fear or dread when exposed to people or cultural items perceived to be different
- Apparent hostility toward people or cultures perceived to be different
- Distrust aimed specifically toward cultures perceived to be different
- Rash generalizations and stereotypes aimed at a set of people based on superficial qualities

Like all phobias, there is no universally specific cause that leads to the development of xenophobia. It can be caused by unique experiences or can simply be the result of alienation from people and cultures different than one's own.

Like many phobias, treatment focuses on first targeting the initial inciting factor that caused the irrational and extreme fear. Therapy includes talking about why the fear was unfounded and addressing any traumatic experiences that caused the phobia, as well as identifying ways to deal with symptoms. Sometimes behavioral techniques are used to systematically and gradually confront the source of fear and learning to control the physical and mental reactions to it. By facing the phobia directly, it is possible to realize that fears are not grounded in real or imminent danger.

Test-Taking Strategies Applied

This is a recall question which relies on social workers understanding terminology related to cultural competence and its barriers. Social workers should promote conditions that encourage respect for cultural, racial, and/or ethnic diversity and promote policies and practices that demonstrate respect for difference; support the expansion of relevant knowledge and resources; advocate for programs and institutions that demonstrate cultural, racial, and/or ethnic competence; and promote policies that safeguard the rights of all people.

If the definition of xenophobia is not known, it may be possible to narrow the choices through eliminating other answers.

Ephebiphobia, also known as hebephobia, is the fear of young people or teenagers.

Trypanophobia is the fear of needles, which can lead to potential health issues, especially when important vaccines and medications that require injections are refused.

Mysophobia, also known as germophobia, is a common fear of general contamination which can lead to extreme anxiety of contact with others.

Knowledge Area

Unit II—Intervention Processes and Techniques for Use Across Systems (Content Area); Intervention Planning and Implementation (Competency); The Criteria Used in the Selection of Intervention/Treatment Modalities (e.g., Client/Client System Abilities, Culture, Life Stage) (KSA)

122. C

Rationale

Social workers recognize the serious consequences of **work-related stress**. Many social workers enter the profession because they have a desire to help others and contribute to the betterment of society. They are drawn to a line of work wherein they can assist individuals, groups, families, and communities to address hardships and challenges. This work can take a huge toll on emotional well-being, physical health, and interpersonal functioning.

Burnout is a process involving increasing emotional exhaustion, coupled with a negative attitude toward clients and reduced commitment to the profession.

Vicarious or secondary trauma is a transformation of worldview as a result of empathic engagement with survivor clients and their trauma material.

Compassion fatigue refers to a set of physical and psychological symptoms which develop due to being exposed to client suffering.

Self-regulation is the ability to control emotions, thoughts, and behavior.

Self-care refers to activities to address emotional, physical, and psychological health.

Self-efficacy is the belief in the capability to achieve a goal or an outcome.

Self-determination is the power or ability to make decisions without outside influence.

In conceptualizing the process of self-care, the importance of self-awareness, self-regulation, and self-efficacy are emphasized.

Test-Taking Strategies Applied

This is a recall question which relies on social workers knowing key words related to self-care and social work practice. While the social worker in the case scenario appears to have some signs of burnout, her belief in being successful demonstrates self-efficacy. Self-efficacy is critical to self-care. The scenario does not describe her taking any action which may be associated with self-care; instead, she has an outlook that is positive, perhaps due to some intrinsic qualities. Self-efficacy is a belief while self-care is an action. There is no mention of the social worker controlling her behavior or exercising her ability to make decisions, eliminating self-regulation and self-determination, respectively.

Knowledge Area

Unit IV—Professional Relationships, Values, and Ethics (Content Area); Professional Development and Use of Self (Competency); Social Worker Self-Care Principles and Techniques (KSA)

123. C

Rationale

Central to required **social work documentation** are case notes. Case notes are an integral and important part of practice. Record-keeping practices have an impact on client outcomes such that poor case notes can result in poor decision making and adverse client outcomes. *A case note is a chronological record of interactions, observations, and actions relating to a particular client.*

The guiding principle for deciding what information should be included in case notes is whether it is relevant to the service or support being provided. Case notes can include, but are not limited to:

- Biopsychosocial, environmental, and systemic factors
- Considerations of culture, religion, and spirituality
- Risk and resilience present
- Facts, theories, or research underpinnings that impact on assessments and/or treatment
- Summaries or all discussions and interactions
- Persons/services involved in the provision of supports including referral information, telephone contacts, and email/written correspondence
- Attendance/nonattendance at scheduled sessions

- Discussions of legal and ethical responsibilities (client rights, responsibilities, and complaints processes; parameters of the service and support being offered and agreed to; issues relating to informed consent, information sharing, confidentiality, and privacy; efforts to promote and support client self-determination and autonomy)
- Details of reasons for and outcomes leading up to or following the termination or interruption of a service or support

Test-Taking Strategies Applied

The question contains a qualifying word—primary. Unlike other questions, the qualifying word in this question is not capitalized. Qualifying words may be capitalized or not, so it is important to read questions carefully.

While case notes may have multiple functions, the correct answer is the one that highlights their usefulness in ensuring efficient and effective client care. Using case records for worker development, reimbursement, and/or regulatory compliance is not the main reason that social workers keep case or progress notes. These notes are used mainly by social workers to help them recall what was done in prior meetings or sessions so that future work can pick up there. It helps to ensure that time is not wasted talking about issues that were already resolved. Additionally, by reviewing case notes prior to sessions, social workers reduce the likelihood that important next steps in discussions take place and therapeutic gaps do not emerge. Case notes also help social workers look back to initial and other past sessions to see progress made. This progress should be regularly reviewed with clients.

Knowledge Area

Unit III—Intervention Processes and Techniques for Use With Larger Systems (Content Area); Record-Keeping and Reporting (Competency); The Principles of Case Recording, Documentation, and Management of Practice Records (KSA)

124. A

Rationale

The mission of the social work profession is rooted in a set of **professional values**. These core values—service, social justice, dignity and worth of the person, importance of human relationships, integrity, and competence—are the foundation of social work's unique purpose and perspective.

These core values reflect what is unique to the social work profession. Core values, and the principles that flow from them, must be balanced within the context and complexity of the human experience.

When providing **service**, social workers' primary goal is to help people in need and to address social problems. *Social workers elevate service to others above self-interest.* Social workers are encouraged to volunteer some portion of their professional skills with no expectation of significant financial return (pro bono service).

Social workers value **social justice**, challenging social inequities on behalf of vulnerable and oppressed individuals and groups of people. *Social workers' social change efforts are focused primarily on issues of poverty, unemployment, discrimination, and other forms of social injustice.*

Social workers respect the inherent **dignity and worth of the person**, treating each person in a caring and respectful fashion, mindful of individual differences and cultural and ethnic diversity. Social workers promote clients' socially responsible self-determination. *Social workers seek to enhance clients' capacity and opportunity to change and to address their own needs.*

Social workers recognize the central **importance of human relationships**, as relationships between and among people are an important vehicle for change. Social workers engage people as partners in the helping process. *Social workers seek to strengthen relationships among people in a purposeful effort to promote, restore, maintain, and enhance the well-being of individuals, families, social groups, organizations, and communities.*

Integrity means that social workers behave in a trustworthy manner. *Social workers act honestly and responsibly and promote ethical practices on the part of the organizations with which they are affiliated.*

Social workers practice within their areas of **competence** and develop and enhance their professional expertise. *Social workers continually strive to increase their professional knowledge and skills and to apply them in practice.*

Test-Taking Strategies Applied

Social workers should uphold all social work values. However, this case scenario contains a qualifying word—most—that is not capitalized. The problem of finding an appropriate provider presents a barrier to fulfilling the client's wish to die at home. Thus, the social worker must focus on developing creative solutions to promoting the client's need for self-determination.

Competence involves practicing within one's expertise and developing as a professional, which are not prevailing issues in this case scenario. Integrity, being honest or trustworthy, is also not directly related to the situation presented. Lastly, pursuing social change or justice for those who are oppressed and disenfranchised does not apply as there is no indication that the barrier encountered results from oppression or unequal treatment.

Knowledge Area

Unit IV—Professional Relationships, Values, and Ethics (Content Area); Professional Values and Ethical Issues (Competency); Legal and/or Ethical Issues Related to Death and Dying (KSA)

125. D

Rationale

Defense mechanisms are unconscious processes that protect clients from unacceptable or painful ideas or impulses.

Denial involves blocking external events from awareness. If some situation is just too much to handle, a client may refuse to experience it. It is a primitive defense, operating by itself or, more commonly, in combination with other, more subtle mechanisms that support it.

Projection involves clients attributing their own thoughts, feelings, and motives to others. Thoughts most commonly projected onto another are the ones that would cause guilt. For instance, a client might hate someone, but his or her superego tells him or her that such hatred is unacceptable. Thus, the client solves the problem by believing that the other person hates him or her.

Displacement is the redirection of an impulse (usually aggression) onto a powerless substitute target. The target can be a person or an object that can serve as a symbolic substitute. A client who is frustrated by his or her superiors on the job may go home and kick the dog or yell at a family member.

Reaction formation is actually a mental process, transforming anxiety-producing thoughts into their opposites in consciousness. A client goes beyond denial and behaves in the opposite way to which he or she thinks or feels. By using reaction formation, the id is satisfied while keeping the ego in ignorance of the true motives. In short, reaction formation means expressing the opposite of inner feelings in outward behavior.

Test-Taking Strategies Applied

The question contains a qualifying word—MOST. While the client may be using more than one of the defense mechanisms listed, it is likely the behavior constitutes reaction formation. There is no evidence that the client denies having an Alcohol Use Disorder or fails to recognize the implications of this disorder, which are both indications of denial. The client's actions go beyond denial as the client is engaging in actions, outrage, and advocacy, which are counter to his inner beliefs of appreciation for his own mandated services.

Knowledge Area

Unit I—Human Development, Diversity, and Behavior in the Environment (Content Area); Effects of the Environment on Systems' Behavior (Competency); Psychological Defense Mechanisms and Their Effects on Behavior and Relationships (KSA)

126. B

Rationale

Social workers must be familiar with various **research techniques** which are applied to practice. **Case-mix adjustment** is the process of statistically controlling for group differences when comparing nonequivalent groups on outcomes of interest. It is done on a post hoc basis, after the treatment groups have been formed and the performance measures collected. The groups may be treatment agencies, consumers, providers, programs, regions, or states. Any time these groups are to be compared on performance indicators, case-mix adjustment must be considered.

For example, mental health authorities and providers in both the public and private sectors are increasingly interested in measuring outcomes of mental health care. Performance measurement is mandated by some state public mental health systems and managed care organizations. By using comparative performance indicators, mental health systems can track the effects of changes within their systems and the effectiveness of routine care provision across sites. They can identify sites providing the highest quality care and sites that may need to improve the quality of care they provide.

However, populations of mental health consumers served by different behavioral health care agencies can be vastly different. Agencies serving individuals with severe and comorbid impairment cannot equitably be compared using raw outcome scores to agencies serving individuals with less challenging mental health concerns. The outcomes that providers or agencies strive for, and for which they are held accountable, are only partly under their control; many individual and environmental variables affect outcomes independently of care. These critical case-mix variables are not evenly distributed across groups.

Case-mix adjustment attempts to identify the individual and environmental variables that influence outcomes, measure those variables, correct for their influence through post hoc statistical methods, and display the case-mix adjusted results in ways that allow for ease of interpretation and use.

Case-mix adjustment is a partial correction that cannot create perfectly equivalent groups or duplicate the rigor of experimental assignment. In a true experiment, the researcher assigns people randomly to different treatment groups, controls the administration of the treatment, and measures the outcome or dependent variable. Statistical laws dictate that, with enough people, the average characteristics will be equal in all groups; the only systematic variation is the treatment. So if the results show that the groups are unequal on the dependent variable, one concludes that the treatment caused the difference. Case-mix adjustment is a post hoc effort to correct for differences among the groups served by the agencies since random selection does not take place.

Case-mix adjustment has an additional function in setting appropriate reimbursement rates in capitation contracts. Adequately and fairly compensating providers on the basis of how much service will be needed, as indicated by case-mix adjustment, removes the incentive for providers to attract only those who are relatively healthy and avoid those with more severe conditions that will require more services.

There may be situations where case-mix adjustment is unnecessary. This situation will occur when the case-mix adjusted results lead to the same conclusions as the unadjusted results regarding group level performance. It may also occur when the gain from doing case-mix adjustment is considered to be small relative to the costs, or when the potential case-mix indicators that are available in a limited dataset do not correlate with the outcome. In the latter case, it is important to recognize that any results to be compared among groups are unadjusted and therefore potentially misleading.

Random sampling assists with creating equivalent treatment and control groups prior to the delivery of interventions.

Inter-rater or interobserver reliability assesses the degree to which different raters/observers give consistent estimates of the same phenomenon.

Descriptive statistics describe the basic features of data in a study. They provide simple summaries and form the basis of virtually every quantitative analysis of data.

Test-Taking Strategies Applied

This is a recall question which relies on social workers being able to apply research principles to practice. Social workers should be able to correctly interpret empirical findings. Understanding whether outcomes are related to differences in sample selection or client characteristics rather than interventions is critical as social workers may inappropriately conclude that services are effective or ineffective when they are not.

Knowledge Area

Unit III—Intervention Processes and Techniques for Use With Larger Systems (Content Area); Program Development and Research (Competency); The Effects of Program Evaluation Findings on Services (KSA)

127. A

Rationale

A valuable source for data is **collateral contacts or informants**—relatives, friends, teachers, physicians, and others who possess insight into clients' lives. Collateral sources are particularly important when, because of developmental capacity or functioning, clients' ability to generate information may be limited or distorted. For example, assessments of clients with memory or cognitive limitations will be enhanced with data that collaterals (family members and friends) can provide.

Social workers must exercise discretion when deciding that such information is needed and in obtaining it. Clients can assist in this effort by suggesting collateral contacts who may provide useful information. Social workers must weigh the validity of information obtained from collateral sources. It is important to consider the nature of their relationships with clients and the ways in which that might influence these contacts' perspectives. Family members may be emotionally involved in client difficulties, skewing their perceptions. Other service providers may have limited contact with clients, with narrow views of their situations. As with other sources of information, input from collateral contacts must be critically viewed and weighed against other information.

Test-Taking Strategies Applied

The question contains a qualifying word—MOST. While all of the sources listed may provide some useful information, it is likely that the client's adult son will be able to provide the most detailed and accurate information as he lives with her. The case scenario states that the client is disoriented. Additionally, clients often overrate their functioning. Therefore, the client herself is not the best person to provide information on her safety. While she is getting visiting nurse services and home delivered meals, agency staff involvement in the home is limited to medication administration and delivery of meals. The social worker's concern about her safety does not focus on her day program as she is constantly supervised there. The client's functioning at the day program may also be different than at home. Staff in the home will not be able to comment on her ability to perform activities of daily living (ADLs) like bathing, toileting, and cooking. Similarly, her physician will only be familiar with her medical status.

Collateral contacts who live with clients—in this scenario, her adult son—are usually very good sources of information regarding clients' functioning as they have the opportunity to observe them for extended periods while performing all tasks which are required for safe, daily living.

Knowledge Area

Unit II—Intervention Processes and Techniques for Use Across Systems (Content Area); Assessment Methods and Techniques (Competency); Methods of Involving Clients/Client Systems in Problem Identification (e.g., Gathering Collateral Information) (KSA)

128. A

Rationale

Social workers must be familiar with **ethical standards related to payment for services**. There are many practices which are not ethical such as setting unreasonable fees, bartering in most instances, and soliciting extra fees from clients when services can be provided by agencies at no additional cost. In addition, an arrangement where social workers accept a percentage of other independent providers' fees for professional services that they have not directly provided is not ethical. Receiving money for referrals made to other professionals constitutes "fee splitting" and is strictly prohibited. Costs of social work services should be established at market value and paid per agreement or contract with clients for services actually received.

"Fee splitting" represents a conflict of interest which may adversely affect client care and well-being. For example, clients may not necessarily be referred to the most appropriate professionals, but instead those with whom referring social workers have "fee splitting" or commission payment type arrangements.

Fee splitting is not only prohibited for social workers, but other professionals as well.

Test-Taking Strategies Applied

This is a recall question which relies on social workers understanding the ethical issues regarding payment for services, and specifically the term "fee splitting."

Knowledge Area

Unit IV—Professional Relationships, Values, and Ethics (Content Area); Professional Values and Ethical Issues (Competency); Legal and/or Ethical Issues Related to the Practice of Social Work, Including Responsibility to Clients/Client Systems, Colleagues, the Profession, and Society (KSA)

129. D

Rationale

A **multidisciplinary team** is a group of individuals from different disciplines, each with unique skills and perspectives, who work together toward a common purpose or goal. The benefits of this approach are well documented. Multidisciplinary teams are often seen as advantageous to clients because they do not have the burden of navigating multiple service systems and communicating to multiple providers who are involved in their care.

Test-Taking Strategies Applied

The question contains a qualifying word—FIRST. While more than one response choice may be helpful throughout the process, the order in which they are to occur is critical. The first answer is incorrect as the team should be involved in determining what assessment information is needed and helping to gather it. Additionally, a biopsychosocial history may not be needed or appropriate as the goal is to determine the current and future needs of the young man. The second response choice is also incorrect. While it may be useful to have professionals who have treated the client in the past on the team, identifying actual individuals comes after the unique skills and perspectives needed have been articulated. It is also premature to outline the timeline for moving as the specific goals and objectives which need to be accomplished before the move have not been set. Thus, the third response choice is incorrect.

The initial action must be to identify the requisite skills needed. Without knowing what other disciplines need to be represented, a social worker will be unable to understand his or her role, as well as those of others, on interdisciplinary teams. Central to effective multidisciplinary team approaches is seeking to establish common ground with other professionals, including commonalities in goals. Professionals should also acknowledge the differences within the field and across other disciplines.

Knowledge Area

Unit III—Intervention Processes and Techniques for Use With Larger Systems (Content Area); Supervision and Administration

(Competency); The Process of Interdisciplinary and Intradisciplinary Team Collaboration (KSA)

130. A

Rationale

Social workers should respect clients' right to privacy or **confidentiality**. In addition, social workers may only disclose confidential information when appropriate with valid consent from a client or a person legally authorized to consent on behalf of a client. Social workers should protect the confidentiality of all information obtained in the course of professional service, except for compelling professional reasons. The general expectation that social workers will keep information confidential does not apply when disclosure is necessary to prevent serious, foreseeable, and imminent harm to a client or other identifiable person.

Social workers should also provide clients with reasonable **access to records**. Social workers who are concerned that clients' access to their records could cause serious misunderstanding or harm to a client should provide assistance in interpreting the records and consultation with a client regarding the records. *Social workers should limit clients' access to their records, or portions of their records, only in exceptional circumstances when there is compelling evidence that such access would cause serious harm to a client*. Both clients' requests and the rationale for withholding some or all of the record should be documented in clients' files. When providing clients with access to their records, social workers should take steps to protect the confidentiality of other individuals identified or discussed in such records.

Test-Taking Strategies Applied

The case scenario clearly states that "the social worker is not worried about the client seeing the information in the record." Thus, there is no compelling reason to limit the client's access to her record. The client's lack of explanation about what will be done with the information does not change the social worker's duty to send a copy of the entire record to the client.

It is inappropriate for the social worker to meet with the former client to do an assessment. Termination has already occurred and the former client has the right to withhold the reason for the request. The social worker also should not remove information from the record as there is no concern with having the client see it. The client can decide whether she will share all, some, or none of the information with others once she receives and reviews it. It is always good to have requests put in writing, but the reason for the request is not needed. In addition, this response is incorrect as it is concerned more with administrative procedure than the issues of record access.

Knowledge Area

Unit III—Intervention Processes and Techniques for Use With Larger Systems (Content Area); Record-Keeping and Reporting (Competency); The Principles of Case Recording, Documentation, and Management of Practice Records (KSA)

131. B

Rationale

Positive psychology is the scientific study of the strengths that enable individuals, families, and communities to thrive. The field is founded on the belief that people want to lead meaningful and fulfilling lives, to cultivate what is best within themselves, and to enhance their experiences of love, work, and play.

It is a reaction against psychoanalysis and behavioral analysis, which focus on negative thinking and emphasize maladaptive behavior. It builds further on the humanistic movement, which encouraged an emphasis on happiness, well-being, and positivity, thus creating the foundation for what is now known as positive psychology.

Positive psychology is concerned with eudaimonia, "the good life," or flourishing, living according to what holds the greatest value in life—the factors that contribute the most to a well-lived and fulfilling life. While not attempting a strict definition of the good life, positive psychologists agree that one must live a happy, engaged, and meaningful life in order to experience "the good life" or use signature strengths every day to produce authentic happiness and abundant gratification.

Psychoanalysis refers both to a theory of how the mind works and a treatment modality. It is based on the belief that people could be cured by making conscious their unconscious thoughts and motivations, thus gaining insight. The aim is to release repressed emotions and experiences, (i.e., make the unconscious conscious).

Behaviorism is an approach to the understanding of human and animal behavior. It assumes that all behaviors are either reflexes produced by a response to certain stimuli in the environment, or a consequence to antecedents. Thus, behaviorists focus primarily on environmental factors which serve as reinforcers or punishers of behavior.

Psychoeducation refers to the process of providing education and information to those seeking or receiving services and their family members.

Test-Taking Strategies Applied

This is a recall question which requires social workers to be familiar with a type of psychology which is rooted in the humanistic movement and has many similarities to the strengths perspective used by social workers. Positive psychology is a strengths-based approach to working with clients.

When the names of diagnoses, theories, or approaches are listed as response choices, it is often wise to think about each of the answers listed *before* looking at the question. Getting the question correct relies on knowing about all four of the answers. Whenever there is a gap in knowledge about one of the diagnoses, theories, or approaches listed, the likelihood of getting the question wrong increases. Knowledge should be used to try to narrow down the possibilities by eliminating incorrect answers, leaving response choices that are candidates for selection.

Knowledge Area

Unit I—Human Development, Diversity, and Behavior in the Environment (Content Area); Human Growth and Development (Competency); Strengths-Based and Resilience Theories (KSA)

132. B

Rationale

Often, **values** and **ethics** are terms that are used interchangeably. Though different, together they form the basis for making decisions. *Values are beliefs that a person holds about aspects of life and serve as guiding principles that influence behavior*. Every individual has a set of values through which he or she looks at all things and also at the world.

Ethics refers to the guidelines for conduct or a system of moral principles. For example, killing and rape are acts which violate a code of conduct which dictates what is wrong and what is right. When these ethics were not in place, no human behavior could be categorized as good or bad, which is what led to the development of these standards to guide human behavior in a society.

Test-Taking Strategies Applied

The question contains a qualifying word—BEST. While the incorrect answers contain some true assertions about values and/or ethics, they do not contain the basic distinction that values are principles held by people to help guide behaviors while ethics are moral codes of conduct that decide what is wrong and what is right about these behaviors.

There is incomplete or inaccurate information contained in many of the incorrect answers. For example, ethics can be unwritten and do not only apply to professional behavior. Values can be customs, beliefs, standards of conduct, and principles considered by a culture, a group of people, or an individual. Thus, they are not only customs of individuals. In addition, values and ethical beliefs can both change over time, though such changes often occur slowly.

Knowledge Area

Unit IV—Professional Relationships, Values, and Ethics (Content Area); Professional Values and Ethical Issues (Competency); Professional Values and Principles (e.g., Competence, Social Justice, Integrity, and Dignity and Worth of the Person) (KSA)

133. B

Rationale

According to psychologist Jean Piaget, children progress through a series of four critical stages of **cognitive development**. Each stage is marked by shifts in how kids understand the world.

- The sensorimotor stage, from birth to age 2
- The preoperational stage, from age 2 to about age 7
- The concrete operational stage, from age 7 to 11
- The formal operational stage, which begins at age 11 and spans into adulthood.

According to Piaget, children in the preoperational stage of cognitive growth (ages 2–7) use magical thinking until they learn the properties of physics and reality—a trial and error process that takes years. Little children do indeed have a hard time drawing the distinction between what is real and what is not, and they sometimes get confused and think that what occurs in their heads is happening in the outside world. Children do not make these errors because they are delusional or confused about the rules of the physical world. The more likely reason that imagination and fact can blend together is that little kids have acute powers of perception—they are experts at seeing, hearing, feeling, thinking, and imagining—but they cannot reflect on those perceptions. In other words, they think a lot, but they do not yet think about thinking.

When adults wake up from a scary dream, the primitive brain feels the emotion, but advanced reasoning puts it in context. Kids, on the other hand, operate more from the gut, with less contemplation or insight about what they have experienced.

Around the age of 4, kids turn a corner and become more aware of their own perceptions and more astute about distinguishing appearance and reality, even though it is a process that takes time to truly sink in. One theory for why this happens is that the right brain, which processes perceptions, and the left brain, which analyzes them, start to communicate better with each other, leading to a higher level of insight for kids in the later preschool years.

Test-Taking Strategies Applied

This is a recall question which relies on social workers understanding stages of cognitive development. Even when theorists are not explicitly stated in questions, correct answers require knowledge of their specific work. For example, being familiar with the work of Kohlberg on moral reasoning, Piaget on cognitive development, and Erikson on psychosocial development can assist with narrowing down response choices to identify the correct answers to questions in their areas.

Knowledge Area

Unit I—Human Development, Diversity, and Behavior in the Environment (Content Area); Human Growth and Development (Competency); Theories of Human Development Throughout the Lifespan (e.g., Physical, Social, Emotional, Cognitive, Behavioral) (KSA)

134. C

Rationale

The diagnosis formerly known as Gender Identity Disorder was changed in the *DSM-5* to **Gender Dysphoria**.

In order for a client to be diagnosed with Gender Dysphoria, he or she must exhibit a strong and persistent cross-gender identification (not merely a desire for any perceived cultural advantages of being the other sex).

In children, the disturbance is manifested by six (or more) of the following for at least 6-months:

- Repeatedly stated desire to be, or insistence that he or she is, the other sex *(must be present)*
- In boys, preference for cross-dressing or simulating female attire; in girls, insistence on wearing only stereotypical masculine clothing

- Strong and persistent preferences for cross-gender roles in make-believe play or persistent fantasies of being the other gender
- A strong rejection of toys/games typically played by one's gender
- Intense desire to participate in the stereotypical games and pastimes of the other gender
- Strong preference for playmates of the other gender
- A strong dislike of one's sexual anatomy
- A strong desire for the primary (e.g., penis, vagina) or secondary (e.g., menstruation) characteristics of the other gender

In adolescents and adults, the disturbance is manifested by symptoms such as a stated desire to be the other gender, frequently passing as the other gender, desire to live or be treated as the other gender, or the conviction that he or she has the typical feelings and reactions of the other gender.

Gender Dysphoria causes clinically significant distress or impairment in social, occupational, or other important areas of functioning.

Gender Dysphoria is not concurrent with a physical intersex condition.

There is a specifier for Gender Dysphoria in the *DSM-5*—posttransition, that is, the client has transitioned to full-time living in the desired gender (with or without legalization of gender change) and has undergone (or is undergoing) at least one medical procedure or treatment regimen, namely, hormone treatment or gender reassignment surgery—confirming the desired gender.

Test-Taking Strategies Applied

The question contains a qualifying word—must—even though it is not capitalized. Dislike of one's sexual anatomy and preference for clothing and playmates of the other gender are indicators of Gender Dysphoria, but do not have to be present. The only criterion that must be present is that the client must want to be the other gender or believe that he or she is the other gender.

"Gender nonconforming" is a broader term that can include clients with Gender Dysphoria, but it can also describe those who feel that they are neither only male or only female. "Transgender" is an umbrella term for clients whose gender identity and/or expression is different from cultural expectations based on the gender they were assigned at birth.

Being transgender does not imply any specific sexual orientation. Clients may be straight, gay, lesbian, bisexual, and so on.

Knowledge Area

Unit II—Intervention Processes and Techniques for Use Across Systems (Content Area); Assessment Methods and Techniques (Competency); The Use of the Diagnostic and Statistical Manual of the American Psychiatric Association (KSA)

135. B

Rationale

Effective **discharge planning** and appropriate postdischarge care are key for client well-being. Discharge planning usually begins early in treatment or clients' inpatient stays. In general, discharge planning is conceptualized as having four steps: (a) assessment; (b) development of plans; (c) provision of service,including providing family education and making service referrals; and (d) follow-up/evaluation. Discharge summaries serve as the primary documents communicating clients' care plans. Often discharge summaries are the only communication with subsequent client care settings. High-quality discharge summaries are generally thought to be essential for promoting client safety when returning home or going to other settings.

While the format of discharge summaries varies across settings, there are some *required components*:

1. Reason for admission
2. Significant findings
3. Procedures and treatment provided
4. Discharge condition and prognosis
5. Client and family instructions (as appropriate)—including needed follow-up services by other providers

Discharge summaries also should be signed by medical or other treating professionals.

Test-Taking Strategies Applied

The question contains a qualifying word—TRUE. It is even capitalized to assist with identifying the distinguishing factor of the correct response from the rest. Each statement must be read carefully and evaluated as to its accuracy. The correct answer is identified through the process of elimination, with each false assertion being excluded.

Knowledge Area

Unit II—Intervention Processes and Techniques for Use Across Systems (Content Area); Intervention Planning and Implementation (Competency); Discharge, Aftercare, and Follow-Up Planning (KSA)

136. C

Rationale

Mirroring is a technique used to gain rapport at the unconscious level. Mirroring, as the name suggests, means copying another person's gestures, tone of voice, or even catchphrases. Mirroring has numerous benefits provided social workers carry it out properly.

One reason that spiders are hated, but other mammals are not, is that mammals look much more similar to people than insects. Individuals are hard-wired to like and feel comfortable around other humans.

When mirroring, social workers try to convince the subconscious mind of clients that they are similar to them. If it works, clients feel comfortable without knowing why. In mirroring, social workers copy the gestures of clients consciously with the goal of making them feel comfortable, even if they didn't feel that way initially. Mirroring requires copying their gestures, using the same tone, or talking about common interests in a manner that is slow enough to make it unnoticeable to their conscious mind. There are other features that can be mirrored using neurolinguistic programming such as blinking rate, facial expressions, or tension in the muscles of the person. Even repeating words can lead to successful mirroring. For instance, if clients say "yes" social workers say "yes," if they say "no" social workers say "no," and so on. The key is to do it very moderately and occasionally, without making clients suspicious.

If social workers want to make sure that mirroring was successful and clients are feeling comfortable, they can assume a new gesture. If clients unconsciously copy, then mirroring has been successful.

There are other verbal communication techniques.

Questioning includes open- and closed-ended formats to *get relevant information in a nonjudgmental manner.*

Clarifying uses questioning, paraphrasing, and restating to *ensure full understanding of clients' ideas and thoughts*, including formulation of the existing problem.

Reframing shows clients that there are different perspectives and ideas that can *help to change negative thinking patterns and promote change.*

Test-Taking Strategies Applied

Selecting the correct answer requires knowledge of the verbal and nonverbal communication techniques listed. The question is asking about a "nonverbal technique." Mirroring is the only nonverbal technique provided. In addition, the sole function of mirroring is rapport building, while the other techniques focus more on gathering information, ensuring understanding of information provided, or challenging negative thinking.

Knowledge Area

Unit II—Intervention Processes and Techniques for Use Across Systems (Content Area); Intervention Planning and Implementation (Competency); Verbal and Nonverbal Communication Techniques (KSA)

137. A

Rationale

Social workers must be aware of the effects **policies, procedures, regulations, and laws** have on practice. Many of these impacts concern choices made based on equality and equity. While there is a common misconception that equity and equality mean the same thing and that they can be used interchangeably, they cannot as there is an important distinction between them. The idea of **equality** is that everyone should receive the same treatment and opportunities, a notion that is fundamental to democracy and the belief that everyone should benefit from the fruits of a good society.

However, when a society is stratified into poles of advantage and disadvantage, with the inevitable consequences of privilege and exclusion, the notion of equal access is just an ideal and does not exist in reality. Fair access, then, may take on a different meaning than equal access and opportunity. Rather than fairness occurring from uniform distribution (equality), where there is an entitlement to the same amount, there may be a need to level the playing field. In other words, **equity** is concerned with fairness by remedying historic injustices that have prevented or diminished access in the first place.

Policies aimed at ensuring that everyone can have access to the same opportunities (equity) provide more resources to those who need them.

Sustainability is the ability to continue over time.

Fidelity is the quality of being loyal or faithful.

Test-Taking Strategies Applied

This is a recall question which relies on social workers understanding the values used in making decisions about policies, procedures, regulations, and laws. It requires knowing the definitions of each of the words listed as response choices.

Knowledge Area

Unit III—Intervention Processes and Techniques for Use With Larger Systems (Content Area); Supervision and Administration (Competency); The Effects of Policies, Procedures, Regulations, and Legislation on Social Work Practice and Service Delivery (KSA)

138. D

Rationale

Transference refers to redirection of client feelings from significant persons to social workers. Transference is often manifested as an erotic attraction toward social workers, but can be seen in many other forms such as rage, hatred, mistrust, parentification, dependence, or even placing social workers in a god-like status. When Freud initially encountered transference, he felt it was an obstacle to treatment success, but he learned that the analysis of the transference was actually the work that needed to be done. Psychodynamic psychotherapy focuses on social workers and clients recognizing transference relationships and exploring their meaning. Because transference between clients and social workers happens on an unconscious level, social workers using psychodynamic models are concerned with using clients' unconscious material (transference) to reveal unresolved conflicts from childhood.

When transference occurs, social workers should:

1. *Normalize*—Clients may feel ashamed for having loving, sexual, or other feelings toward social workers, but transference happens all the time. Social workers interested in relational issues expect transference and are comfortable talking about it.
2. *Talk about it*—Speaking about transference makes uncomfortable feelings more manageable and even help them diminish. Once feelings are raised by clients, social workers should know where to go next.
3. *Find the root*—Transference reactions usually point to some deeper issue or unfinished business from the past. When these deeper issues are identified, discussed, and resolved, growth occurs.
4. *Document*—Clients' feelings are both clinically significant and have potential legal or ethical implications. Documenting can also provide protection and is appropriate given the clinical

significance of the feelings. Precautions should also be taken to avoid misunderstandings. Precautions may include not doing home visits or not being alone with clients if appropriate.

Social workers often jump to transferring the client as the solution, which is often not necessary and may not be in the client's best interests. Clients and social workers need to maintain boundaries and process feelings as part of important clinical work.

Test-Taking Strategies Applied

The question contains a qualifying word—FIRST. While many of the response choices can be helpful, social workers must begin by making clients understand that their feelings are typical. If clients feel badly about their feelings, it may interfere with the helping relationship. After they are normalized, they can be explored therapeutically. The feelings should never be ignored and clients should not be referred to other workers as transference provides valuable opportunities for growth and deeper understanding.

Knowledge Area

Unit IV—Professional Relationships, Values, and Ethics (Content Area); Professional Development and Use of Self (Competency); The Impact of Transference and Countertransference in the Social Worker–Client/Client System Relationship (KSA)

139. B

Rationale

Ethnography affords social workers a powerful and unique vehicle for obtaining an in-depth, contextualized understanding of clients' perspectives and experiences necessary for effective social work practice and advocacy. Unlike other forms of social inquiry such as surveys, interviews, and analysis of administrative databases, a hallmark of ethnographic research is sustained engagement in clients' lives. **Participant observation** is a qualitative method with roots in traditional ethnographic research, whose objective is to help social workers learn the perspectives held by clients. As qualitative researchers, social workers presume that there will be multiple perspectives within any given community. They are interested both in knowing what those diverse perspectives are and in understanding the interplay among them. Qualitative researchers accomplish this through observing and participating, to varying degrees, in a acommunity's daily activities. Participant observation always takes place in community settings, in locations believed to have some relevance to the issues at hand. The method is distinctive because social workers approach participants in their own environment. Generally speaking, social workers who engage in participant observation try to learn what life is like for "insiders" while remaining, inevitably, as "outsiders."

While in these community settings, social workers make careful, objective notes about what they see, recording all accounts and observations as field notes in a field notebook. Informal conversation and interaction with members of the study population are also important components of the method and should be recorded in the field notes, in as much detail as possible. Information and messages communicated through mass media such as radio or television may also be pertinent and thus desirable to document.

Test-Taking Strategies Applied

The question contains a qualifying word—BEST. The question asks for the method which is used with "an ethnographic approach." Social workers need to know the meaning of "ethnographic," including basic research methods which would be consistent with this inquiry. Participant observation approaches have historically been important components of ethnographic research.

The incorrect answers are all research terms, but do not relate to ethnography in any way.

Statistical regression is a statistical process for estimating the relationships among variables. It includes many techniques for modeling and analyzing several variables, when the focus is on the relationships between dependent variables and one or more independent variables (or predictors).

Experimental design is a blueprint that enables the testing of hypotheses by reaching valid conclusions about relationships between independent and dependent variables. It refers to the conceptual frameworks within which experiments are conducted.

Self-administered questionnaires are data collection instruments, either in paper or electronic form, which respondents complete on their own.

Knowledge Area

Unit III—Intervention Processes and Techniques for Use With Larger Systems (Content Area); Program Development and Research (Competency); Data Collection and Analysis Methods (KSA)

140. C

Rationale

The mission of the profession is rooted in a set of **social work core values**. These core values, embraced by social workers throughout the profession's history, are the foundation of social work's unique purpose and perspective and include:

- Service—providing help and resources to help others achieve their maximum potential
- Social justice—ensuring equal rights, protections, and opportunities for all
- Dignity and worth of the person—believing everyone is valuable
- Importance of human relationships—understanding how interactions can be used
- Integrity—being trustworthy
- Competence—providing services within skills and abilities

This constellation of core values reflects what is unique to the social work profession.

Unconditional positive regard is a term used by humanist psychologist Carl Rogers to describe a technique used in his nondirective, client-centered therapy. According to Rogers, unconditional positive regard involves showing complete support and acceptance of a client no matter what that person says or does. It is the ability to view a client as being worthy of caring about and as someone who has strengths and achievement potential. It is built on respect and is usually communicated nonverbally.

Social workers accept and support clients, no matter what they say or do, placing no conditions on this acceptance. It means caring for clients as separate people, with permission to have their own feelings and experiences. Rogers firmly believed every person was born with the potential to develop in positive, loving ways. Through the provision of services, social workers become clients' next chance, maybe their last chance, to be welcomed, understood, and accepted. Acceptance creates the conditions needed for change.

Test-Taking Strategies Applied

This is a recall question which relies on social workers knowing both the core social work values and the meaning of unconditional positive regard. Self-determination is not a core social work value so it must be eliminated as a possible correct response. The correct answer distinguishes itself from the other choices as the dignity and worth of an individual are directly related to the notion of unconditional acceptance and support. Social workers must accept and support clients, no matter what they say or do, placing no conditions on this acceptance. This goal can only be accomplished if there is true belief in the dignity and worth of all humans.

Knowledge Area

Unit IV—Professional Relationships, Values, and Ethics (Content Area); Professional Values and Ethical Issues (Competency); Professional Values and Principles (e.g., Competence, Social Justice, Integrity, and Dignity and Worth of the Person) (KSA)

141. A

Rationale

Social workers shall acknowledge their **responsibility and privilege in professional relationships** and the potential for harm to others should that privilege be misused. Social workers shall consider the potential risk to others based on the nature of the professional relationship prior to entering any dual/multiple role relationship. *Social workers shall assume full responsibility to ensure that professional relationships maintain the integrity of professional standards in their practice at all times.*

Test-Taking Strategies Applied

The question asks about responsibility for integrity (i.e., honesty and having strong moral principles) in helping relationships. Social workers are solely responsible for establishing and maintaining these standards. Social workers must role model appropriate professional behavior—being honest and establishing boundaries—even when clients may not be acting appropriately. While social workers want to share power and decision making in helping relationships, the responsibility for integrity always lies with them. This is a recall question.

Knowledge Area

Unit IV—Professional Relationships, Values, and Ethics (Content Area); Professional Development and Use of Self (Competency); The Social Worker's Role in the Problem-Solving Process (KSA)

142. B

Rationale

Object permanence is the understanding that objects continue to exist even when they cannot be observed (seen, heard, touched, smelled, or sensed in any way). Object permanence occurs during the first of Piaget's four stages, the sensorimotor stage.

Piaget assumed that a child could only search for a hidden toy if she or he had a mental representation of it. Piaget found that infants searched for hidden toys when they were around 8 months old.

Object permanence typically starts to develop between 4 and 7 months of age and involves a baby's understanding that when things disappear, they are not gone forever. Before a baby understands this concept, things that leave his view are gone, completely gone. Developing object permanence is an important milestone. It is a precursor to symbolic understanding (which a baby needs to develop language, pretend play, and exploration) and helps children work through separation anxiety.

Test-Taking Strategies Applied

The question requires knowledge of cognitive development, including key milestones. Understanding that object permanence is part of Piaget's sensorimotor stage can assist with narrowing down possible correct answers as this stage ends at age 2, thereby eliminating two incorrect choices. Recent research suggests that development of object permanence may begin before 4 months and be in place earlier than Piaget originally hypothesized. However, 8 months is the best answer as object permanence is clearly developed by 18 months and "typically" associated with infancy, rather than toddlerhood.

Knowledge Area

Unit I—Human Development, Diversity, and Behavior in the Environment (Content Area); Human Growth and Development (Competency); Theories of Human Development Throughout the Lifespan (e.g., Physical, Social, Emotional, Cognitive, Behavioral) (KSA)

143. A

Rationale

Techniques of interviewing should be tailored to the specifics of a client, not generic, "one size fits all" inquiries. The focus is on the uniqueness of a client and his or her unique situation.

The purpose of the social work interview can be informational, diagnostic, or therapeutic. The same interview may serve more than one purpose.

Communication during a social work interview is interactive and interrelational. A social worker's questions will result in specific responses by a client that, in turn, lead to other inquiries. The message is formulated by a client, encoded, transmitted, received, processed, and decoded. The importance of words and messages may be implicit (implied) or explicit (evident).

There are a number of techniques that a social worker may use during an interview to assist clients.

Confrontation occurs when social workers *call attention to clients' feelings, attitudes, or behaviors*, often when there is inconsistency in them. Confrontation can be very effective when there is a need to highlight feelings, attitudes, or behaviors which may be useful to the therapeutic process.

Interpretation occurs when social workers pull together patterns of behavior to *get a new understanding* of client situations or problems.

Universalization helps social workers reassure clients about the "normality" of their feelings regarding their own situation. This technique is used to demonstrate that client *feelings and experiences are shared by others*.

Clarification uses questioning, paraphrasing, and restating to *ensure full understanding of clients' ideas and thoughts*, including formulation of the existing problem.

Test-Taking Strategies Applied

This is a recall question that relies on social workers knowing techniques of interviewing. The question contains part of the definition of confrontation by stating that the social worker "calls attention to an observation."

In the case scenario, there is a lack of congruence between the wife's beliefs and actions. Congruence is the matching of awareness and experience with communication. It is essential that a client is able to express himself or herself and that this communication is reflective of his or her feelings. Congruence is essential for the vitality of a relationship and to facilitate true helping as part of the problem-solving process.

In the case scenario, confrontation of the wife's actions by the social worker may assist her in seeing that her perceptions are not supported by the observed interactions during the sessions.

Knowledge Area

Unit II—Intervention Processes and Techniques for Use Across Systems (Content Area); Intervention Planning and Implementation (Competency); The Principles and Techniques of Interviewing (e.g., Supporting, Clarifying, Focusing, Confronting, Validating, Feedback, Reflecting, Language Differences, Use of Interpreters, Redirecting) (KSA)

144. B

Rationale

The **problem-solving model** is based on the belief that an inability to cope with a problem is due to some lack of motivation, capacity, or opportunity to solve problems in an appropriate way. Clients' problem-solving capacities or resources are maladaptive or impaired.

The goal of the problem-solving process is to enhance the client's mental, emotional, and action capacities for coping with problems and/or making accessible the opportunities and resources necessary to generate solutions to problems.

A social worker engages in the problem-solving process via the following steps—engaging, assessing, planning, intervening, evaluating, and terminating.

Test-Taking Strategies Applied

The question contains a qualifying word—FIRST—that is capitalized to stress the importance of the order in which the actions should occur. When answers represent actions that social workers would take throughout the helping process, using the problem-solving model (also called the planned change or helping process) can be extremely helpful in determining their order.

Exploring options for treatment is a task which occurs during planning, and providing therapy is an intervention. The correct answer, determining what has been done before to address the problem, takes place during engagement and assessment—both of which precede planning and intervention. Anxiety Disorders do not go away and require psychotherapy, medication, or both. It is likely that the client in the case scenario has a treatment history that can be useful in learning about what has worked and not worked in the past.

There is no indication of risk for self-harm as the client states that he wants to change and is relying on the social worker to help him start the process.

Knowledge Area

Unit II—Intervention Processes and Techniques for Use Across Systems (Content Area); Intervention Planning and Implementation (Competency); Problem-Solving Models and Approaches (e.g., Brief, Solution-Focused Methods or Techniques) (KSA)

145. A

Rationale

Professional objectivity in social worker–client relationships is critical. This objectivity can be compromised if there is a conflict of interest in relationships with clients. A conflict of interest is a situation where regard for one duty may lead to disregard of another. When faced with potential or actual conflicts of interest, it is important that social workers consider the perceptions of others (clients, colleagues, the community, employers, etc.). It is important, therefore, that social workers are proactive in avoiding conflicts of interest and discuss any actual conflicts of interest with supervisors or employers so that they can be resolved. Dual relationships should never be entered into knowingly even if social workers feel that they can manage the potential conflicts or feel that there are no significant issues.

Test-Taking Strategies Applied

While the mother in this case scenario has considerable confidence in the child's social worker, there is an apparent conflict of interest for the social worker in supervising the child's visits with the father. The social worker will be expected to provide feedback to the court concerning the need for ongoing supervision of the dad's contact with his daughter. The objectivity in writing the report may actually be or could be perceived as being impaired by virtue of the pre-existing treatment role with the child.

Thus, even if the child and father are comfortable with the social worker taking on this additional role, it is inadvisable for legal and ethical reasons. The divorce may have a profound impact on the child, but exploring the effects is not related to the request at hand, so the last answer is a distractor.

Knowledge Area

Unit IV—Professional Relationships, Values, and Ethics (Content Area); Professional Values and Ethical Issues (Competency); Professional Objectivity in the Social Worker–Client/Client System Relationship (KSA)

146. B

Rationale

Reflective listening is a valuable **method used to facilitate communication**. Reflective listening is at times used interchangeably with active or empathic listening. It is a way of listening and responding to clients that improves mutual understanding and trust. It is an essential skill and critical to the therapeutic process. Empathic listening builds trust and respect with clients by enabling them to share their emotions and reduce tensions. It encourages the surfacing of information and creates "safe" environments that are conducive to collaborative problem solving. When engaging in empathic listening, social workers should:

- **Concentrate on not talking** and pay attention while looking directly at clients
- **Prepare their replies**
- **Ask for time to respond** if needed
- **Pay attention** to how the person is behaving nonverbally (e.g., yelling or screaming, not making eye contact, etc.)
- **Demonstrate listening** by nodding or shaking head
- **Paraphrase** or translate what is said; reflect it back
- **Recognize client feelings** ("you seem to be frustrated," "you sound angry," "you seem to be upset")
- **Be attentive**, interested, nonjudgmental, and noncritical
- **Avoid interrupting**, changing the subject, interrogating, teaching, and giving advice

Test-Taking Strategies Applied

Selecting the correct answer requires knowledge that reflective listening is a communication strategy involving two key steps: seeking to understand client ideas and then offering the ideas back to them to confirm they have been understood correctly. It attempts to reconstruct what clients are thinking and feeling and to relay this understanding back. While used interchangeably at times with active listening, reflective listening is a more specific strategy than the more general method of active listening. It arose from Carl Rogers' school of client-centered therapy in counseling theory.

The incorrect answers either do not reflect good listening skills (thinking about what should be said next or directing discussion toward other topics) or are not related to listening at all (helping clients to understand social workers' roles).

Knowledge Area

Unit IV—Professional Relationships, Values, and Ethics (Content Area); Professional Development and Use of Self (Competency); The Principles and Techniques for Building and Maintaining a Helping Relationship (KSA)

147. B

Rationale

Interdisciplinary collaboration is a necessary, yet challenging social work activity. When multiple agencies which work with clients act independently of each other, the result is that clients are subject to fragmented services, none of which address clients as whole individuals. A shared vision among collaborators facilitates strategies to achieve common goals. The biggest benefit of collaboration among agencies is the improved well-being of clients.

Collaboration among agencies is the key to preventing fragmentation. In addition to reducing the likelihood of clients falling through the cracks between disparate and unconnected agencies, collaboration fosters a more holistic view of clients. With effective collaboration, service providers recognize differing viewpoints through their contact with professionals with expertise in different areas. In addition to decreasing paperwork and minimizing fragmentation, this process could help to strengthen linkages and communication among various agencies providing different services to meet clients' varying needs.

Test-Taking Strategies Applied

The question contains a qualifying word—primary—though it is not capitalized. While the benefits listed in the incorrect response choices may result from collaborations between service providers, the correct answer to any question on the examination is always the one which speaks to enhancing the well-being of clients.

Interdisciplinary service collaborations can reduce duplication, foster innovation, and lead to enhanced effectiveness. However, they predominantly exist to bring together professionals from different professions or disciplines. The multifaceted training and experience of these providers helps to ensure that all client needs are addressed. The correct answer is the only one that references the needs of clients across life domains, which is the principal reason for taking an interdisciplinary approach.

Knowledge Area

Unit III—Intervention Processes and Techniques for Use With Larger Systems (Content Area); Supervision and Administration

(Competency); The Process of Interdisciplinary and Intradisciplinary Team Collaboration (KSA)

148. B

Rationale

A **phobia** is an Anxiety Disorder involving a persistent fear of an object, place, or situation disproportional to the threat or danger posed by the object of the fear. The person who has the phobia will go to great lengths to avoid the object of the fear and experience great distress if it is encountered. These irrational fears and reactions must result in interference with social and work life to meet the *DSM-5* criteria. There are five subtypes of Specific phobia: Animal (including the fear of snakes, spiders, rodents, and dogs), Natural Environment (including the fear of heights, storms, water, and the dark), Blood-Injection-Injury (including the fear of blood, injury, needles, and medical procedures), Situational (including the fear of enclosed spaces, flying, driving, tunnels, and bridges), and Other. Social Phobia, involving fear of social situations, is a separate disorder.

Under *DSM-5*, several changes have been made to prevent the over-diagnosis of Specific Phobias based on the overestimation of danger or occasional fears. A client no longer has to demonstrate excessive or unreasonable anxiety for a diagnosis of Specific Phobia. Instead, the anxiety must be "out of proportion" to the threat, considering the environment and situation.

A client who has a **Specific Phobia Disorder** experiences significant and persistent fear when in the presence of, or anticipating the presence of, the object of fear, which may be an object, place, or situation.

The *DSM-5* criteria for a Specific Phobia are:

- There is a marked and out-of-proportion fear within an environmental or situational context to the presence or anticipation of a specific object or situation.
- Exposure to the phobic stimulus provokes an immediate anxiety response, which may take the form of a situationally bound or situationally predisposed panic attack.
- Recognition exists that the fear is out of proportion.
- The phobic situation(s) is avoided or else is endured with intense anxiety or distress.

- The avoidance, anxious anticipation, or distress in the feared situation(s) interferes significantly with the person's normal routine, occupational (or academic) functioning, or social activities or relationships, or there is marked distress about having the phobia.

The new *DSM-5* criteria states that the symptoms for all ages must have a duration of at least 6 months.

The anxiety, panic attack, or phobic avoidance associated with the specific object or situation must not be better accounted for by another mental disorder.

Many different types of medications are used in the treatment of Anxiety Disorders, including traditional **antianxiety drugs** such as benzodiazepines. Because they work quickly—typically bringing relief within 30 minutes to an hour—they are very effective when taken during a panic attack or another overwhelming anxiety episode. However, they can be physically addictive and need to be closely monitored.

Test-Taking Strategies Applied

This question requires determining the correct diagnosis for the client in the case scenario. Based on the information provided, it appears that the client has Specific Phobia, natural environment type. This diagnosis, which is an Anxiety Disorder, is best treated with antianxiety medications. Thus, the response choices must be reviewed and the drugs must next be classified into one of four major types—antipsychotics, mood stabilizers, antidepressants, or antianxiety medications. Ativan is the only antianxiety drug listed, making it the correct response choice.

Mellaril and Risperdal are antipsychotic medications which are used to control hallucinations and delusions. Tegretol is a mood stabilizer used for the treatment of Bipolar Disorder.

Knowledge Area

Unit II—Intervention Processes and Techniques for Use Across Systems (Content Area); Biopsychosocial History and Collateral Data (Competency); Common Psychotropic and Non-Psychotropic Prescriptions and Over-the-Counter Medications and Their Side Effects (KSA)

149. C

Rationale

There are many formats for the recording of **case notes**. Case notes document activity and client progress. They help social workers identify effective and ineffective treatment strategies. In addition, if auditors, advocates, or supervisors look at files, they need to be able to get clear pictures of clients, and learn what has been done, what is working, and what areas need attention. In addition, without good, clear case notes, it can be next to impossible for successful client transition to other professionals should it be needed.

Narrative notes are summaries about client interactions which provide an overview of what occurred during meetings or conversations. There are no means for organizing these notes and they may vary in specificity and topic, depending upon the pressing issues. While they are open-ended, social workers should make sure that they contain all relevant information, summarizing what has occurred and what will be the focus of treatment in the future.

Subjective, objective, assessment, plan (**SOAP**) is a format used predominantly in health care facilities. The subjective section includes clients' reported symptoms and the objective section contains test and exam results. The assessment section includes conclusions and impressions based on the first two sections. The plan section explains the next steps, including the need for treatment, medication, and/or further testing.

Another format is referred to as **DAP**. This format is similar to SOAP except that both subjective and objective data are included in the same section. DAP is an acronym that stands for data, assessment, and plan. The data section includes contact information for clients, subjective and objective data, and observational notes. Subjective data is a summary of information given by clients and may include direct quotes. Objective data includes information often gleaned from direct observation or other sources, including body movements, facial expressions, test results, and so on. The assessment is a summary based on subjective and objective information collected. The last section is the treatment plan, including any referrals or interventions that have been completed or are recommended.

Another popular problem-based case recording format is assessed information, problem addressed, interventions provided, and evaluation (**APIE**). The first section includes documentation of assessed information with regard to clients' problems while the second is an explanation of problems that are to be addressed. These sections are followed by intervention descriptions and plans and evaluations of problems once interventions are complete, respectively.

Test-Taking Strategies Applied

The question contains a qualifying word—MOST. While the client may be using another model, the case scenario only describes three distinct sections, making DAP the probable model.

Narrative recording does not have distinct sections, but is an overall summary of the details which are thought to be important. SOAP includes both the assessment and plan as separate sections, but also separates the subjective information from the objective data. Therefore, there are four separate components of a case record. APIE contains information on evaluation findings, which are not mentioned in the social worker's notes in this question.

Knowledge Area

Unit III—Intervention Processes and Techniques for Use With Larger Systems (Content Area); Record-Keeping and Reporting (Competency); The Principles of Case Recording, Documentation, and Management of Practice Records (KSA)

150. D

Rationale

Confidentiality is a cornerstone of healthy therapeutic relationships and effective treatment and is based upon the ethical principles of autonomy and fidelity, and to a lesser degree beneficence and nonmaleficence. Autonomy assumes clients have the right to decide to whom they will reveal information, and confidentiality is based upon respect for clients' ability to choose what they disclose. Fidelity refers to social workers' faithfulness and loyalty to keep promises to clients, including not revealing information clients disclose. Social workers are also honest about limits of confidentiality so clients are able to make informed decisions about self-disclosure. Beneficence and nonmaleficence have an important role in confidentiality. Clients benefit when information is kept confidential and trusting relationships can be achieved. The disclosure of private information without client consent can do harm to therapeutic relationships even when such disclosures are mandated by law.

Issues of confidentiality are often complex, especially when group therapy is provided. Group psychotherapy is a powerful and curative method of psychological treatment, but issues of confidentiality are magnified at least as many times as there are group members. Not only is information revealed to social workers, it is also revealed to other group members, and there is no guarantee that other group members will maintain confidentiality. However, group members expect complete confidentiality and do not fully understand how confidentiality in group settings differs from confidentiality in individual therapy.

Informed consent is the process whereby clients learn about confidentiality. When group treatment is being provided, education regarding confidentiality should begin prior to entering group. Potential group members should be informed that social workers may have to break confidentiality in certain circumstances, and those circumstances should be fully explained. They should also be informed that social workers can assure confidentiality on their part (within the constraints of the law), but cannot promise that other group members will maintain confidentiality. Another important issue to discuss is the probable lack of privileged communication. In most states, privileged communication does not exist in group settings due to the third-party rule, which states that information revealed in front of a third party was not intended to be private and is not privileged. Therefore, group members may be called to testify against their peers regarding information obtained in group sessions.

Confidentiality should be discussed openly, thoroughly, and often among group members. Maintaining confidentiality should be the goal for group members, and consequences for participation for those who breach confidentiality should be openly discussed. A common phrase used in group therapy is, "What is said in group—stays in group." However, absolute confidentiality in groups is difficult and often unrealistic.

Test-Taking Strategies Applied

This is a recall question which relies on social workers understanding the ethical standards related to the provision of group versus individual therapy. In order for clients to make informed choices about what they disclose, it is critical that they understand confidentiality standards which apply.

The social worker cannot assure the client in this case scenario that information disclosed will be kept confidential as there are no legal mandates which prohibit group members from sharing it with others. The client is participating in group therapy, not individual treatment, so it is not appropriate for the social worker to ask about the nature of the information and provide "guidance" to the client. The group is the helping agent and concerns should be shared with all members, not the social worker individually. The client should also not be discouraged from sharing sensitive information with others as doing so is the basis of group therapy.

The correct answer provides the client with accurate information about confidentiality in group treatment and lets him make the decision on his own about whether to share it during the next session.

Knowledge Area

Unit II—Intervention Processes and Techniques for Use Across Systems (Content Area); Intervention Planning and Implementation

(Competency); Group Work Techniques and Approaches (e.g., Developing and Managing Group Processes and Cohesion) (KSA)

151. A

Rationale

Contracts in social work specify goals to be accomplished and tasks to be performed to achieve these aims. They also set **time frames for interventions** and deadlines for completion of goals. They are agreements between social workers and clients and essential for positive outcomes.

It is essential that goals contained in contracts be feasible. Unachievable goals set clients up for failure, which can lead to continued disappointment, disillusionment, and defeat. Chosen goals must be able to be accomplished. In instances where clients may have unrealistic expectations, social workers must assist them in realizing what is realistic.

Test-Taking Strategies Applied

There are many reasons that desired goals need to be examined and revised in order to be realistically achievable. In the case scenario, the client has a limited number of sessions which will be paid by insurance coverage. It is premature for the social worker to advocate for additional sessions as there is no new information which would cause the insurance company to alter its decision. It is unfair for the client to think that the changes desired will occur in the time frame allotted. The client may become increasingly discouraged when goals are not achieved, jeopardizing motivation to reach desired outcomes. Lastly, making progress toward the target problem should not be abandoned completely as it was identified and prioritized through the assessment process. Instead, the social worker must tactfully work with the client to temper expectations about the amount of change that is possible in the fixed time frame.

Knowledge Area

Unit II—Intervention Processes and Techniques for Use Across Systems (Content Area); Intervention Planning and Implementation (Competency); The Criteria Used in the Selection of Intervention/Treatment Modalities (e.g., Client/Client System Abilities, Culture, Life Stage) (KSA)

152. A

Rationale

Bartering arrangements, particularly involving services, create the potential for conflicts of interest, exploitation, and inappropriate boundaries in social workers' relationships with clients. Social workers should avoid accepting goods or services from clients as payment for professional services. *Social workers should explore and may participate in bartering only in very limited circumstances* when it can be demonstrated that such arrangements are an accepted practice among professionals in the local community, considered to be essential for the provision of services, negotiated without coercion, and entered into at the client's initiative and with the client's informed consent. *Social workers who accept goods or services from clients as payment for professional services assume the full burden of demonstrating that this arrangement will not be detrimental to the client or the professional relationship.*

Test-Taking Strategies Applied

While bartering in social work is extremely rare, the 2008 *NASW Code of Ethics* provides specific guidance about the criteria which must be met in order for it to occur. While these standards are located in provisions about payment for services, they speak to the potential that such financial arrangements have for inappropriate professional boundaries between social workers and clients.

The question contains a qualifying word—EXCEPT—that requires social workers to select the response choice which is not specified in the 2008 *NASW Code of Ethics* with regard to bartering. When EXCEPT is used as a qualifying word, it is often helpful to remove it from the question and eliminate the three response choices which must be done as per ethical standards. This approach will leave the one response choice which is not required.

Social workers—not clients—must demonstrate that bartering relationships are not detrimental.

Knowledge Area

Unit IV—Professional Relationships, Values, and Ethics (Content Area); Professional Values and Ethical Issues (Competency); Legal and/or Ethical Issues Related to the Practice of Social Work, Including Responsibility to Clients/Client Systems, Colleagues, the Profession, and Society (KSA)

153. C

Rationale

Family systems theory views issues and problems within a circular fashion, using what is described as a systemic perspective; this means that the event and the problem exist within the context of the relationship, where each influences the other. Family systems theory aims to assess these patterns of interactions and look at why things may be happening, instead of why they happened.

Family systems theory considers the nature of relationships to be bidirectional, and moves away from seeking blame of one person for the dynamic of the relationship. *The exception to this theory is within abusive relationships, where the responsibility and blame lay clearly with the perpetrator of the abuse.*

Within family systems theory, behaviors are believed to arise due to the interrelated nature and connectedness of various family members. For example, to seek understanding of children in distress, their behavior would be viewed through the lens of their **family (parent–child) behaviors** and family systems rather than looking at young persons in isolation.

Polygamy or the act of having more than one spouse at a time is based on cultural beliefs or traditions. There is no blame associated with polygamy.

Adultery or infidelity, using a family systems approach, is seen as a "family affair" that must be understood and treated within the marital system rather than from an individual perspective. Social workers use marital therapy to understand the relational dynamics that led to and/or sustain affairs. They shy away from blame and focus on issues of intimacy, communication, expectations, agreements, and conflict management in the marriage.

Test-Taking Strategies Applied

This is a recall question about family dynamics and functioning. Social workers must understand family systems theory, as well as the dynamics of abuse. *Victims should never be seen as contributing to or responsible for their abuse.* As the question asks about "blame for the dynamics" resting with specific individuals as opposed to resulting from the action of all parties, a belief contrary to a family systems approach, the correct answer must involve abuse of one person by another.

Knowledge Area

Unit I—Human Development, Diversity, and Behavior in the Environment (Content Area); Functioning of Various Systems (Competency); Family Dynamics and Functioning and the Effects on Individuals, Families, Groups, Organizations, and Communities (KSA)

154. A

Rationale

Cultural sensitivity refers to a set of skills used in social work practice that facilitates learning about and understanding clients whose cultural background may not be the same. Social workers must operate with the awareness that cultural differences exist between them and clients without assigning these differences a value. These differences are positive—not better or worse, right or wrong.

Being culturally sensitive does not mean being an expert in each culture's values. It simply means a willingness to ask honest questions, seek understanding, and demonstrate empathy rather than judging. It also means that, when knowingly entering spaces in which there will be cultural differences at play, social workers should do a bit of homework beforehand and avoid jumping to conclusions.

The most important thing when being culturally sensitive is remembering to ground interactions in the understanding that clients' background, experiences, and values naturally vary from those of social workers. These differences should lead to understanding and empathy, rather than judgment.

Test-Taking Strategies Applied

This is a recall question which relies on social workers understanding the effect of culture, race, and ethnicity on behaviors, attitudes, and identity. In the case scenario, the social worker is demonstrating respect and not assuming that the client would like to be called by his or her first name. Such action is an example of cultural sensitivity. Professional boundaries are the invisible structures which are imposed in therapeutic relationships. The question to the client is not indicative of a limit placed on the interactions between the client and social worker. Objectivity concerns examining issues truthfully and impartially. The social worker is not examining or viewing information—he or she is simply asking a question. Ethnocentrism is viewing others' cultures solely by the values and standards of one's own culture. The social worker is doing the opposite in the case scenario.

Knowledge Area

Unit I—Human Development, Diversity, and Behavior in the Environment (Content Area); Diversity, Discrimination, and Stereotypes (Competency); The Effect of Culture, Race, and Ethnicity on Behaviors, Attitudes, and Identity (KSA)

155. D

Rationale

Social workers must have basic **research knowledge** in order to evaluate the appropriateness of interventions and assist in decision making. The promotion of evidence-based research within social work is widespread.

Evidence-based research gathers evidence that may be informative for clinical practice or clinical decision making. It also involves the process of gathering and synthesizing scientific evidence from various sources and translating it to be applied to practice.

The use of evidence-based practices (EBPs) places the well-being of clients at the forefront, desiring to discover and use the best practices available. The use of evidence-based practice requires social workers to only use services and techniques that were found effective by rigorous, scientific, empirical studies— that is, outcome research.

Social workers must be willing and able to locate and use evidence-based interventions. In areas in which evidence-based interventions are not available, social workers must still use research to guide practice. Applying knowledge gleaned from research findings will assist social workers in providing services informed by scientific investigation and lead to new interventions that can be evaluated as EBPs.

When reading and interpreting experimental research findings, social workers must be able to identify **independent variables** (or those that are believed to be causes) and **dependent variables** (which are the impacts or results). In many studies, the independent variable is the treatment provided and the dependent variable is the target behavior that is trying to be changed. The **reliability** and **validity** of research findings should also be assessed. Reliability is concerned with obtaining the same findings repeatedly when conditions are not altered. Validity focuses on accuracy. There are two types of validity—internal validity and external validity. **Internal validity** is the confidence that exists that the independent variable is the cause of the dependent variable and not extraneous factors. **External validity** is the extent to which the same results will be produced if the context or population is altered. It determines to what extent an intervention can be generalized.

Measurement error is the difference between what assessments indicate and actual constructs (knowledge and abilities). These errors are often introduced when collecting data.

Test-Taking Strategies Applied

This is a recall question which relies on social workers understanding key research terms and concepts. Such knowledge is essential to having a sufficient understanding of KSAs related to the use of measurable objectives, subjective and objective data, applying research to practice, and so on. In addition to being able to understand and explain the meaning of important research terminology, social workers must be versed in experimental and single-subject research designs.

Knowledge Area

Unit III—Intervention Processes and Techniques for Use With Larger Systems (Content Area); Program Development and Research (Competency); Methods to Assess Reliability and Validity in Social Work Research (KSA)

156. D

Rationale

Interdisciplinary collaboration in social work practice is often difficult and requires great skill. Social science research brings understanding that each person in a collaborative process has a set of biases, values, and assumptions. Individuals have maps or mental models inside their heads that create meaning for experiences. These mental models carry many assumptions, values, and expectations which result in individuals having somewhat different mental models of how collaborative processes will proceed.

Shared values and goals are a foundational part of the overarching mental structure that drives collaborative efforts. *Therefore, it is important to evaluate personal goals and values, and to make them explicitly conscious as part of a dualistic pursuit of self-knowledge and knowledge of others' mental models.* Reflection or frequent inquiry to recognize personal and professional values and priorities is critical. Lack of awareness of these hot buttons, or emotional drivers, limits the ability to proactively respond to difficult situations in constructive ways.

Test-Taking Strategies Applied

The question contains a qualifying word—MOST. While the incorrect response choices may be useful, they are not as important as understanding that differences in opinion, work style, and so on, stem from diversity in values and should not be viewed negatively. Conflict is inevitable in any group process, but "successful engagement" is not contingent on the development of conflict resolution skills. It is helpful if social workers use their resources to advance group goals and understand that not all decisions are made jointly. However, these actions are not as critical as acknowledging the value differences which will exist.

Knowledge Area

Unit IV—Professional Relationships, Values, and Ethics (Content Area); Professional Development and Use of Self (Competency); The Influence of the Social Worker's Own Values and Beliefs on Interdisciplinary Collaboration (KSA)

157. B

Rationale

Erikson's psychosocial theory of development considers the impact of various "crises" on **personality development** from childhood to adulthood. According to Erikson's theory, everyone must pass through a series of eight interrelated stages over the entire life cycle.

1. **Infancy**
   Basic Trust Versus Mistrust
   During the first or second year of life, the major emphasis is on nurturing, especially in terms of visual contact and touch. A child will develop optimism, trust, confidence, and security if properly cared for and handled. If a child does not experience trust, he or she may develop insecurity, worthlessness, and general mistrust of the world.
2. **Toddler/Early Childhood Years**
   Autonomy Versus Shame and Doubt
   At this point, a child has an opportunity to build self-esteem and autonomy as he or she learns new skills and right from wrong. The well-cared-for child is sure of himself or herself, carrying himself or herself with pride rather than shame. Children tend to be vulnerable during this stage, sometimes feeling shame and low self-esteem during an inability to learn certain skills.
3. **Preschooler**
   Initiative Versus Guilt
   During this period, a child experiences a desire to copy adults and take initiative in creating play situations. A child also begins to use that wonderful word for exploring the world—"Why?" If a child is frustrated over natural desires and goals, he or she easily experiences guilt. The most significant relationship is with the basic family.
4. **School-Age Child**
   Industry Versus Inferiority
   During this stage, a child is capable of learning, creating, and accomplishing numerous new skills and knowledge, thus developing a sense of industry. This is also a very social stage of development; if there are unresolved feelings of inadequacy and inferiority, there can be serious problems in terms of competence and self-esteem. As the world expands a bit, the most significant relationship is with the school and neighborhood. Parents are no

longer the complete authorities they once were, although they are still important.

5. **Adolescence**
   Identity Versus Role Confusion
   An adolescent must struggle to discover and find his or her own identity, while negotiating and struggling with social interactions and "fitting in," as well as developing a sense of morality and right from wrong. Some attempt to delay entrance to adulthood and withdraw from responsibilities. Those unsuccessful with this stage tend to experience role confusion and upheaval. Adolescents begin to develop a strong affiliation and devotion to ideals, causes, and friends.
6. **Young Adulthood**
   Intimacy Versus Isolation
   At the young adult stage, people tend to seek companionship and love. Young adults seek deep intimacy and satisfying relationships, but if unsuccessful, isolation may occur. Significant relationships at this stage are with marital partners and friends.
7. **Middle Adulthood**
   Generativity Versus Stagnation
   During this time, adults strive to create or nurture things that will outlast them, often by parenting children or contributing to positive changes that benefit other people. Contributing to society and doing things to benefit future generations are important. *Generativity* refers to "making a mark" on the world through caring for others, as well as creating and accomplishing things that make the world a better place. *Stagnation* refers to the failure to find a way to contribute. Those who are successful during this phase will feel that they are contributing to the world by being active in their homes and communities. Others may feel disconnected or uninvolved. Some characteristics of stagnation include being self-centered, failing to get involved with others, not taking an interest in productivity, exerting no efforts to improve the self, and placing one's concerns above all else. It is at this point in life that some experience what is often referred to as a "midlife crisis" and feel regret. This might involve regretting missed opportunities such as going to school, pursuing a career, or having children. In some cases, this crisis is an opportunity to make adjustments that will lead to greater fulfillment.

8. **Late Adulthood**
   Integrity Versus Despair—Wisdom
   The last stage involves much reflection. Some older adults look back with a feeling of *integrity*—that is, contentment and fulfillment—having led a meaningful life and valuable contribution to society. Others have a sense of despair during this stage, reflecting upon their experiences and failures. They may fear death as they struggle to find a purpose to their lives, wondering "What was the point of life? Was it worth it?"

Test-Taking Strategies Applied

This is a recall question which relies on social workers understanding the stages of psychosocial development. The case scenario provides the age of the client, as well as his struggles—both of which can assist with distinguishing the correct answer from the incorrect ones.

Knowledge Area

Unit I—Human Development, Diversity, and Behavior in the Environment (Content Area); Human Growth and Development (Competency); Theories of Human Development Throughout the Lifespan (e.g., Physical, Social, Emotional, Cognitive, Behavioral) (KSA)

158. C

Rationale

An **ethical dilemma** is a predicament when a social worker must decide between two viable solutions that seem to have similar ethical value. Sometimes two viable ethical solutions can conflict with each other. Social workers should be aware of any conflicts between personal and professional values and deal with them responsibly. In instances where social workers' ethical obligations conflict with agency policies or relevant laws or regulations, they should make a responsible effort to resolve the conflict in a manner that is consistent with the values, principles, and standards expressed in the 2008 *NASW Code of Ethics*.

In order to resolve this conflict, ethical problem solving is needed. There are six essential steps in ethical problem solving:

1. Identify ethical standards, as defined by the professional code of ethics, that are being compromised (always go to the code of ethics first—do not rely on a supervisor or coworkers).
2. Determine whether there is an ethical issue or dilemma.

3. Weigh ethical issues in light of key social work values and principles as defined by the code of ethics.
4. Suggest modifications in light of the prioritized ethical values and principles that are central to the dilemma.
5. Implement modifications in light of prioritized ethical values and principles.
6. Monitor for new ethical issues or dilemmas.

Test-Taking Strategies Applied

The question contains a qualifying word—NEXT. Its use indicates that the order in which the response choices should occur is critical. Knowledge of the sequential steps in the ethical problem-solving process is needed. The question states that there is already a realization that an ethical dilemma exists. Once the issue has been identified, social workers must next weigh ethical issues in light of key social work values and principles.

Seeking supervision is a practical answer which is incorrect as it does not represent a step in the ethical problem-solving model. Social workers often seek supervision when they are not sure of the correct course of action. The examination expects social workers to have knowledge about the proper actions to take based on best practices in the field.

Social workers cannot choose a correct course of action based on prioritized ethical values until they have been weighed in light of existing principles. Thus, this action will occur after the one specified in the correct answer.

Determining the root cause of problems is critical, but the question is asking for the sequential steps in ethical problem solving. The issues cannot be eradicated until all steps have been taken, making this answer also incorrect.

Knowledge Area

Unit IV—Professional Relationships, Values, and Ethics (Content Area); Professional Values and Ethical Issues (Competency); Techniques to Identify and Resolve Ethical Dilemmas (KSA)

159. A

Rationale

Alcohol Withdrawal is a potentially life-threatening condition that can occur in clients who have been drinking heavily for weeks, months, or years and then either stop or significantly reduce their alcohol consumption. Alcohol Withdrawal symptoms can begin as early as 2 hours after the last drink, persist for weeks, and range from mild anxiety and shakiness to severe complications, such as seizures and **delirium tremens** (also called DTs). DTs are characterized by confusion, rapid heartbeat, and fever.

Because Alcohol Withdrawal symptoms can rapidly worsen, it is important for clients to seek medical attention even if symptoms are seemingly mild. Appropriate Alcohol Withdrawal treatments can reduce the risk of developing withdrawal seizures or DTs.

Prescription drugs of choice include benzodiazepines, such as diazepam (Valium), chlordiazepoxide (Librium), lorazepam (Ativan), and so on. Such medications can help control the shakiness, anxiety, and confusion associated with alcohol withdrawal and reduce the risk of withdrawal seizures and DTs. In clients with mild to moderate symptoms, anticonvulsant drugs may be an effective alternative to benzodiazepines, because they are not sedating and have low potential for abuse.

Because successful treatment of Alcohol Withdrawal does not address the underlying disease of addiction, it should be followed by treatment for alcohol abuse. Relatively brief outpatient interventions can be effective, but more intensive therapy may be required. Services range from 12-step groups—such as Alcoholics Anonymous and Narcotics Anonymous—to residential treatment that offers a combination of cognitive behavioral and family therapy.

Test-Taking Strategies Applied

The question is asking about Alcohol Withdrawal—not the treatment of the underlying disorder. Alcohol Withdrawal focuses on reducing the effects of the symptoms and medically monitoring them for serious health implications. Medications are used to help shakiness, anxiety, and confusion. Thus, psychopharmacology is the treatment of choice to address them. The incorrect response choices are effective treatments for the underlying disease and relapse prevention which occur after withdrawal symptoms have been addressed.

Knowledge Area

Unit II—Intervention Processes and Techniques for Use Across Systems (Content Area); Intervention Planning and Implementation (Competency); The Criteria Used in the Selection of Intervention/Treatment Modalities (e.g., Client/Client System Abilities, Culture, Life Stage) (KSA)

160. A

Rationale

Privileged communication is a legal right, existing by statute or common law, that protects the client from having his or her confidences revealed publicly from the witness stand during legal proceedings. Certain professionals, including social workers, cannot legally be compelled to reveal confidential information they received from their clients. The privilege protects clients, and the right to exercise privilege belongs to clients, not to professionals.

There are four conditions that are generally accepted as being necessary for a communication to be considered privileged:

1. The communication must originate in the confidence that it will not be disclosed.
2. The element of confidentiality must be essential to the full and satisfactory maintenance of the relationship between the parties.
3. The relationship must be one that in the opinion of the community ought to be fostered.
4. The injury to the relationship caused by disclosure must be greater than the benefit gained through disclosure for the correct disposal of litigation.

The landmark Supreme Court decision on the protection of psychotherapist–client privilege is *Jaffee v. Redmond*, 518 U.S. 1 (1996). The case created by common law the right for federal litigants and witnesses to keep their private psychotherapy records out of the courtroom, rejecting an approach that would have permitted federal judges to review and weigh the value of the potential evidence excluded under the privilege.

The *Jaffee* decision is notable in several respects. For social workers, it is a landmark ruling recognizing the professionalism and relevance of social workers providing psychotherapy in today's mental health treatment milieu. For trial lawyers and their clients, *Jaffee* presented a new rule of evidence, drawing a bright line around a certain type of evidence that is inaccessible for legal probing. For mental health clients, the case bolsters the wall of protection afforded the intimacy of the therapeutic relationship. *Jaffee* has also contributed to the treatment of health privacy in the Health Insurance Portability and Accountability Act of 1996 (HIPAA) regulations.

Although *Jaffee* is only directly applicable to cases filed in federal court, many states have had occasion to review the *Jaffee* decision as they decide similar matters under their jurisdiction.

Test-Taking Strategies Applied

The question contains a qualifying word—BEST. While all of the response choices relate to client privacy, only the correct answer mentions privilege being a legal term which aims to keep communication from being disclosed in court proceedings.

It is best practice for social workers to get clients' written consent when releasing information, though verbal consent is acceptable in certain situations. Social workers must report suspected child abuse and neglect, but such a mandate is not related to the definition of privilege, making the third answer listed incorrect. Lastly, often treatment information of minors cannot be withheld from parents, though laws vary across states given the ages of minors and types of treatment received. This answer is also incorrect as it is not related to privilege, but concerns instead another important privacy topic.

Knowledge Area

Unit IV—Professional Relationships, Values, and Ethics (Content Area); Confidentiality (Competency); Legal and/or Ethical Issues Regarding Confidentiality, Including Electronic Information Security (KSA)

161. C

Rationale

A **forensic interview** of a child is a developmentally sensitive and legally sound method of gathering factual information regarding allegations of abuse or exposure to violence. This interview is conducted by a competently trained, neutral professional, such as a social worker, utilizing research and practice.

The forensic interview is one component of a comprehensive child abuse investigation, which includes, but is not limited to, the following disciplines: law enforcement and child protection investigators, prosecutors, child protection attorneys, victim advocates, and medical and mental health practitioners. *Forensic interviewing is a first step in most child protective services investigations, one in which a professional interviews a child to find out if he or she has been maltreated.*

In addition to yielding the information needed to make a determination about whether abuse or neglect has occurred, this approach produces evidence that will stand up in court if the investigation leads to criminal prosecution. Properly conducted forensic interviews are legally sound in part because they ensure the interviewer's objectivity, employ nonleading techniques, and emphasize careful documentation of the interview.

A fuller understanding of forensic interviewing and its role in child welfare can be gained by comparing it with social work interviewing, another type of interviewing commonly used by child welfare workers. The social work interview allows social workers to assess and identify a family's strengths and needs and develop a service plan with the family. This broad, versatile approach incorporates the use of a variety of interviewing techniques. Social work interviewing is used at every step of child welfare, from intake through case closure; it is used with individuals and groups, children and adults.

Although it employs some of the same techniques as the social work interview, such as open-ended and forced choice questions, the forensic interview is much more focused. Generally, it is used only during the assessment portion of an investigation, and involves only the children who are the subject of the investigation.

Test-Taking Strategies Applied

Forensic denotes the scientific methods and techniques used in the investigation of crime. Its use relates to the collection of evidence used for prosecution. This question requires social workers to be knowledgeable about legal terms and the distinction between forensic and social work interviewing.

Knowledge Area

Unit IV—Professional Relationships, Values, and Ethics (Content Area); Confidentiality (Competency); Legal and/or Ethical Issues Regarding Mandatory Reporting (e.g., Abuse, Threat of Harm, Impaired Professionals, etc.) (KSA)

162. A

Rationale

Maslow's hierarchy of needs is a motivational theory comprising a five-tier model of human needs, often depicted as hierarchical levels within a pyramid.

Maslow stated that people are motivated to achieve certain needs and that some needs take precedence over others. The most basic need is for physical survival, which will be the first thing that motivates behavior.

This five-tier model can be divided into **deficiency needs** and **growth needs**. The first four levels are often referred to as deficiency needs and the top level is known as growth needs. Growth needs can never be satisfied completely. They consist of the need to know and understand. They are linked to **self-actualization**.

Deficiency needs are said to motivate people when they are unmet. Also, the need to fulfill such needs will become stronger the longer the duration they are denied.

Lower level deficit needs must be satisfied before progressing on to meet higher level growth needs. When a deficit need has been satisfied it will go away and activities become habitually directed toward meeting the next set of needs that we have yet to satisfy. These then become salient needs. However, growth needs continue to be felt and may even become stronger once they have been engaged.

Test-Taking Strategies Applied

Often the names of theorists are not mentioned in questions. However, reasoning using their work is essential to successfully select the correct answers. Maslow's hierarchy of needs can be divided into basic (or deficiency) needs (i.e., physiological, safety, social, and esteem) and growth needs (i.e., self-actualization). "Deficiency needs" arise due to deprivation, according to Maslow.

The question contains a qualifying word—NOT—that requires social workers to select the response choice which is not a deficiency need. When NOT is used as a qualifying word, it is often helpful to remove it from the question and eliminate the three response choices which are deficiency needs. This approach will leave the one response choice which is NOT a deficiency need, but instead a growth need.

Knowledge Area

Unit I—Human Development, Diversity, and Behavior in the Environment (Content Area); Human Growth and Development (Competency); Basic Human Needs (KSA)

163. C

Rationale

Social workers' **ethical responsibilities** include those related to payment for services.

When setting fees, social workers should ensure that the fees are fair, reasonable, and commensurate with the services performed. Consideration should be given to clients' ability to pay.

Social workers should avoid accepting goods or services from clients as payment for professional services. Bartering arrangements, particularly involving services, create the potential for conflicts of interest, exploitation, and inappropriate boundaries in social workers' relationships with clients. Social workers should explore and may participate in bartering only in very limited circumstances when it can be demonstrated that such arrangements are an accepted practice among professionals in the local community, considered to be essential for the provision of services, negotiated without coercion, and entered into at the client's initiative and with the client's informed consent. Social workers who accept goods or services from clients as payment for professional services assume the full burden of demonstrating that this arrangement will not be detrimental to the client or the professional relationship.

Social workers in fee-for-service settings may terminate services to clients who are not paying an overdue balance if the financial contractual arrangements have been made clear to the client, if the client does not pose an imminent danger to self or others, and if the clinical and other consequences of the current nonpayment have been addressed and discussed with the client. Social workers should not terminate services to pursue a social, financial, or sexual relationship with a client.

Social workers should not solicit a private fee or other remuneration for providing services to clients who are entitled to such available services through the social workers' employer or agency.

Test-Taking Strategies Applied

This is a recall question which requires social workers to select the unethical action "according to the professional code of ethics." While the examination will never refer directly to the 2008 *NASW Code of Ethics* as there are other professional organizations with ethical mandates, it is helpful to read the 2008 *NASW Code of Ethics* and remember its standards when choosing between answers. Most questions on the examination will focus on the first section which addresses social workers' ethical responsibilities to clients. The correct answer is always the one which most closely mirrors the standard which is explicitly stated in the 2008 *NASW Code of Ethics*.

Knowledge Area

Unit IV—Professional Relationships, Values, and Ethics (Content Area); Professional Values and Ethical Issues (Competency); Legal and/or Ethical Issues Related to the Practice of Social Work, Including Responsibility to Clients/Client Systems, Colleagues, the Profession, and Society (KSA)

164. D

Rationale

According to the *DSM-5*, to meet the criteria for diagnosis of **Schizophrenia**, a client must have experienced at least two of the following symptoms:

- Delusions
- Hallucinations

- Disorganized speech
- Disorganized or catatonic behavior
- Negative symptoms

At least one of the symptoms must be the presence of delusions, hallucinations, or disorganized speech.

Continuous signs of the disturbance must persist for at least 6 months, during which the client must experience at least 1 month of active symptoms (or less if successfully treated), with social or occupational deterioration problems occurring over a significant amount of time. These problems must not be attributable to another condition.

The APA removed Schizophrenia subtypes from the *DSM-5* because they did not appear to be helpful for providing better-targeted treatment or predicting treatment response.

Treatments for Schizophrenia are aimed at reducing or eliminating symptoms of Schizophrenia, including hallucinations, delusions, and jumbled speech. There is, however, no cure for Schizophrenia. Most clients will require both medications and psychotherapy. **Antipsychotics** are a class of psychiatric medication primarily used to manage psychosis (including delusions, hallucinations, paranoia, or disordered thought), principally in Schizophrenia. However, their long-term use is associated with significant side effects such as involuntary movement disorders and metabolic syndrome.

Test-Taking Strategies Applied

This question requires determining the correct diagnosis for the client in the case scenario. Based on the information provided, it appears that the client has Schizophrenia. This diagnosis is listed in the *DSM-5* with Schizophrenia Spectrum and Other Disorders, such as Delusional Disorder, Brief Psychotic Disorder, Schizophreniform Disorder, Schizoaffective Disorder, and so on. These disorders are generally treated with antipsychotic medications. Thus, the response choices must be reviewed and the drugs must next be classified into one of four major types—antipsychotics, mood stabilizers, antidepressants, or antianxiety medications. Clozaril is the only antipsychotic drug listed, making it the correct response choice.

Paxil and Prozac are antidepressant medications while Lithium is a mood stabilizer used for the treatment of Bipolar Disorder.

Knowledge Area

Unit II—Intervention Processes and Techniques for Use Across Systems (Content Area); Biopsychosocial History and Collateral Data (Competency); Common Psychotropic and Non-Psychotropic Prescriptions and Over-the-Counter Medications and Their Side Effects (KSA)

165. A

Rationale

From the structural perspective, **roles** are the culturally defined norms—rights, duties, expectations, and standards for behavior—associated with a given social position. In other words, social position is seen as influencing behaviors. In addition, statuses such as gender, ethnicity, sexual orientation, and social class also shape roles.

For example, as a mother, a woman is expected to place the care of her child above all other concerns. However, this normative expectation varies across cultures, with some cultures expecting mothers to be paid workers as well. Many cultures believe that women with preschool-age children should not work outside of the home and that their children will suffer if they do.

The actual enactment of role behavior, however, may not correspond to the **role expectations**. **Role competence**, or success in carrying out a role, can vary depending on social contexts and resources. In countries with strong normative expectations for women to be full-time mothers, single mothers and low-income mothers often have to violate these role expectations and have been criticized as less competent mothers as a result.

Indeed, there is pressure to conform successfully to roles. Sanctions are used as tools of enforcement. Punishments for not following the role of mother can range from informal sanctions, such as rebukes from family members, to formal sanctions, such as divorce.

Test-Taking Strategies Applied

Social workers must be aware of social role theory and view problems as emerging from interactions between clients and their environments. Person-in-environment perspectives are sensitive to role conflicts experienced by clients.

In the case scenario, the client is facing conflicting demands and expectations—as a mother, wife, professional, and so on. The client is the woman and the problem should not be viewed as a family issue.

Family problems are best resolved by family therapy in which the interactions of members are the focus of intervention.

Cultural bias involves a prejudice or highlighted distinction in viewpoint that suggests a preference of one culture over another. There are cultural differences in views between the client and her husband's family, but the problem does not stem from cultural bias. If cultural bias existed, intervention would focus on education of the client about diverse perspectives. The client recognizes the views of her husband's family and does not appear to see her views as superior. However, she is unhappy due to the conflict that exists between the fulfillment of her various roles.

Social injustice is an unfair practice that results in violation of human rights. Her problem is a personal one and not an indicator of social injustice.

Knowledge Area

Unit I—Human Development, Diversity, and Behavior in the Environment (Content Area); Effects of the Environment on Systems' Behavior (Competency); Role Theories (KSA)

166. B

Rationale

A **doorknob disclosure** is an uncomfortable, painful, or embarrassing revelation offered at the end of a session, usually by a client who is leaving. Social workers often see clients reveal their most painful conflicts during the last 30 seconds of sessions, just when they are ready to leave. Often they already have their hands on the door knobs. These revelations may be new issues or other aspects of problems already discussed.

The two main reasons for doorknob disclosures are (a) the need to gauge reactions because of fear, rejection, or judgment about the disclosed material and (b) the need to prolong the helping relationship by extending the session or number of sessions due to fear of not being able to cope without support.

Doorknob disclosures are often a form of resistance. Bringing up important material or intense emotions at the end of sessions, rather than earlier, ensures that there will not be enough time to deal with it.

Social workers must be skilled in the principles of communication—encouraging clients to raise all issues early in the session and therapeutic process. Social workers should also help manage the time in sessions—giving clients ample notice of when sessions are drawing to an end, which is an inappropriate time to bring up new concerns or topics.

Immediate responses to doorknob disclosures need to be to reassure clients that they will get to discuss material at the next sessions (once ruling out that there is an immediate safety issue that requires immediate attention). If the disclosure comes from a fear of coping alone or ending the therapeutic relationship, time should be spent discussing this issue—rather than the disclosure itself.

Test-Taking Strategies Applied

The question contains a qualifying word—MOST. While clients may use doorknob disclosures for more than one purpose, revealing information in this manner clearly stems from fear. Clients want the safety of gauging social workers' reactions to the material and/or lack time to discuss revelations more fully. It can be comforting to clients to bring up painful or sensitive topics in this manner as they have the knowledge that they will not have to explore them in more depth until the next session, giving them time to feel content with even saying the information out loud.

Knowledge Area

Unit II—Intervention Processes and Techniques for Use Across Systems (Content Area); Intervention Planning and Implementation (Competency); Verbal and Nonverbal Communication Techniques (KSA)

167. B

Rationale

Death is just one **life event or crisis** which impacts families. When deaths of family members occur, children go through a series of stages in trying to understand its meaning. For example, preschool children usually see death as reversible, temporary, and impersonal. Watching cartoon characters on television miraculously rise up whole again after having been crushed or blown apart tends to reinforce this notion. In order to identify when death is truly understood by children, it is necessary to outline the complex concepts associated with death, including:

- Irreversibility or finality, the understanding that the dead cannot come back to life
- Universality or applicability, the understanding that all living things (and only living things) die

- Personal mortality, the understanding that death applies to oneself
- Inevitability, the understanding that all living things must die eventually
- Cessation or nonfunctionality, the understanding that bodily and mental functions cease after death
- Causality, the understanding that death is ultimately caused by a breakdown of bodily functions
- Unpredictability, the understanding that the timing of (natural) death is not known in advance

Piaget's cognitive developmental stages indicate that these death concepts cannot really be understood until age 7 years at the absolute earliest. Using Piaget's model, child understanding emerges as follows:

- First stage—Preoperational (2–7 years)—Children think of death as a temporary or reversible state, and tend to characterize death with respect to concrete behaviors such as being still or having closed eyes or departing.
- Second stage—Concrete operational (7–11 years)—Children recognize that all living things must die and that death is irreversible; however, they consider death to be caused by concrete elements originating from outside the body and do not recognize death as an intrinsic and natural part of the life cycle.
- Final stage—Formal operational (11 years and older)—Children hold an adult view of death as an inevitable, universal final stage in the life cycle of all living things, characterized by the cessation of bodily functions.

Thus, children's understanding of death is truly linked to cognitive developmental maturation.

Test-Taking Strategies Applied

If the age of a client is mentioned in a case scenario, it is usually relevant in selecting the correct response choice. The age is a useful hint of where a client is in the life course and what might be expected with regard to his or her cognitive, emotional, and/or social development.

This case scenario requires knowledge about the complex concepts associated with death as well as child development. Most questions, like this one, require an integration of several knowledge areas.

Memorization is not needed when studying, but instead the ability to apply knowledge learned.

All of the response choices listed, except the first one, concern the child's ability to comprehend death. As the child is only 4 years old, each answer must be evaluated based on the theoretical knowledge about cognition at this age. As the beginning of abstract thought does not occur until age 7, the child would see death as a temporary or reversible state, like being asleep.

The first answer is incorrect as children find death to be an emotionally charged issue, reacting with sadness, anxiety, and fear over separation.

Knowledge Area

Unit I—Human Development, Diversity, and Behavior in the Environment (Content Area); Human Growth and Development (Competency); Theories of Human Development Throughout the Lifespan (e.g., Physical, Social, Emotional, Cognitive, Behavioral) (KSA)

168. A

Rationale

Social workers should respect clients' right to **privacy and confidentiality**. Social workers may disclose confidential information when appropriate with valid consent from a client or a person legally authorized to consent on behalf of a client. Social workers should protect the confidentiality of all information obtained in the course of professional service, except for compelling professional reasons. The general expectation that social workers will keep information confidential does not apply when disclosure is necessary to prevent serious, foreseeable, and imminent harm to a client or other identifiable person such as duty to warn, child abuse, and so on.

In these instances, social workers should inform clients, to the extent possible, about the disclosure of confidential information and the potential consequences, when feasible *before* the disclosure is made (*NASW Code of Ethics, 2008—1.07 Privacy and Confidentiality*). This applies whether social workers disclose confidential information on the basis of a legal requirement or client consent.

In all instances, social workers should disclose the least amount of confidential information necessary to achieve the desired purpose; only information that is directly relevant to the purpose for which the disclosure is made should be revealed.

Test-Taking Strategies Applied

The 2008 *NASW Code of Ethics* explicitly acknowledges social workers' ethical obligation to inform clients, to the extent possible, of the need to make mandatory reports due to suspected child maltreatment. This obligation should not result in delays in reporting. Additionally, informing clients does not mean that social workers should be deterred in any way from reporting based upon clients' reactions. Social workers must be honest with clients throughout the problem-solving process. Clients should be aware of social workers' obligations for mandatory reporting since it is to be discussed as soon as possible in social worker–client relationships and as needed throughout the course of these relationships.

Knowledge Area

Unit IV—Professional Relationships, Values, and Ethics (Content Area); Confidentiality (Competency); Legal and/or Ethical Issues Regarding Mandatory Reporting (e.g., Abuse, Threat of Harm, Impaired Professionals, etc.) (KSA)

169. B

Rationale

The 2008 *NASW Code of Ethics* explicitly acknowledges that social workers should not provide clinical services to individuals with whom they have had a prior sexual relationship. Providing clinical services to a former sexual partner has the potential to be harmful to the individual and is likely to make it difficult for a social worker and individual to maintain **appropriate professional boundaries**. In addition, social workers should not engage in sexual activities or sexual contact with current or former clients or clients' relatives or other individuals with whom clients maintain a close personal relationship when there is a risk of exploitation or potential harm to a client (*NASW Code of Ethics, 2008—1.09 Sexual Relationships*).

Test-Taking Strategies Applied

In the case scenario, the social worker is aware that the referral is for a woman with whom he had a prior intimate relationship. According to the 2008 *NASW Code of Ethics*, it is unethical to provide clinical services to this client. Since there should be no therapeutic relationship between them, meeting with the client to discuss her problem or scheduling an intake are both inappropriate. Informing a supervisor is advisable, but not a sufficient action to properly "act ethically in this situation." The social worker must decline the referral even if he is the only Spanish-speaking clinician. Services may need to be located for the client at another agency if there is no one linguistically competent to counsel her at the existing one.

Knowledge Area

Unit IV—Professional Relationships, Values, and Ethics (Content Area); Professional Values and Ethical Issues (Competency); Professional Boundaries in the Social Worker–Client/Client System Relationship (e.g., Power Differences, Conflicts of Interest, etc.) (KSA)

170. D

Rationale

Cognitive bevaioral therapy (CBT) combines cognitive and behavioral therapies. The basic premise of CBT is that emotions are difficult to change directly, so CBT targets emotions by changing thoughts and behaviors that are contributing to the distressing emotions. CBT builds a set of skills that enables an individual to be aware of thoughts and emotions; identify how situations, thoughts, and behaviors influence emotions; and improve feelings by changing dysfunctional thoughts and behaviors. The process of CBT skill acquisition is collaborative. Skill acquisition and homework assignments are what set CBT apart from "talk therapies." Brief CBT is the compression of CBT material and the reduction of the average 12 to 20 sessions into four to eight sessions. In brief CBT, the concentration is on specific treatments for a limited number of client problems. Specificity of the treatment is required because of the limited number of sessions and because a client is required to be diligent in using extra reading materials and homework to assist in his or her therapeutic growth. Brief CBT can range in duration from client to client and provider to provider.

Certain problems are more appropriate for brief therapy than others. Problems amenable to brief CBT include, but are not limited to, Adjustment, Anxiety, and Depressive Disorders. Therapy also may be useful for problems that target specific symptoms (e.g., depressive thinking) or lifestyle changes (e.g., problem solving, relaxation), whether or not these issues are part of a formal psychiatric diagnosis. Brief CBT is particularly useful in a primary care setting for clients with anxiety and depression associated with a medical condition. Because these clients often face acute rather than chronic mental health issues and have many coping strategies already in place, brief CBT can be used to enhance adjustment. Issues that may be addressed in primary care include, but are not limited to, diet, exercise, medication compliance, mental health issues associated with a medical condition, and coping with a chronic illness or new diagnosis.

Other problems may not be suitable for the use of, or may complicate, a straightforward application of brief CBT. Bipolar Disorder or Antisocial Personality Disorder typically are not appropriate for a shortened therapeutic experience because of the pervasive social, psychological, and relational problems individuals with these disorders experience. Long-standing interpersonal issues often require longer treatment durations. Clients exhibiting comorbid conditions or problems also may not be appropriate because the presence of a second issue may impede progress in therapy. For example, a client with a Substance Use Disorder comorbid with Major Depressive Disorder may not be appropriate because the substance use requires a higher level of care and more comprehensive treatment than is available in a brief format. However, brief CBT could be used with Personality Disorders and comorbid clients in dealing with specific negative behaviors or in conjunction with more intensive treatment. Lastly, conditions such as serious mental illness require focused and more intensive interventions.

Test-Taking Strategies Applied

Central to selecting the correct response choice is recognizing that the intervention modality mentioned in the question is brief therapy. Brief therapy is a systematic, focused process that relies on assessment, client engagement, and rapid implementation of change strategies. Brief therapy providers can effect important changes in client behavior within a relatively short period.

Substance Use Disorders are chronic, requiring long-term support. Brief therapy for substance abuse treatment can be a valuable, but limited, approach and it should not be considered a standard of care.

Personality Disorders form a class of mental disorders that are characterized by long-lasting, rigid patterns of thought and behavior.

Personality Disorders are seen as an enduring pattern of inner experience and behavior that deviates markedly from the expectations of the culture of the individual who exhibits it. These patterns are inflexible and *pervasive* across many situations. Thus, they are not optimally treated by brief therapy.

Dissociative Identity Disorder (DID), formerly called Multiple Personality Disorder, is a condition that is characterized by the presence of at least two clear personality states, called alters, which may have different reactions, emotions, and body functioning. While there's no "cure" for DID, long-term treatment is very successful. Effective treatment includes talk therapy or psychotherapy, medications, hypnotherapy, and adjunctive therapies to help clients with DID improve their relationships with others, prevent crises, and experience uncomfortable feelings. Because oftentimes the symptoms of Dissociative Disorders occur with other disorders, such as anxiety and depression, Dissociative Disorders may be treated using the same drugs prescribed for those disorders.

Knowledge Area

Unit II—Intervention Processes and Techniques for Use Across Systems (Content Area); Intervention Planning and Implementation (Competency); The Criteria Used in the Selection of Intervention/ Treatment Modalities (e.g., Client/Client System Abilities, Culture, Life Stage) (KSA)

Evaluation of Results

These tables assist in identifying the content areas and competencies needing further study. Within each of the competencies, there are specific Knowledge, Skills, and Abilities (KSAs) that social workers should reference to assist with locating appropriate study resources. As there is tremendous overlap in the material that could be contained across the KSAs within a given competency, all KSAs for the competency should be reviewed to make sure of an adequate breadth of knowledge in the content area. A listing of the KSAs for each content area and competency can be found in Appendix A.

The results of this evaluation should be the basis of the development of a study plan. Social workers should get to a level of comfort with the material so that they can summarize relevant content, including key concepts and terms. Social workers do not need to be experts in all of the KSAs, but should understand their relevancy to social work practice. They should be able to describe how each of the KSAs specifically impact assessment, as well as decisions about client care.

Appendix B provides useful information on learning styles that can assist when determining the best ways to study and retain material. Success on the Association of Social Work Boards (ASWB®) examination does not require a lot of memorization of material, but rather the ability to recall terms and integrate multiple concepts to select the best course of action in hypothetical scenarios. Thus, time is best spent really understanding the KSAs and not just being able to recite definitions.

Analysis of Advanced Generalist Practice Test Unit I: Human Development, Diversity, and Behavior in the Environment (23%)					
Competency	**Question Numbers**	**Number of Questions**	**Number Correct**	**Percentage Correct**	**Area Requiring Further Study?**
1. Human Growth and Development	18, 26, 74, 86, 89, 91, 92, 99, 116, 119, 131, 133, 142, 157, 162, 167	16	8/16	50 %	
2. Functioning of Various Systems	3, 8, 29, 153	4	4/4	100 %	
3. Effects of the Environment on Systems' Behavior	15, 37, 39, 46, 66, 104, 105, 125, 165	9	5/9	__%	
4. Diversity, Discrimination, and Stereotypes	2, 21, 44, 55, 61, 67, 78, 102, 118, 154	10	9/10	90%	

Analysis of Advanced Generalist Practice Test Unit II: Intervention Processes and Techniques for Use Across Systems (32%)					
Competency	**Question Numbers**	**Number of Questions**	**Number Correct**	**Percentage Correct**	**Area Requiring Further Study?**
5. Biopsychosocial History and Collateral Data	1, 7, 12, 28, 31, 32, 36, 52, 79, 96, 100, 106, 108, 148, 164	15	__/15	__%	
6. Assessment Methods and Techniques	14, 33, 57, 62, 71, 72, 94, 97, 127, 134	10	__/10	__%	
7. Intervention Planning and Implementation	4, 5, 10, 17, 20, 27, 40, 41, 47, 58, 60, 68, 81, 84, 85, 88, 109, 113, 114, 121, 135, 136, 143, 144, 150, 151, 159, 166, 170	29	__/29	__%	

Analysis of Advanced Generalist Practice Test Unit III: Intervention Processes and Techniques for Use With Larger Systems (18%)					
Competency	**Question Numbers**	**Number of Questions**	**Number Correct**	**Percentage Correct**	**Area Requiring Further Study?**
8. Program Development and Research	6, 50, 115, 117, 126, 139, 155	7	3/7	__%	
9. Methods for Social Change	45, 48, 54, 59, 83	5	4/5	80%	
10. Supervision and Administration	11, 13, 22, 23, 34, 35, 38, 65, 110, 129, 137, 147	12	9/12	__%	
11. Record-Keeping and Reporting	16, 51, 53, 63, 123, 130, 149	7	2/7	__%	

Analysis of Advanced Generalist Practice Test
Unit IV: Professional Relationships, Values, and Ethics (27%)

Competency	Question Numbers	Number of Questions	Number Correct	Percentage Correct	Area Requiring Further Study?
12. Professional Values and Ethical Issues	9, 24, 56, 73, 77, 80, 101, 111, 112, 120, 124, 128, 132, 140, 145, 152, 158, 163, 169	19	16/19	__%	
13. Confidentiality	19, 25, 30, 42, 49, 64, 69, 75, 82, 87, 90, 107, 160, 161, 168	15	12/15	__%	
14. Professional Development and Use of Self	43, 70, 76, 93, 95, 98, 103, 122, 138, 141, 146, 156	12	11/12	__%	

Overall Results of Advanced Generalist Diagnostic Practice Test

	Content Area	Number of Questions	Number Correct	Percentage Correct
Unit I (23%)	Human Development, Diversity, and Behavior in the Environment	39	26/39	67%
Unit II (32%)	Intervention Processes and Techniques for Use Across Systems	54	38/54	70%
Unit III (18%)	Intervention Processes and Techniques for Use Across Larger Systems	31	19/31	61%
Unit IV (27%)	Professional Relationships, Values, and Ethics	46	39/46	85%
Overall Knowledge	ASWB® Advanced Generalist Examination	170	122/170	72%

Appendix A

Content Areas, Competencies, and KSAs for the ASWB® Advanced Generalist Examination

Human Development, Diversity, and Behavior in the Environment (Content Area)

1. Human Growth and Development (Competency)

KSAs

Theories of human development throughout the lifespan (e.g., physical, social, emotional, cognitive, behavioral)

The indicators of normal and abnormal physical, cognitive, emotional, and sexual development throughout the lifespan

Theories of sexual development throughout the lifespan

Theories of spiritual development throughout the lifespan

Theories of racial, ethnic, and cultural development throughout the lifespan

The effects of physical, mental, and cognitive disabilities throughout the lifespan

Basic human needs

The principles of attachment and bonding

The effect of aging on biopsychosocial functioning

The impact of aging parents on adult children

Gerontology

Personality theories

Theories of conflict
Factors influencing self-image (e.g., culture, race, religion/spirituality, age, disability, trauma)
Parenting skills and capacities
Feminist theory
Addiction theories and concepts
Systems and ecological perspectives and theories
Strengths-based and resilience theories
Crisis intervention theories
Psychoanalytic and psychodynamic approaches
Indicators and dynamics of abuse and neglect throughout the lifespan

2. Functioning of Various Systems (Competency)

KSAs
The family life cycle
Family dynamics and functioning and the effects on individuals, families, groups, organizations, and communities
Models of family life education in social work practice
Theories of couples development
Theories of group development and functioning

3. Effects of the Environment on Systems' Behavior (Competency)

KSAs
Person-in-environment (PIE) theory
The interplay of biological, psychological, social, and spiritual factors
The dynamics of interpersonal relationships
Psychological defense mechanisms and their effects on behavior and relationships
The indicators of psychosocial stress
The effect of poverty on individuals, families, groups, organizations, and communities
The impact of the environment (e.g., social, physical, cultural, political, economic) on individuals, families, groups, organizations, and communities
Role theories
Social and economic justice
The impact of globalization on clients/client systems (e.g., interrelatedness of systems, international integration, technology, environmental or financial crises, epidemics)

4. Diversity, Discrimination, and Stereotypes (Competency)

The effect of disability on biopsychosocial functioning throughout the lifespan
The effect of culture, race, and ethnicity on behaviors, attitudes, and identity
The effects of discrimination and stereotypes on behaviors, attitudes, and identity
The influence of sexual orientation on behaviors, attitudes, and identity
The impact of transgender and transitioning process on behaviors, attitudes, identity, and relationships
Systemic (institutionalized) discrimination (e.g., racism, sexism, ageism)
The principles of culturally competent social work practice
Sexual orientation concepts
Gender and gender identity concepts

Intervention Processes and Techniques for Use Across Systems (Content Area)

5. Biopsychosocial History and Collateral Data (Competency)

KSAs
The components of a biopsychosocial assessment
The components and function of the mental status examination
Biopsychosocial responses to illness and disability
Biopsychosocial factors related to mental health
Basic medical terminology
The indicators of mental and emotional illness throughout the lifespan
Co-occurring disorders and conditions
Symptoms of neurologic and organic disorders
The types of information available from other sources (e.g., agency, employment, medical, psychological, legal, or school records)
The impact of caregiving on families
The dynamics and effects of loss, separation, and grief
The impact of physical and mental illness on family dynamics
The indicators of behavioral dysfunction
The indicators of feigning illness
The indicators of somatization
Body image and its impact (e.g., identity, self-esteem, relationships, habits)
The indicators of traumatic stress and violence
The effects of life events, stressors, and crises on individuals, families, groups, organizations, and communities

The impact of out-of-home placement (e.g., hospitalization, foster care, residential care, criminal justice system) on clients/client systems
The impact of out-of-home displacement (e.g., natural disaster, homelessness, immigration) on clients/client systems
The indicators and risk factors of the client's/client system's danger to self and others
The impact of stress, trauma, and violence
The effects of physical, sexual, and psychological abuse on individuals, families, groups, organizations, and communities
The indicators, dynamics, and impact of exploitation across the lifespan (e.g., financial, immigration status, sexual trafficking)
The characteristics of perpetrators of abuse, neglect, and exploitation
The indicators of addiction and substance abuse
The effects of addiction and substance abuse on individuals, families, groups, organizations, and communities
Criminal justice systems
Common psychotropic and non-psychotropic prescriptions and over-the-counter medications and their side effects

6. Assessment Methods and Techniques (Competency)

KSAs
The factors and processes used in problem formulation
Methods of involving clients/client systems in problem identification (e.g., gathering collateral information)
Techniques and instruments used to assess clients/client systems
Methods to incorporate the results of psychological and educational tests into assessment
Methods to assess ego strength
Methods to assess organizational functioning (e.g., agency assessments)
Methods to obtain sensitive information (e.g., substance abuse, sexual abuse)
Communication theories and styles
Risk assessment methods
Methods to assess the client's/client system's strengths, resources, and challenges (e.g., individual, family, group, organization, community)
The indicators of motivation, resistance, and readiness to change
Methods to assess motivation, resistance, and readiness to change
Methods to assess the client's/client system's communication skills
Methods to assess the client's/client system's coping abilities
The indicators of the client's/client system's strengths and challenges

Methods used to assess trauma
Placement options based on assessed level of care
The use of the Diagnostic and Statistical Manual of the American Psychiatric Association

7. Intervention Planning and Implementation (Competency)

KSAs
The principles and techniques of interviewing (e.g., supporting, clarifying, focusing, confronting, validating, feedback, reflecting, language differences, use of interpreters, redirecting)
Methods to involve clients/client systems in intervention planning
Cultural considerations in the creation of an intervention plan
The criteria used in the selection of intervention/treatment modalities (e.g., client/client system abilities, culture, life stage)
The components of intervention, treatment, and service plans
Psychotherapies
The impact of immigration, refugee, or undocumented status on service delivery
Discharge, aftercare, and follow-up planning
The phases of intervention and treatment
The client's/client system's role in the problem-solving process
Problem-solving models and approaches (e.g., brief, solution-focused methods or techniques)
Methods to engage and motivate clients/client systems
Methods to engage and work with involuntary clients/client systems
Methods to obtain and provide feedback
The principles of active listening and observation
Verbal and nonverbal communication techniques
The concept of congruence in communication
Limit setting techniques
The technique of role play
Role modeling techniques
Techniques for harm reduction for self and others
Methods to teach coping and other self-care skills to clients/client systems
Client/client system self-monitoring techniques
Methods of conflict resolution
Crisis intervention and treatment approaches
Theories of trauma-informed care
Methods and approaches to trauma-informed care
Anger management techniques

Stress management techniques
Cognitive and behavioral interventions
Strengths-based and empowerment strategies and interventions
Client/client system contracting and goal-setting techniques
Partializing techniques
Assertiveness training
Task-centered approaches
Psychoeducation methods (e.g., acknowledging, supporting, normalizing)
Group work techniques and approaches (e.g., developing and managing group processes and cohesion)
Family therapy models, interventions, and approaches
Couples interventions and treatment approaches
Permanency planning
Mindfulness and complementary therapeutic approaches
Techniques used for follow-up
Techniques used to evaluate a client's/client system's progress
The indicators of client/client system readiness for termination
Consultation approaches (e.g., referrals to specialists)
Methods to assess the availability of community resources

Intervention Processes and Techniques for Use With Larger Systems (Content Area)

8. Program Development and Research (Competency)

KSAs
Methods to establish program objectives and outcomes
Methods of service delivery
Methods to establish service networks or community resources
The effects of program evaluation findings on services
Methods to evaluate agency programs (e.g., needs assessment, formative/summative assessment, cost-effectiveness, cost-benefit analysis, outcomes assessment)
The principles and features of objective and subjective data
Basic and applied research design and methods
Data collection and analysis methods
Methods to assess reliability and validity in social work research
Methods to develop and evaluate measurable objectives for client/client system intervention, treatment, and/or service plans
Methods, techniques, and instruments used to evaluate social work practice
Evidence-based practice

9. Methods for Social Change (Competency)

KSAs

Theories of social change and community development
Community organizing and social planning methods
Techniques for mobilizing community participation
The impact of social institutions on society
The impact of the political environment on policy-making
Concepts of social policy development and analysis
Techniques to inform and influence organizational and social policy
Theories and methods of advocacy for policies, services, and resources to meet clients'/client systems' needs
Primary, secondary, and tertiary prevention strategies

10. Supervision and Administration (Competency)

KSAs

Governance structures
Theories of organizational development and structure
The effects of policies, procedures, regulations, and legislation on social work practice and service delivery
Leadership and management techniques
Fiscal management techniques
Fund-raising and development
Asset-building approaches (e.g., collaborative relationships, human capital, resources)
The relationship between formal and informal power structures in the decision-making process
Educational components, techniques, and methods of supervision
Methods to identify learning needs and develop learning objectives for supervisees
Case recording for practice evaluation or supervision
Methods to create, implement, and evaluate policies and procedures for social worker safety
Models of supervision and consultation (e.g., individual, peer, group)
The supervisee's role in supervision (e.g., identifying learning needs, self-assessment, prioritizing, etc.)
Employee recruitment, training, retention, performance appraisal, evaluation, and discipline
The impact of transference and countertransference within supervisory relationships

The components of a safe and positive work environment
The components of case management
The elements of a case presentation
Time management approaches
Methods of networking
The process of interdisciplinary and intradisciplinary team collaboration
The basic terminology of professions other than social work (e.g., legal, educational)
Methods to create, implement, and evaluate policies and procedures that minimize risk for individuals, families, groups, organizations, and communities
Methods to develop, review, and implement crisis plans
Quality assurance, including program reviews and audits by external sources
Accreditation and/or licensing requirements
Professional development activities to improve practice and maintain current professional knowledge (e.g., in-service training, licensing requirements, reviews of literature, workshops)

11. Record-Keeping and Reporting (Competency)

KSAs
The principles of case recording, documentation, and management of practice records
The elements of client/client system reports
The principles and processes for developing formal documents (e.g., proposals, letters, brochures, pamphlets, reports, evaluations)

Professional Relationships, Values, and Ethics (Content Area)

12. Professional Values and Ethical Issues (Competency)

KSAs
Legal and/or ethical issues related to the practice of social work, including responsibility to clients/client systems, colleagues, the profession, and society
Professional values and principles (e.g., competence, social justice, integrity, and dignity and worth of the person)
Techniques to identify and resolve ethical dilemmas
Client/client system competence and self-determination (e.g., financial decisions, treatment decisions, emancipation, age of consent, permanency planning)

Techniques for protecting and enhancing client/client system self-determination
The client's/client system's right to refuse services (e.g., medication, medical treatment, counseling, placement, etc.)
Professional boundaries in the social worker–client/client system relationship (e.g., power differences, conflicts of interest, etc.)
Ethical issues related to dual relationships
Professional objectivity in the social worker–client/client system relationship
Self-disclosure principles and applications
Legal and/or ethical issues regarding documentation
Legal and/or ethical issues regarding termination
Legal and/or ethical issues related to death and dying
Research ethics (e.g., institutional review boards, use of human subjects, informed consent)
Ethical issues in supervision and management

13. Confidentiality (Competency)

KSAs
The principles and processes of obtaining informed consent
The use of client/client system records
Legal and/or ethical issues regarding confidentiality, including electronic information security
Legal and/or ethical issues regarding mandatory reporting (e.g., abuse, threat of harm, impaired professionals, etc.)

14. Professional Development and Use of Self (Competency)

KSAs
The components of the social worker–client/client system relationship
The social worker's role in the problem-solving process
Methods to clarify the roles and responsibilities of the social worker and client/client system in the intervention process
The principles and techniques for building and maintaining a helping relationship
The concept of acceptance and empathy in the social worker–client/client system relationship
The dynamics of power and transparency in the social worker–client/client system relationship
The impact of transference and countertransference in the social worker–client/client system relationship

The impact of domestic, intimate partner, and other violence on the helping relationship
The dynamics of diversity in the social worker–client/client system relationship
The effect of the client's developmental level on the social worker–client relationship
Social worker self-care principles and techniques
Burnout, secondary trauma, and compassion fatigue
The influence of the social worker's own values and beliefs on the social worker–client/client system relationship
The influence of the social worker's own values and beliefs on interdisciplinary collaboration

Appendix B

Learning Styles

The following are some suggested techniques for each learning style that can help to fill in content gaps that may exist.

VISUAL LEARNERS

Visual learners learn best through what they see. Although lectures can be boring for visual learners, they benefit from the use of diagrams, PowerPoint slides, and charts.

- Use colored highlighters to draw attention to key terms
- Develop outlines or take notes on the concepts
- Write talking points for each of the Knowledge, Skills, and Abilities (KSAs) on separate white index cards
- Create a coding schema of symbols and write them next to material and terms that require further study
- Study in an environment that is away from visual distractions such as television, people moving around, or clutter

AUDITORY LEARNERS

Auditory learners learn best through what they hear. They may have difficulty remembering material, but can easily recall it if it is read to them.

- Tape-record yourself summarizing the material as you are studying it—listen to your notes as a way to reinforce what you read
- Have a study partner explain the relevant concepts and terms related to the KSAs
- Read the text aloud if you are having trouble remembering it
- Find free podcasts or YouTube videos on the Internet on the content areas that are short and easy to understand to assist with learning
- Talk to yourself about the content as you study, emphasizing what is important to remember related to each KSA

KINESTHETIC OR HANDS-ON LEARNERS

Kinesthetic learners learn through tactile approaches aimed at experiencing or doing. They need physical activities as a foundation for instruction.

- Make flashcards on material because writing it down will assist with remembering the content
- Use as many different senses as possible when studying—read material when you are on your treadmill, use highlighters, talk aloud about content, and/or listen to a study partner
- Develop mnemonic devices to aid in information retention (e.g., EAPIET or *EAt PIE T*oday is a great way to remember the social work problem-solving process [Engaging, Assessing, Planning, Intervening, Evaluating, and Terminating])
- Write notes and important terms in the margins
- Ask a study partner to quiz you on material—turn it into a game and see how many KSAs you can discuss or how long you can talk about a content area before running out of material